HEIRLOOM FLOWERS

VINTAGE FLOWERS FOR MODERN GARDENS

TOVAH MARTIN

CONSULTANTS:

DIANE WHEALY

AT THE FLOWER AND HERB EXCHANGE
AND MARILYN BARLOW OF SELECT SEEDS

PHOTOGRAPHS BY

DAVID CAVAGNARO

The dark chenille-like tassels of Love-lies-bleeding, *Amaranthus caudatus*, have been appreciated in gardens since the 17th century

FIRESIDE
Rockefeller Center
1230 Avenue of the Americas
New York, NY 10020

Designed by Kitty Crossley
Edited by Charlie Ryrie

10 9 8 7 6 5 4 3 2 1

Library of Congress Cataloging-in-Publication Data
available on request

Printed & bound in Singapore

PUBLISHER'S ACKNOWLEDGMENTS

*The publisher would like to thank
David Cavagnaro for supplying wonderful photographs which bring the
pleasures of heirloom gardening to life.
Many thanks also go to Diane
Whealy who offered her help and
knowledge readily and with charm even
though we gave her extra work at her
most frantic time of year.*

*Thanks to all the people at Gaia
Books who helped in the production of
this book, particularly Patrick
O'Halloran for administrative
assistance, and Caroline Sheldrick for
additional research and copyediting;
thanks to Lyn Bresler for compiling the
Index, and to Julia Rowntree for her
illustration on pages 11 and 99.*

CONTENTS

THE AUTHOR

Tovah Martin is the garden editor for Victoria magazine as well as The Litchfield County Times. She has authored many gardening books, most notably *Tasha Tudor's Garden*, recipient of the Garden Writer's Association of America's award for Best Book of the Year in 1995. She lectures frequently, she has appeared on several TV shows and was awarded the Massachusetts Horticultural Society's Gold Medal in 1995. Her 1810 Roxbury, Connecticut home is fronted by a cottage garden filled with heirlooms.

THE PHOTOGRAPHER

David Cavagnaro is a naturalist, plantsman, writer and photographer whose words and pictures have appeared in books and magazines worldwide. His house in Iowa lies among acres of meadows which he has reclaimed from arable land to turn into a wildflower paradise, and his own large gardens are filled with heirloom flowers and vegetables.

THE CONSULTANTS

Diane Whealy and her husband Kent founded the Seed Savers Exchange in Iowa in 1975, which has grown to be a vitally important international organization for promoting and conserving the genetic diversity of the world's food crops. In 1989 Diane developed the work of SSE further by starting the Flower and Herb Exchange, dedicated to preserving heirloom flowers, and distributing them widely through a flourishing seed exchange. The Flower and Herb Exchange ensures that old-fashioned flowers are kept alive for future generations.

Marilyn Barlow founded and runs Select Seeds, a small company specialising in heirloom and hard-to-find flowers.

AUTHOR'S ACKNOWLEDGMENTS

Innumerable preservationists helped with this book. In particular I would like to thank Marilyn Barlow of Select Seeds, Scott Kunst of Old House Gardens, Diane and Kent Whealy of the Seed Savers Exchange and the Flower and Herb Exchange, Tasha Tudor, Rob Girard, Joy Logee Martin, Nancy McDonald, Rand B. Lee, Denis Garrett, Ed Rasmussen of the Fragrant Path, Renee Shepherd of Shepherd's Garden Seeds, Howard Shapiro and Allan Kapuler of Seeds of Change, Geo. Park Seed Co., Peggy Newcomb of the Thomas Jefferson Center for Historic Plants, Dick Meiners of Pinetree Garden Seeds, Jeff McCormack Ph.D. of Southern Exposure Seed Exchange, Thelma Crawford, Adrian Kencik, Peter Grayson, Marlyn Sachtjen, Antonia Russo, Bill Brumback and Barbara Pryor of the New England Wildflower Society, Mary Jane Hatfield, Rev. Douglas Seidel, Bill Shepherd of the Arkansas Native Plant Society, Craig Freeman, Eric Sundell and Mark Bridgen Ph.D. of the University of Connecticut, as well as the horticultural historians that have come before us.

Foreword

....

The morning glories that cover the south side of the barn at Heritage Farm each summer are a living link to my great-grandparents, who passed away long before I was born. Grandchildren are sometimes lucky enough to inherit their grandfather's rocking chair or grandmother's candy dish, but I was given the seeds of Grandpa Ott's beautiful morning glory and a huge German Pink tomato – living heirlooms that continue to provide unbroken links to my ancestors. Because of their love of flowers and their foresight, when Grandpa Ott's parents, my great-grandparents, immigrated from Bavaria to the United States in 1867, morning glory seeds were thoughtfully packed in their trunk along with other belongings needed to start a new life in the wooded hills near St. Lucas, Iowa.

The thousands of gardeners and farmers who immigrated to North America invariably brought along some treasured seeds of vegetables and flowers from their homelands, and they are responsible for the cornucopia of garden plants that we enjoy today. Often these seeds were hidden under bands of hats and in the linings of suitcases, or sewn into the hems of dresses to avoid confiscation by immigration officials. Because we are a nation of immigrants, these living heirlooms form a unique heritage of seeds that has been steadily accumulating for four centuries. First arriving with passengers on the Mayflower, traditional varieties continue to accompany gardeners and farmers who are immigrating today from Cambodia, Laos, Haiti and Cuba. The vast majority of this heritage of seeds come from northern Europe, and sometimes these living heirlooms have been grown on the same farm by different generations of a family for more than 150 years. Dedicated gardeners must continue to steward and replant these seeds, otherwise these living heirlooms will become extinct. Then future generations will never enjoy the rich fragrances of grandmother's Sweet Peas or Evening Scented Stock, or be able to taste the juicy deliciousness of a Rainbow Tomato. Histories as well as irreplaceable genetic characteristics are rapidly being lost forever to gardeners and plant breeders.

My great-grandparents' morning glories flourished in the early sunlight of North American summer mornings, just as the large heart-shaped green leaves and hundreds of small purple flowers had greeted them each morning in Bavaria. Like other cherished belongings that surrounded them in their log home, these velvety purple morning glories with red stars in their throats must have provided familiar feelings and warm memories of home. My great-grandparents gave seeds to each of their nine children, but my grandfather - Baptist John Ott - was the only one who kept them going. Grandpa Ott was an ornery, colorful old character, full of vivid stories and mischievous laughter, and my husband and I feel quite lucky to have spent the last year of his life leaning from him in his garden. After my grandfather passed away, Kent and I realized that the survival of my family's seeds was up to us. We immediately started trying to locate other gardeners who were also keeping heirloom seeds in an attempt to collect, maintain and distribute these rare varieties before they were lost.

In 1975 Kent and I founded the Seed Savers Exchange (SSE), a non-profit education and conservation organization, and for more than two decades we have continued to locate other gardeners who are keeping the seeds of heirloom food crops, flowers and herbs that have been passed down in their families. We have used SSE's publications to weave together a network of thousands of gardeners who are willing to share their family's treasured seeds through an annual seed exchange. In 1975 there were only 29 members offering about 50 varieties though in a six page newsletter that included vegetables, flowers and herbs. But the number of listings in *Seed Savers Yearbook* has been growing at such a rapid rate that today 1,000 member annually offer seeds of 11,000 endangered varieties through a 460 page yearbook. By 1990 SSE's yearbook was be coming to large to print, so we decided to no longer list flowers and herbs.

As you can imagine, however, many of SSE's members were disappointed because they are also keeping large collections of heirloom of flowers and herbs, which are an equally important part of our garden heritage. So in 1990, we founded and began publishing *The Flower and Herb Exchange* (FHE) to make certain that our member' heirloom flowers and herbs also were not lost. We soon discovered that a unique heritage of old-time flowers and herbs are still being maintained by gardeners throughout the world, and many of these rare varieties have never been available through commercial catalogs. Nine years later, *The 1998 Flower and Herb Exchange* has grown to nearly 350 members who are offering 3,000 listings of heirloom flowers and herbs.

Although a significant number of flowers and herbs have been lost during the past years, much still remains because of the foresight of so many dedicated gardeners who were wise enough to save their family's living treasure. For many of us, some of our favorite childhood memories are in our grandparents gardens where delicately beautiful old-time flowers grew that evoke such wonderful memories. Fragrance is also an important trigger for our memories. The sweet smell of Lily of the Valley will always carry me back to my grandparents yard, enclosed by a white picket fence that held in all of the incredible beauty and fragrance of their flowers.

The members of *The Flower and Herb Exchange* have become plant detectives. The are beginning to reconstruct their horticultural pasts from the clues that have been left for us to discover: summer photos taken in grandmother's yard and garden; peonies and roses discovered in old cemeteries;

daffodils, lilies and iris that continue to mark the stone remains of foundations and picket fences that rotted away long ago around abandoned homesteads. Details of local legend and lore associated with gardening can often be sifted out of conversations with elderly gardeners who can still describe their gardens in vivid detail. Even when other memories are fading, elderly gardeners can clearly remember the garden flowers that filled their lives with beauty.

I have read many times about the hard lives of early pioneer women who were often able to sustain their energy and spirit with flowers. After all of the farm chores were done, after the vegetable garden was weeded and harvested, and after the daily bread was secured, their attention would turn to the flowers that brightened the house, porch, yard and gardens. And they shared this incredible beauty and rich fragrances with everyone who came to their homes. There was a section of grandmother's garden that she called her friendship garden. Usually the neighbors and relatives who visited would always leave with a slip of some plant wrapped in a handkerchief that was dampened with water.

I am deeply pleased that *The Flower and Herb Exchange* has quickly become a valuable tool that gardeners can use to re-create and replant the flower gardens of the past. One or two generations temporarily lose sight of the beauty that graced our families' homesteads and gardens, and helped sustain our grandparents during time that were harder than we can imagine. It is now our turn and our responsibility to re-create the garden landscapes of the past by reintroducing many of the plants that bloomed in our grandparents' gardens and yards.

In this book Tovah Martin does us all a service by reminding us of the long histories and the beauties of our heirloom flowers. Our children must be able to share our eager anticipation of the rich beauty of each new spring. They need to be filled with the beautiful memories that are brought to life each year by the fragrance of the lilacs or the beauty of Grandpa Ott's morning glories.

Diane Whealy

Diane Whealy 1998

Co-founder of the Seed Savers Exchange
Director of The Flower and Herb Exchange

Part One

Our floral heritage

1

What are heirloom flowers?

I know a cottage perched on the summit of a hill with winding paths crisscrossing in and out of hollyhocks and foxgloves, under arbors smothered in rambling roses. The gardener in residence is an octogenarian who sold her car long ago and only sees people when they come to her. She went into the city a few years ago on an errand and wasn't much pleased with what she found, so she came home resolved not to venture there again. Instead, she takes a goat or two on the mile walk down to her mailbox on fair days. And when the weather's bad, she sits by the fire and reads. I tried bringing her the newest 'Jolly Joker' pansy one year, and found it on the compost when I visited next. Pansies had no business being orange and purple, she curtly explained. She prefers the muted shades of Viola 'Irish Molly' which is planted not far from the lettuce poppies she broadcasts out the back door each year – from seed that originated with her Scottish nanny, and probably before. Time never seems to touch that little garden in northern New England.

ABOVE: Bedding violas were developed from pansies crossed with *V. cornuta* and *V. lutea* from Western and Central Europe

LEFT: The exuberant Oriental poppy was first introduced into France from Armenia in the early18th century

One of the many beauties of the cottage garden on the hill is that I always know where to go if I lose my 'Mrs Sinkins' dianthus. It will be growing there along with other fragrant clove pinks – and you can't always find it at a garden center. At the moment, most folks favor long stemmed carnation hybrids or multi-flowered alpine varieties, neither of which emit the heavenly clove scent that floats from the petals of many heirloom pinks. True, 'Mrs Sinkins' doesn't have a long stem custom made for easy bunching in a bouquet. And it ceases to bloom in the heat of the summer. But where else can you find such a fantastic scent?

Among the many little quirks and attributes that make old-fashioned plants different from their modern counterparts, heirloom flowers often excel in the aromatic realm. Although aroma isn't a prime selling point for most mainstream nurseries or plant centers right now, if gardeners start requesting the old scented flowers, we may be able to revive the fragrant gardens enjoyed for centuries.

Delicate flowers of Gypsophila – baby's breath – contrast with the generous blossoms of this beautifully scented 'Seven Sisters' rambler rose

FASHION AND PLANTS

Thank heavens for the tides of fashion. If it weren't for their influence, we would all still be running around in corsets or miniskirts. Our homes might be swathed in dark, velvet draperies with overstuffed fainting couches placed wherever they might be of service, or we could be sitting stiffly on ladderback chairs around a beehive oven. Fashion dictates everything, from the curves on table legs to the prevalence of kneebones seen on the street. It alters the etiquette of dinner party conversation and sways the syllabus of university courses. Fashion sets the trends, and the scene changes accordingly. Ten years from now, cars might be bigger or smaller, they might be aerodynamic, feature tailfins or even be rendered obsolete altogether. But one thing is certain – they'll be different from the way they were yesterday.

Although we tend to associate the term 'fashion' with skirt lengths and tie widths, its influence reaches far wider. So it should come as no great surprise to learn that flowers have changed with time. For all sorts of reasons, flowers have come and gone over decades and centuries. The double green zinnia sitting in your window box this summer would definitely raise Thomas Jefferson's eyebrows. And he, no doubt, grew a taller, leaner snapdragon than the varieties modern seed houses favor.

Heirloom flowers aren't necessarily ancient history; when gardening is popular, the landscape changes drastically from one decade to the next. Flower fashions are nearly as volatile as the cycles of couture, and flowers have felt and been affected by the fluctuations of clothing styles, and the whims of milliners. If lapel buttonholes disappear from men's jackets, then boutonnières rapidly slip out of vogue. As a result, bachelor's buttons are no longer hybridized in petal colors or with stem lengths appropriate for that purpose. If stockings stop

Change is inevitable, and we welcome the introduction of a new phlox that promises to be mildew resistant, or a hardy strain of sage from Germany with rich, zesty, evergreen leaves. We want our plant repertoire to expand, we lust after lacier artemisias and hardier rosemarys. If we're putting in moon gardens, we hunger for 'Alba' forms. When we're following the latest solenostemon trend, we welcome hybrids created to tolerate full sun.

When you're changing your beds to keep abreast of current trends, remember that the world witnessed a rampant coleus craze during the Victorian era (solenostemons were then known as coleus; plant names change even more rapidly than skirt lengths). And the only named solenostemon to survive from the 19th century into the 1990s is 'Pineapple Queen'. The cycles of fashion are fascinating, but it's a pity when everyone rushes out to purchase coleus only to find the benches lacking in older hybrids. Perhaps those cast-offs didn't boast the sun tolerance of the newest modern strain. Perhaps they were dowdy compared to the latest introductions. And their names were definitely not as trendy as 'Betelgeuse' or 'Towering Inferno'. But they had their virtues. They shouldn't be lost. Someone's got to keep the past alive.

RIGHT: *Camellia japonica* had been cultivated in Japan and the East for millennia before their introduction to Britain in 1730

being held up by garters, then the blossoms that were once tucked into those bands have no role to play. Half a year later, garter adornments might be replaced by flowers perfectly suited for adorning your hairstyle, or something. The flowers in question find new uses, or they simply disappear from florists' shops.

Women's clothing fashions have proved particularly fickle for flowers. Camellia corsages were once worn at the waist to accentuate a lady's hourglass figure. But when everyone threw off their corsets and fashions fell straight from the shoulder or were drop-waisted, the corsage was positioned more prominently on the shoulder and composed of eye-catching blossoms such as orchids. No one bemoaned the passing of the corset, you could even stitch one up today based on 19th century patterns if the inclination arose or the fashion returned, but flowers aren't that easily whipped together. If the flowers that were grown for those corsages disappear, especially if they happen to be hybrids, there's little chance that they'll ever surface again. The quirk of nature that produced many-petaled parma violets is unlikely to happen twice. As far as flowers are concerned, tides of fashion can be unrelenting.

Of course, it's not all negative. Fashions (especially trends in the florist trade) have sometimes harmed flower futures, but cycles have also led to all sorts of innovations in the flower world. Fashions have sent explorers wandering around the globe, collecting plants from the tropics and introducing them to the hot houses of Europe and North America. Trends in garden design have increased the legions of pansy hybrids, and brought more white forms of flowers into cultivation. Fashion means that a certain flower may suddenly enjoy a flurry of hybridization, and ever-increasing interest in gardening means that the rosters of plants in cultivation increase accordingly.

In 1975, the Hardy Plant Society began publishing *The Plant Finder*, a volume listing all known cultivars available in the United Kingdom, with their sources. The first edition listed 22,000 plants. In 1994, that number rose to 65,000 different cultivars. However, over 700 hybrids were also listed as missing – Oriental poppies and crocus in particular lost large numbers of hybrids from their ranks. Similarly, if you happen to look through horticultural classifieds with any regularity, or if you read letters to the editor in your favorite horticultural periodical, you're bound to come across quite a few botanical losts and founds placed by gardeners.

A flower's legions might swell due to whims of fashion. Or, by the same token, it might slip into oblivion when the beat moves on.

Exuberant canna lilies were highly popular in Victorian gardens, grown as exotic focal points in elaborately designed borders

FROM WHENCE THEY CAME

Fashion was one factor affecting the coming and going of flowers. Transportation, communication and technology are also responsible. At one time, people knew the wildflowers indigenous to their region, and little else. That was fine, because until relatively recent times the average citizen had little time for cultivating flowers, as the enemy was forever pounding at the gates and every ounce of energy was expended in keeping plagues at bay and cultivating crops that might sustain the family during the cold seasons. Clearly, there would have been few opportunities for playing around with petunias, even if petunias were available.

Once trade routes were established, plants began to move around. Of course, plants had traveled before that time, on winds and tides and randomly in horses' hooves and wagon wheels of conquering armies and suchlike, but they didn't always take hold, and they weren't necessarily embraced. Needless to say, useful plants (crops, vegetables and herbs) were the

ABOVE: Many American plants including common milkweed *Asclepias syriaca* arrived in England via John Tradescant the younger

first to be carried deliberately from one place to another. With the creation of monasteries, and within the relative calm of their walled gardens, herbs such as chamomile, sage, lemon balm, southernwood, yarrow, winter savory and betony arrived on British shores in the late 900s and became "essentials". With expanded trade routes, more herbs arrived from far afield, but a plant's fate was only sealed favorably if it could be put to service. Beside native flowers, some of the oldest plants in cultivation are herbs.

Things began to improve for flowers from the 12th century onward. Flowers moved from purely functional household or kitchen uses and also became used for strewing, and to decorate monasteries, halls and churches to mark special occasions. With the Crusades, Mediterranean plants such as coronilla and gladiolus began filtering into British gardens. The Crusades explained the early introduction of hollyhocks from Persia and lavender from the Mediterranean. They were introduced, but kept primarily cloistered until calmer times.

By the 16th century, well recovered from the turmoil of the aftermath of the Black Death, the economic and housing situations had changed in Europe, prompting more of the populace to look twice at – and embrace – plants that might not be absolutely crucial to their family's well-being. Many pretty little flowers such as lungwort *Pulmonaria,* honesty *Lunaria,* and periwinkle *Vinca major* and *Vinca minor* came into popular cultivation, but people still found creative uses for the plants whenever it was possible – in *Adam in Eden* (1657) William Coles recommends periwinkle for cramps, and lungwort (grown under the name of Jerusalem cowslip) was billed as a general remedy for the respiratory system. Until quite recently, flowers were most often adopted and widely grown if they were useful – leaving their beauties and esthetic delights to be made famous by poets and artists rather than gardeners.

Although the British were by no means the first enthusiastic gardeners – we know that garden design and flower development had been important for centuries in the Middle East and the Orient – introduction dates traditionally mark the year that a plant arrived in Britain. Not only did British gardeners and herbalists faithfully document new botanical immigrants, but they proved conscientious hosts to botanical strangers arriving on their shores. Moreover, they generously kept the chain moving, sharing their finds with other kindred spirits. British were great adopters, employers, chroniclers, stewards and disseminators of new arrivals.

Not long after Europeans arrived in North America, the Brave New World was explored for horticultural treasures. Some of the earliest and most fruitful collecting sprees were accomplished by the John Tradescants, a father (1570-1638) and son (1608-1662) team. The Elder became a shareholder in the Virginia Company, receiving plants through their efforts. His son journeyed personally to collect in Virginia. They were responsible for the introduction of plants such as the coneflower *Rudbeckia laciniata,* the Jamestown lily *Zephyranthes atamasca,* goldenrod *Solidago canadensis,* spiderwort *Tradescantia virginiana,* Prince's feather *Amaranthus hypochondriacus,* American cowslip *Dodecatheon meadia,* milkweed *Asclepias syriaca,* foamflower *Tiarella cordifolia,* trumpet vine *Campsis radicans,* yellow passionflower *Passiflora lutea,* Virginia creeper *Parthenocissus quinquefolia,* and turtle head *Chelone glabra,* as well as many other North American plants.

John Bartram (1699-1776) and his son William (1739-1823) were also important early plant collectors, sending finds to their English liaison, Peter Collinson, a fellow Quaker and an astute businessman. He in turn disseminated the newly supplied American novelties amongst eager gentlemen collectors in Britain, from whence they passed into wide circulation.

Moss phlox *Phlox subulata,* growing here with vivid green *Euphorbia*, were introduced to England from North America in 1745

The exchange went the other way as well. The first pilgrims to settle in North America arrived with seeds of plants that they deemed critical for their survival. The emphasis was on vegetables, of course, but non-native herbs and flowers also arrived early on North American shores. And American settlers struggled to keep abreast of botanical introductions from that moment onward. The pioneer life wasn't easy, but it became a little more comfortable when accompanied by favorite plants from the Old Country. As the years progressed and communication improved, more and more plants arrived, fueled by prominent and globe-trotting citizens such as Thomas Jefferson. Through correspondence abroad, they heard of rarities that were arriving in Europe regularly from further and further flung places and were eager to pay the price necessary to receive the objects of their desire.

As technology improved and with the introduction of heated glasshouses into North America in the late 1700s (the very first version was reputedly built in 1736, similar structures didn't follow for many years), both hardy and tender plants came to America and survived to become integrated into the cultivated landscape.

With the advent of steam travel in the early 1800s, quantities of plants began to return with explorers from the tropics. At first, wealthy aristocrats and monarchs footed the bills and hid the plants away in their own personal botanical gardens. Eventually the hardier of the new arrivals filtered into the public domain, although tender tropicals remained the property of wealthy citizens who could afford their protection in glasshouses over the winter. Tropicals weren't adopted by the general populace until late in the 19th century when glass became cheaper and more readily available. By then, even if a glasshouse was out of reach for many, homes were brighter, with more windows, allowing tender plants to survive between growing seasons.

FLOWERS VERSUS THE ELEMENTS

A newly imported plant introduction can only take root, thrive and persist from season to season if it can tolerate the conditions in its new residence. Not all the green immigrants brought back by explorers found their adoptive homes hospitable. Some tropicals simply curled up their roots and perished when they witnessed their first bitter winter in captivity. Even indoors (especially when exposed to the fits and starts of stoves in primitive greenhouses), it has always proved difficult to host foreigners in unaccustomed conditions.

Many heirloom species have developed highly defined physical characteristics to deal with the climate at hand. Plants are survivors. And survival tactics include adapting rather skillfully to native regions, leading to some astonishingly handsome traits. Species bristle with small, waxy leaves as protection from burning sun if necessary, or they brandish big, furry foliage to soak up stray light if shade happens to be the prevailing condition in the understory of their native jungle. They develop root systems to soak up tiny droplets of moisture if that's all nature normally provides in their native habitat, or they sink a network of roots adapted to aquatic conditions if they normally grow in the muck beside bogs. Some of the most fascinating heirlooms hail from severe habitats. When faced with a challenge, their solutions are feats of engineering.

Hybridizers tinker with plants to lengthen their stems or render them dwarf, but few man-made alterations can equal the incredible gimmicks that plants devise unaided to survive in a stressful environment. Flowers use all sorts of ploys including fragrance, gaudily colored petals, long-throated blooms, pollen streaks or throat blotches to attract their pollinators. Leaves are shaped in forms likely to facilitate existence in the wild. Seedcasings are often

RIGHT: Common desert plants, numerous species of cacti exist, all excellently adapted to thrive in arid regions

aerodynamically designed to disperse just where germination is likely to be effective. Seeds might be contrived to crack only when seared by fire or when dashed against rocks. Diversity makes the botanical world go round.

Plants that are deprived of rain for several months of the year sometimes develop bulbous or tuberous roots to store moisture during their time of dearth. Desert plants often have plump, succulent leaves and stems to hold water when little is provided. Alpine plants tend to hug the ground with creeping stems and tough, little leaves to protect them from brutally windy conditions at high altitudes and minimize the moisture they'll need when wedged between rock crevices. When the rocks sweat as temperatures fluctuate, a few precious drops of water become available. Mediterranean and arid-land plants often have small, aromatic leaves rich in essential oils. Scented leaves baffle predators, and the oils that evaporate in the heat of the sun linger briefly after sunset to act as a blanket, protecting the plant from the sudden temperature drop.

Regionality is a wonderful thing. Your local weeds might seem rather provincial compared to exotics from afar, but take a second look. Upon closer inspection, all sorts of hidden secrets might be revealed. And remember that those plants have adapted to living happily in your region. They are your true heirlooms.

And yet, gardeners have traditionally hungered after the heirlooms of other regions. We love a challenge. There's nothing wrong with inviting strangers to dwell on your turf. But before you transplant an heirloom or sow its seeds, study its native habitat. Fads and fashions come and go, but if you can't provide enough water to support a calla lily in your backyard, a struggle for survival will ensue unless you can alter the conditions accordingly. Soil amendments help. Hoses and drip irrigation also come to your aid. In addition to learning about the history of a newly adopted plant, also study its roots. Find out its soil preferences and the rainfall typical of its native region, and experiment.

Old-fashioned sweet peas are descended from *Lathyrus odoratus*, sent to Britain from Sicily in 1699 by Father Cupani, a Franciscan monk

FASHION IN THE GARDEN

For centuries most plant development depend-
ed on fate, chance introductions, or serendipity.
In fact, plant breeding didn't begin in earnest
until the ramifications of Mendel's famous pea
experiments (published in 1865) truly hit home.
Before that time, plants were selected – for
example, seed was saved of a chance poppy discovered with a white hem around its edge and
all its ordinary neighbors were destroyed until a
stable strain of Shirley poppies was established.
If gardeners were striving toward a specific goal,
the process took many growing seasons. You
chose plants that naturally portrayed the qualities that you needed, you didn't try to mold
plants to fit your design.

However, every decade or generation favors
a different style of garden design, and garden
fashions drastically affect the repertoire of plants
on everyone's wish lists. In the 19th century
nurseries really began tinkering with plants, to
the advantage of those who followed the latest
trends, but much to the peril of the original
species that parented the hybrids. Columbines,
astilbes, pelargoniums, lupines, verbenas and
many other popular garden plants have strayed
so far from their ancestral roots that few modern gardeners give the species garden space.
The hybrids display "superior" qualities and
their parents disappear from cultivation. Who
wants to host an inferior form? Unfortunately,
this has meant that the parents of many
common garden hybrids are no longer available.

As plants were introduced and travel broad-
ened, garden fads were adopted and abandoned
with ever-increasing rapidity. At one time or
another, Britain fell head over heels for knot
gardens of herbs shorn to look like a carpet,
formal gardens loaded with blossoms, landscape
parks with very few flowers, "natural" gardens
with native plants incorporated, ribbon borders
composed primarily of annuals and herbaceous

ABOVE: Native to China, hollyhocks *Alcea
rosea* have been popular ever since their
introduction to Britain in the 16th century

borders full of perennials. There have been shrubberies, nutteries, pinetums, and other favorites, or mixtures of different styles worked in tandem. And as each fashion waxed and waned different plants came into play.

The United States saw the coming and going of many of the same fads – usually arriving several years after they climaxed in Britain. It is only recently that North American native plants have been given garden space. Instead, American gardeners have tended to follow foreign trends, from the pioneers' gardens with a few favorite flowers native to their homelands, to the gardens of wealthy citizens who invested considerable time and money to make their grounds blossom. Over the past 200 years, wealthy American gardeners have favored Japanese gardens, Italian gardens, Elizabethan knot gardens and Spanish gardens. Color theme gardens have waltzed with popularity many times. During the Victorian Era, blue or pink gardens were all the rage, and ladies opted for "moon gardens" of white blossoms that could be seen at dusk or admired in the moonlight without marring their complexions.

Fashions continue to change: herbaceous borders make way for naturalistic plantings; fiery colors usurp pastel shades; bedding plants and perennial gardens fall in and out of favor, and every gardening fad has its attendant flowers. Formal gardens have favored tidy plants that could easily be clipped and politely maintained within bounds without encroaching on their bedfellows. Dwarf varieties made neat little mounds whose growth could be easily controlled and predicted while "cottage" gardens allowed less disciplined plants to tumble one on another. And as different gardening styles were embraced, new plants became readily available. But when the next fad arrived, they were dropped just as rapidly. Too often, the latest hybrids superseded older varieties. And plants from the past were forgotten.

FLORISTS AND FLOWERS

Cut flower fashions have also influenced floral changes. Short-stemmed blooms could be threaded into a buttonhole or tucked into your hat while formal bouquets and flowers for deeper vases needed longer flower stems. All common cut flowers – dianthus, sweet peas, violets and roses – were eventually bred or selected for long stems. But all these flowers lost one critical charcteristic – they all lost their fragrance.

Thanks to florists, sweet peas now have large fluttery petals due to a quirk of giganticism that was nurtured and harnessed. Sunflowers come in a broad spectrum of colors, roses have stronger stems capable of keeping heavy buds from nodding, double bouvardias are readily available, double pelargoniums with flowers that won't shatter when you carry them across the street are prevalent and dahlias both great and small are available in a rainbow of hues – to mention only a handful of changes that have occurred at florists' behest.

Sometimes fashions work against florists – marigolds became such popular bedding plants that they lost their original long-stemmed form much loved by florists; cosmos seem to be moving toward shorter stems to fulfill the desires of landscapers. The violets that were once so overbred purely to supply the New York City opera crowd with nosegays eventually fell victim to disease and vanished in a wink from the glasshouses that mushroomed in nearby suburbs for that purpose. The story of florists' flowers hasn't entirely been a bed of roses.

Sunflowers *Helianthus anuus* have always exhibited highly variable forms

Phlox

Talk to Rachel Kane for more than just a few minutes, and phlox are bound to come up in the conversation. Although she sells and seeks out all sorts of perennials for her nursery, Perennial Pleasures in East Hardwick, Vermont, it's phlox that really tug at her heartstrings.

Native to the United States, *Phlox paniculata* wasn't greatly revered in this country, but it was an entirely different story in Europe. Rachel explains: "People in Europe viewed them as rarities, just as the Europeans went into raptures over the goldenrod that we treat like weeds." As a result, much of

there are phlox galore around old foundations, tucked where a long-gone farmyard once stood, but it's hard to identify the plants with any certainty. "One of the troubles is that they set seed so easily. You get something that looks interesting, but it could be a hybrid seedling rather than a named variety." And there is precious little reference material – few farmers kept accurate records of their floral planting, and carefully planned estates with garden lists are few and far between in northern Vermont. Lacking definite documentation, Rachel either has to take a stab at identifying the phlox she finds, or affix tentative names. It's frustrating.

At present, her catalog lists about 25 varieties of phlox, including her favorite which she calls, 'Old Cellar Hole', named because it was found in the abandoned cellar hole of a long-gone house. "It's very fragrant, lavendery-pink, four feet or more in height and a very strong plant. Best of all, it doesn't get mildew," Rachel says.

Phlox are plentiful because they tend to be strong plants, good at looking after themselves. "They can survive wherever it's sunny," Rachel claims. "But they look entirely different when they're well taken care of. The soil makes the biggest difference. They'll live in poor soil. But give them good, slightly sweet soil, water them when it goes dry and divide them every four years, then they'll not only look splendid but will be more resistant to mildew," Rachel explains. "Of course, some varieties come down with mildew no matter what you do. In that case, I abandon them and turn to one of the 150 varieties that I can grow without problems."

ABOVE: Phlox paniculata *is native through much of North America, but first recorded in Britain in 1732*

They are abundant in her neck of the woods because they can endure the prolonged and tempestuous winters typical of northern Vermont.

Phlox were never the aristocrats of the garden, they were the plants of the rank and file, but because they would tolerate the climate, the locals forgave their little quirks – such as a tendency toward mildew and a brief season of glory. They forgave and embraced them. Wherever you see an old farmyard in Vermont, clumps of fragrant phlox won't be far away.

Rachel's collecting takes place in Britain, virtually the only place where she can be certain of finding specific named varieties.

Although Rachel can't seem to keep from collecting, her mission is fraught with difficulties. She studies monographs on the genus, she pores over old catalogs and books, but she can't be certain that she's found the phlox that she seeks. "In the 1940's, when phlox was enjoying its heyday, there were 202 named varieties of *Phlox paniculata*. And yet, I haven't been able to lay my mits on most of those old hybrids," she laments. This isn't for lack of collecting material;

WHICH FLOWERS ARE HEIRLOOMS?

What may be a treasured heirloom to your community may be ignored by another. Some heirlooms are endangered, some are widely grown. Many heirlooms are species, but not all. Some of our earliest heirlooms had been subject to selection for centuries in the Far and Middle East before the plants were carried here on trade routes. The first chrysanthemum to arrive in Europe from China was already far removed from the simple daisy-like *Chrysanthemum indicum*, which had seen human intervention since the T'ang Dynasty (618-902AD). The first azalea to come from China in 1808 was the wild scarlet-flowered form, but whites, oranges, purples, and doubles followed rapidly. And although simplicity is often a trait of ancient heirlooms, not all double flowers are new introductions. Double-flowered and striped camellias could be seen by the earliest explorers in China.

Broad sweeping generalizations are impossible, but a few traits recur. Heirlooms tend to be more fragrant than their modern counterparts. Many are taller and more like their wild predecessors – heirloom narcissus look ill-kempt beside the newest hybrids. Colors may be more subdued in older flowers – for example early clivias were "flesh-colored", a far cry from the screaming oranges we find today. In general, flower palettes have increased with time and interest. Certainly, heirloom roses tend to have a more subtle blush than some of the newer hybrids. They blend easily with one another.

The form of early blossoms may be less finely honed, and heirlooms often sport fewer flowers in an umbel. Bloom span can be brief. Above all, they tend to be more disease resistant. After all, weeds are some of the hailest and hardiest plants known to mankind.

Some would say that heirloom flowers are the plants that time forgot. If you speak to Antonia Russo, one of the key players in the informal little group known as the Solon Heritage Flower Society in Solon, Iowa ("it's really just my elderly neighbor and I, doing all we can to protect what's here"), she'll contend that heirloom flowers tend to survive longest in the nooks and crannies where the tides of fashion never penetrated. In the backyards of the little Iowa towns, beside the clotheslines of the ladies who still wear the same dresses and support-hose they wore forty years ago, that's where you'll find rows of cannas lined out proudly every year like soldiers, as soon as danger of frost is passed.

The straight-lined rows offer the first clue that design trends didn't touch the little community. "I used to think that the rows were plain," Antonia once admitted, "then I began to realize that the rows were part of the tidiness and simplicity of the place." Heirloom flowers grow in Solon not because the residents are particularly keen on preservation, but because they knew nothing else. But no one remembers the names of the flowers in their backyard: "The names aren't important," insists Antonia. "The way of life is important and that's what's slipping away." The wonderfully disheveled backyards are going, along with the clotheslines and rhubarb at the end of the yard. "We're losing the richest element of our lives; it was a life filled with flowers," Antonia worries. She didn't have to describe the scene in Solon, Iowa too long. It was reminiscent of another place. It reminded me of my friend's cottage garden on the hill in New England.

2

Wildflowers: our earliest heirlooms

Long before gardeners corralled plants into gardens, folks were picking fistfuls of daisies and presenting them to sweethearts. Wildflowers were the first flowers everyone knew, the repertoire of familiar faces varying drastically depending on whether you happened to dwell by the seaside, inland, on a mountaintop or in a valley. Your own region was special, it boasted its own distinctive flora, its own heirlooms.

Every region of the globe that can support animal or human habitation can also support plants specially adapted to surviving the conditions at hand. Call many of them weeds if you will, but wildflowers are survivors, brilliantly equipped to endure the rigors of their native domain. Adaptations are ingenious, some wildflowers brandish spines or thorns to fend off predators where forage is sparse, others have succulent leaves to retain water where rainfall is meager. Prairie flowers tend to be long-stemmed and wind-pollinated to take advantage of the gusts that whip through their native wide open spaces. Meadow blossoms are large and colorful, the better to be singled out by roving butterflies, while alpine wildflowers often have modest, ground-hugging blooms that billow with scent to attract their pollinators. Butterfly-pollinated flowers are usually bright, night-blooming moth-pollinated flowers are generally luminous white. The variations go on and on; the ingenuity of nature is fascinating. Although there are undoubtedly many insignificant wildflowers on the globe, many are incredibly handsome, once you take a moment to focus on their charms.

Even dandelions are astonishingly complex, splendid plants, if you forgive the fact that they tend to monopolize your lawn. They are opportunists, but in the greater scheme of things, dandelions are one of nature's ways of ensuring that every field is not usurped only by grasses. The beauty of wildflowers lies in their multiformity, and the way that each flower's unique features are wrought entirely independent of man. When left to its own devices, nature will be infinitely creative.

ABOVE: The dainty trout lily *Erythronium dens-canis* has been recorded in European gardens since 1596

LEFT: Wild forms of the water iris *Iris sibirica* have been found in many areas of Northern Europe for 500 years

The Mayflower story

I remember trailing arbutus, creeping around an old cemetery overgrown with trees and visited once or twice a year by someone with a scythe. The cemetery wasn't the most exciting place on earth from most vantage points, but I would wander up there in spring, clear away fallen leaves from the patch, sit on a toppled tombstone and commune with the Mayflower, trailing arbutus, *Epigaea repens*.

The wildflower was insignificant for much of the year; its thready stems and battered little leaves didn't really beckon during June or July. But in May, every pink-lipped flower of that ground-hugging creeper held a whole perfume bottle of fragrance in its petals. I would crawl on hands and knees, bury my nose in the blossoms and inhale a breathtaking scent that lingered in my memory all year.

Arbutus featured prominently in Native American folklore and legends. They related that, every spring, Seegun (the summer spirit) came to claim the earth from Peboan (the spirit of winter). As Seegun thawed the forest, Peboan slowly withered away until all that remained were the furs that he wore. From those furs, arbutus leaves sprang and Seegun nestled them into the soil, her warm breath forcing the plants to blossom. Although patches of snow were still scattered throughout the forest, arbutus was a symbol that Seegun possessed the earth.

Trailing arbutus was abundant when the Pilgrims came to North America and dubbed it 'the Mayflower' in honor of its month of bloom and also to commemorate the ship that brought them to the New World. For centuries the little flower was prolific throughout the woods in southern New England, where many folks celebrated the first sunny days of spring by trotting off to find a patch of trailing arbutus in the woods, returning home with a bouquet of its aromatic blossoms.

But that's where the problems began. With the Industrial Revolution people moved cityward, but memories of rural roots or traditions encouraged city dwellers to send peddlars and florists to pick trailing arbutus wholesale and bring the flowers to the city. By the end of the 19th century, commercial collectors had grown so greedy that several states deemed it necessary to pass laws protecting the plant. However the laws – largely ignored and unenforceable – were allegedly based primarily on sentiment as the Mayflower was still common enough in 1918 for Massachussetts to declare it their state flower.

At the same time, and more seriously, forests were slipping away. The Mayflower likes shade overhead and an acid soil rich in forest litter underfoot, and it often grew in association with chestnut trees, which disappeared rapidly after chestnut blight began its rampage in the early 1900s. Well-meaning efforts to transplant *Epigaea repens* generally failed due to an essential symbiotic fungus clinging around the roots. It is nearly impossible to dig trailing arbutus without damaging the root fungus, so plants starve to death before the balance can be restored.

People foresaw the demise of the Mayflower, and in March 1925 Massachusetts attempted to save its floral emblem by passing an emergency law levying a $50.00 fine on anyone found collecting blossoms and a $100.00 fine on anyone collecting for profit. Even so, it was astonishing how rapidly the Mayflower slipped away. The Plant Buyer's Index of 1927 listed 25,000 plants of *Epigaea repens* available wholesale. By 1931, there were none on the market. Currently, although *Epigaea repens* is not officially considered an endangered species, few New Englanders have ever seen or smelled the Mayflower.

I consider myself fortunate to have a memory of its fragrance buried in my youth. Once an integral element of local folk heritage and spring traditions, the Mayflower, like so many other heirloom wildflowers, has slipped into obscurity.

WILDFLOWER ROOTS

There are more than 200,000 vascular plants on the globe, and each and every one was once (and still might be) a wildflower somewhere. Ancestors of the pelargoniums that are coddled on our windowsills run rampant around the Cape of Good Hope in South Africa. The poinsettias proffered at festivities during the winter holidays grow unbidden in Mexico. Certain wildflowers are indigenous to only a confined ecological niche, too specialized to adapt comfortably into adjacent locales. Others have been introduced into cultivation and nurtured in gardens beyond their native region. But many quietly remain wildlings, growing only in the woods, tidal pools or rock outcroppings where they are happy, the least adaptable and most specialized among them are most prone to extinction.

The wildflowers that cast seeds and roots merrily over the broadest ranges usually enjoy the greatest popularity. They are the plants that figured strongly in folklore and custom to become part of the universal network of wildflowers. When a wildflower was recognized and loved by significant masses of people, many uses, legends and names grew up around that plant. Some of those customs and associations traveled broadly, others remained unique to an area. Dandelions were called pishamoolags in Ireland, dumble dores in Labrador, pissabeds in Newfoundland, dashalogas in Rhode Island, doonhead clocks in North Carolina, swine-snouts and witch-gowans elsewhere. Other wildflowers were known by even more numerous, but equally inventive epithets. Foxglove, for example, has answered to hundreds of common names throughout its long career. The quantity of common names amassed by a wildflower gives you some indication of how broadly that plant spread and how beloved it was by the people.

FOXGLOVES

At different times, in different parts of Northern Europe, foxgloves rejoiced in the following names, some of which are still common:
Bee catchers, Beehives, Blobs, Bloody bells, Bloody fingers, Bunny rabbit mouths, Clothes pegs, Cowflops, Deadmen's bellows, Deadmen's fingers, Dog's lugs, Dragon's mouth, Fairy cap, Fairy fingers, Fairy's petticoats, Finger cap, Finger boot, Flop a dock, Flop-poppy, Fox-and-leaves, Foxflops, Granny's fingers, Gooseflops, Gapmouth, Hill poppy, King's Elwand, Lady's fingers, Lion's mouth, Long purples, Mary's candle, Popbells, Popdock, Poppers, Rabbit's flower, Scabbit dock, Scotch mercury, Snapjack, Thimble flower, Throatwort, Tiger's mouth, Virgin's fingers, Witch's thimble.

The foxglove was a fairy plant or a goblin's plant in England, Wales and Ireland, a plant of magic, with supernatural powers. Fairies were supposed to have given the corollas of the flower to foxes who wore them as gloves so as to sneak in magic silence up to poultry or away from hunters. Among their many powers, foxgloves were once considered able to bring back children taken away by the fairies.

In many country areas in Northern Europe foxgloves were used for centuries as a purge against fevers, colds and other illnesses. A popular story relates how in 1785 an early physician was believed to be given foxglove as a remedy by a witch, he then researched its properties to find that it acted upon the heart and was a good diuretic, establishing its future importance as an instrument against heart disease. The cardiac drugs digoxin and digitoxin are still extracted from Digitalis lanata.

LEFT: Foxgloves *Digitalis purpurea have long been used in medicine*   RIGHT: Soapwort *Saponaria* is still used in washing fragile textiles

ABOVE: Bluebells *Hyacinthoides non scripta* are a favorite British wildflower   BELOW: Violets are among the 400 species in the Viola family

FROM FIELD TO STORE

By whatever names they were known, wildflowers were once integral to daily life. Most people were intimately familiar with their regional flora and knew the identity, blooming times and particular uses of their botanical neighbors. Individuals, families and whole communities interacted with wildflowers on a regular basis. They were woven into the thread of daily life. Not only were wildflower petals plucked to discern whether he loved you, or loved you not, wild plants were involved in many of the regular tasks necessary to stay alive.

Plenty of wildflowers, including chickweed, dandelion, purslane and stinging nettle, were once considered culinary treats in season. At one time, eating from the wild was an important way of surviving the dearth between the time the last potato was put on the table in late winter and spring and summer harvests. When people were starving, nettles and plantain leaves seemed a delicacy. By necessity, the average man, woman and child could readily distinguish between the poisonous Bad Henry *Mercurialis annua* and the similar looking wild salad herb Good King Henry *Chenopodium bonus-henricus*. This latter plant and its many near relatives now feature in upmarket vegetable seed catalogues, along with dandelions! These days you may walk into an urban supermarket or trendy restaurant to find such plants have become fashionable ingredients, with purchasers paying a high premium for eating pre-packed purslanes or corn salads, or the rather unlovely samphire – humble wild plants.

In Elizabethan times, in England, the salt-tolerant samphire, *Salicornia maritima*, was used as a potherb – Shakespeare mentions 'the dreadful trade' of harvesting samphire from the cliffs of Dover (dangling from strong ropes and undoubtedly with some loss of life). Samphire can still be found around estuaries in some limestone areas, and it is being studied as a possible food crop in desert regions where only brackish water is available for irrigation. But many other ancient wildflowers have been lost to time, and most of their uses long forgotten. Others undoubtedly also hold secrets yet to be rediscovered and harnessed. Only 10 per cent of the world's flora has been tested for possible medicinal value. A smaller percentage has been explored as food crops.

Until relatively recent times, every wildflower was known and valued for its unique qualities; those that weren't edible were put to a multitude of other uses. The delightfully pungent leaves of ambrosia, *Chenopodium botrys*, were tucked into the folds of laundry as a moth-repellant. Wildflowers with strong fibers were woven into cloth – stinging nettles can be used to weave a fabric that is more durable than linen. Detergents were made of numerous wildflowers including soapwort *Saponaria officinalis* which is still used today to clean textiles in museum collections. And even more crucially, wildflowers have always been harvested to furnish medicines – even conventional medicine includes some form of plant drug in many prescriptions, and herbal medicine has never died out but is regaining popularity. We now know that many wild plants contain antibacterial, antifungal and antibiotic agents; others have sedative or stimulant qualities, others relieve pain or restore energy.

Folk medicine has often required liberal gathering of plants, but they used to be respected as part of the wild landscape, their harvest was generally regulated by the laws of nature with a desire to keep the supply sustainable. Perhaps because they were so necessary in times past, wildflowers were cherished and protected. They remain essential today as we explore new uses and exploit ancient employments. We must take care of them all.

Before the Age of Reason folk history was as important in Western life as it remains today in less developed cultures. Legends explained the turning of the seasons, the creation of life and the forces of good and evil to people who had no understanding whatsoever of science. Flowers could fend off dangerous forces. Folk history helped bind the family and community together.

The legends differed depending upon what part of the world you happened to inhabit. Native Americans had one set of talismans, while Europeans had another. During the Middle Ages, foxglove was thought to deter witches in some parts of the world, and superstitious Welsh housewives later used a black dye of the leaves to paint witch-proof black lines on the stone floors of their cottages. In other parts of Britain, picking foxglove was thought to offend the fairies, with dire consequences.

Garlic was introduced into England in 1548 from the Mediterranean, where it was considered an aphrodisiac, while in the Orient, that pungent wildflower was held at arm's length and believed to possess magical qualities. Much later, German miners brought garlic cloves when descending into the mines to ward off the evil spirits underground.

STORIES AND SEASONS

Wildflowers mark the seasons. Just as the Mayflower signaled to the Pilgrims that their first long hard winter would soon be relieved by spring, the blossoming of different wildflowers punctuates the flow of the year. When coltsfoot blossomed, American settlers knew that it was time to put peas in the soil; and it was safe to plant corn when maple leaves were as large as mouse ears. An old English saying proclaims "On St Valentine's day, sow beans in the clay." Henry David Thoreau knew that bird songs would lessen after the dogbane *Amsonia tabernaemontana* leaves turned yellow in autumn. In Cedar Falls, Iowa, the residents traditionally put winter clothes away promptly when "the blue flags bloomed". And British countryfolk once told the time by the pale blue flowers of wild chicory which open at 7 o'clock and close at midday.

Whatever you believed, wherever you dwelled, wildflowers were once part of the language, part of the lore for that region. Where a wildflower was prevalent and its blossoming was a much-anticipated moment, festivals and holidays sometimes accompanied its blooming. In Britain, June 23rd was traditionally St. John's Day when garlands of St. John's wort, *Hypericum perforatum*, were hung on doors and windows as a talisman against evil.

Superstitions are no longer celebrated so outwardly, but wildflowers are still fêted as star attractions during seasonal festivals. It wouldn't be May Day without apple blossoms accompanying the festivities. In the United States, daisies are a crucial fixture on July 4th. Although we pay them only passing acknowledgement and sometimes blame them for reclaiming gardens that were once their domain, wildflowers are still vital. Many of their roles in society's clockwork have not yet been explored.

BELOW: Purple coneflower *Echinacea purpurea* above globe thistle *Echinops ritro*   ABOVE: Monarch caterpillar on *Asclepias tuberosa*

A striking dark form of the traditional annual cornflower *Centaurea cyanus*

WHERE ARE THEY NOW?

People tend to rally around the beady-eyed, soft and furry issues of habitat loss. We may mourn when a familiar flower slips away, yet countless specialized meek and mild wildflowers that most people never encountered are also slipping away. They might not have noteworthy flowers, they might not be sufficiently plentiful to figure in the heirloom traditions handed down through the generations, but they might still be essential to the ecosystem. All too frequently the extinction of one single species of plant can confer the same fate on tens, hundreds, or even thousands of animals, birds and insects. And physically insignificant wild plants could possess virtues as yet unexplored. When any plant slips into oblivion, the bell tolls for us all.

Although wildflowers have been harvested for culinary, medicinal and other uses through-out history, sometimes in considerable quantities, most were still plentiful 250 years ago. Wildflower populations weren't in peril prior to the Industrial Revolution, their colonies weren't greatly stressed until the 1800s. But when populations shifted cityward the new concrete, plant-bereft domain left people with memories of but infrequent access to the native blossoms that figured so firmly in ritual and leg-end. So wildflowers were brought to them. Eager customers paid florists to go into the woods and meadows and pick favorite blossoms or deliver pots of traditional symbols of spring into the great metropolises. That's when it was first noticed that popular wildflowers were beginning to falter.

In the United States, the first conservation law was passed in 1892 in Connecticut to pro-tect the climbing fern, *Lygodium palmatum,* gath-ered wholesale by florists as a bouquet filler. In 1901 the Society for the Protection of Native Plants issued a leaflet addressing the plight of the climbing fern, warning of its impending destruction. Perhaps this warning was not strong enough, or maybe it came too late. Although not globally endangered, the climbing fern now needs protection in New England where it was once plentiful.

For some reason, conservationists rallied around the climbing fern early in its career as a much sought out and frequently poached wild-flower although other wildflowers were also shrinking due to commercial harvest from the wild. And the problem continues. In Britain, the bluebell *Hyacinthoides non-scripta* is one of the national symbols of spring, where whole tracts of woodland used to be carpeted in blue. In 1998 a law had to be passed to protect the once ubiquitous woodland flower, because it was dug so relentlessly from its native habitats.

Some experts suggest that wild animals pose a greater threat and do more damage to wildflower numbers than all the battalions of florists and herbalists that descend upon the woodlands to poach. The number of voracious deer roving parts of the American countryside has increased drastically in recent years and they've taken their toll on wild orchids, gentians and lilies. In Northern Europe rabbit populations are also at an all time high. But the greatest of all current threats to wildflowers is habitat loss. The wanton destruction of wildflower habitats has wreaked incredible havoc with the delicate balance of nature.

As human populations grow, agricultural operations expand, leading to the overgrazing of land once dominated by wildflowers. Large-scale agricultural development wields a worse evil than merely altering the land that it steals for its immediate operations. It changes the entire environment. Its side effects include addi-tional pollution, herbicide run-off and pesticide drift. The wildflowers that survive its immediate encroachment are visited by fewer pollinators and sickened by chemicals.

There are other ramifications to increasing populations. People put up shopping centers, parking lots and airports where wildflowers once dominated. They want roads, leisure facilities, fuel, shelter, tennis courts and lawn-carpeted backyards. As a result, mining operations increase, suburbs sprawl, the natural environment dwindles – wildflowers are squashed and squelched.

To survive fruitfully, many wildflowers require the stretching swathes of land that pre-vailed before the Industrial Revolution. Some wildflowers are especially fond of virgin habitats, and virgin habitats are themselves endangered. In the United States, the imperiled Midwestern prairies tell a particularly poignant story of vanishing lands. Swallowed by agricul-ture, they are virtually gone.

Meanwhile, Europe has even less in the way of natural vegetation left, with destruction of habitats escalating out of control in the last half century – Britain alone has lost 98 per cent of its native flower meadows, 60 per cent of its heaths, half its marshes and half its virgin wood-lands in the last 40 years.

The numbers are frightening. Ten per cent of the world's flora is tottering on the verge of endangerment. In other words, of the 250,000 chronicled species of plants dwelling on the globe, 25,000 are imperiled. Many of these disappearances are occurring in the species-rich, yet over-exploited rainforests of the world, but a horrific number of losses are happening every day right under our own noses. While people are becoming increasingly aware of the plight of some of our most beautiful wildflowers, such as orchids, and of the healing potential of others, many wildings stand no chance of ever becom-ing heirlooms. Of the 250,000 plants reputed to live somewhere on the globe, only a handful of those wildflowers are heirlooms. It's tragic to think that fewer will have the opportunity to reach heirloom status in future generations.

Perhaps you couldn't call Furbish's lousewort an heirloom flower prior to 1976. Virtually no one knew of the existence of that shy snapdragon, indigenous only along the shores of the St. John River in Maine – besides perhaps Miss Kate Furbish who found the flower in 1880. But Pedicularis furbishae would never be seen again if the Dickey-Lincoln hydroelectric project had been built.

The endangered little lousewort took on the United States Army Corps of Engineers. Amazingly, the lousewort won. So now the little plant, a latter day David fighting a powerful Goliath, has earned a place in folk his-tory right alongside Paul Bunyan. The sparse little lousewort has attained heir-loom status.

Unfortunately, there are many other wildflowers out there that will fall victim to the bulldozer before they are discovered.

The giant helleborine orchid *Epipactis gigantea*

The showy orchis *Orchis spectabilis*

PRESERVING WILDFLOWERS

There is no easy fix, but you can help. By adopting wildflowers, planting them in your garden and taking them under your wing, you shelter them from their precarious existence in the wild. Wildflower gardening doesn't take the place of habitat preservation, but it helps wild-flowers survive. And it renders them intimate, strengthening their bond with future generations. It makes strangers into heirlooms.

Planting wildflowers is no new fad. Wildflowers were encouraged along roadsides as early as 1285 when Britain's anti-bandit laws were passed, stipulating that there could be no highwayman-hiding trees, bushes or ditches within 200 feet of roads linking market towns. Before sugar was imported, honey plants were cultivated, before exotics came into cultivation,

people were nurturing wild plants for healing. Not all of those wildflowers remained solid fix-tures in the garden, but many — bred to bear bigger, better flower trusses — have become common garden plants. Primroses, foxgloves, geums, violets and the like are now classified firmly as garden fare. They are now the heirlooms of the garden rather than the heirlooms of the field.

There may be nothing new about planting wildflowers, but native-plant gardening has become increasingly vital as plants left to their own devices slip away. As long as the wildflow-ers sold for garden use are nursery-propagated rather than dug from the wild, the trend has the firm support of wildflower organizations.

However, it isn't quite as easy as it sounds. Don't expect wildflowers to fend for themselves. Prepare the site, amend the soil and

Preserving the Prairie

The prairie will never slip away if Marlyn Sachtjen has anything to do with it. In the height of Wisconsin's gardening season in midsummer, Marlyn is forever watching the weath-er and praying for rain. Without rain, she might have to water the sweeping wildflower meadow in her backyard which entails an awful lot of hose lugging and sprinkler wielding. But if need be, she's perfectly willing to set up the sprinklers to come to the aid of her prairie.

It must be twenty years or more since Marlyn first planted her piece of prairie. She struts around in her wide-brimmed sun hat, treading the pieces of salvaged carpet that she's laid out for paths, addressing each grass and

wildflower as if it is a fond family member — lupines, big bluestem (Marlyn's 'big blue'), little bluestem, blazing stars, milkweeds, prairie clovers and more.

Marlyn has always been a prairie activist, encouraging school groups to return their fields to the wild state, lecturing to all kinds of organizations, saving her seeds and sharing them with others. Summer days slip away invested in the duties of nipping seed-heads if necessary, making certain that aggressive prairie plants don't muscle out their neighbors, marching around the paths, marshalling the plants. Her winters are spent burning the stubble (if snow accumulation permits) to make ready for the next year.

Ask Marlyn to talk about her prairie, how she made it and why, and she'll ask if you've got a couple of years to spend listening. She calls herself 'a crusader to rid the world of lawn grass', accusing lawns of promoting the wanton use of pesticides and chemicals.

The autumn after her longtime husband died, Marlyn decided to embark on another major venture rather than spending her time mourn-ing. "My newest mammoth project is to convert my remaining six acres of land into a shady woodland situation," she explains. "I've got strong motives," she declares with only a slight tremble in her aging voice, "there are wildflowers to preserve."

defend your introductions from encroachment of more aggressive weeds, just as you would maintain any planting. Although it sounds like a contradiction in terms, you can't just plunk wildflowers in the wild and expect them to survive. You've got to give them a fighting chance and care for them until their colonies are established. They tend to be stubborn and headstrong plants with specific needs. Before adopting a wildflower, study its native habitat, then try to replicate that environment as closely as possible. If the right conditions are met, the flowers will thrive.

There is a flip side to wildflower gardening. Not every wildflower is a welcome guest. There can be a fine line between nurturing an exotic wildflower and inviting an aggressive weed into your midst. Without the proper climatic controls and predators, wildflowers can run rampant. Beautiful introductions can have devastating consequences, nudging out indigenous plants that may grow less strongly. In the United States, loosestrife chokes the waterways of the Northeast, kudzu encroaches on the Southeast, honeysuckle engulfs the Midwest and leafy spurge grows roughshod in the West. Nature is a delicate balance, caution is essential. Before you plant, learn as much as you can about the personality of the plant you are inviting into your garden. Choose wildflowers indigenous to your region rather than dabbling in exotics from further afield. One ecosystem's heirloom can become another area's nightmare.

Once established, native plantings should survive with minimal intervention. In arid regions, desert wildflowers will not stress water resources. In damp areas, bog wildflowers will not suffer from the wet underfootings. You'll be saving the native floral wealth, and you'll benefit all the insects, birds and other wildlife that interact with the plant. When you steward wildflowers, the ramifications go beyond the plants you're nurturing.

Many wildflower gardeners will be able to tell you stories for every Joe Pye weed, Indian plantain and symplocarpus in their gardens. One of my favorites is the way Mary Jane Hatfield came by a generous stand of dragonroot Arisaema dracontium: For years, she delivered parcels to a neighbor's shack in Boone County, Iowa ("no running water, but a yard full of plants") and admired the dragonroot growing all around the foundation. "The 84 year old lady who lived in the shack was so poor. She had no family, no friends, her cotton dress was held together with pins and she was constantly swearing."

There were no heirs and, after her neighbor's death, Mary Jane was given permission to dig any plants that she could salvage before the land was sold and the shack razed. So she brought home the rare Arisaema dracuntium which now grows happily around the foundation of her home. Now Mary Jane nurtures one of the last colonies of that Jack-in-the-pulpit relative. "Now there's very little left, except in my yard and the yards of friends."

3

The cottage garden legacy

Many heirloom flowers owe their life to the cottage garden. It was in that little plot of land, tucked in the yard between the house and the lane, that the average citizen first planted a few blossoms to liven up the scenery. And that same modest garden nurtured heirlooms throughout the centuries. The cottage garden kept heirlooms from slipping away, it was their homeground and refuge – far from the fickle winds of fashion.

Cottage gardens can be found among the working class all over the world. The first were not in the country at all but in suburbs of the free cities of Italy and Germany in the early Middle Ages. Here emerged the first free men, craftsmen and tradesmen protected by guilds and rich enough to own their small houses. And it was in the towns that men most needed to cultivate potherbs and salads, away from the wild provisions of the country-side. But the cottage garden in England is generally considered the prototype, so it is there we'll chronicle its rise, fall and rebirth.

ABOVE: Yarrow *Achillea millefolium* was brought into cottage gardens early on as a wound herb

LEFT: Campanulas, often known as bell-flowers, have been cottage garden favorites for around 400 years

In 1349 the Black Death, or bubonic plague, struck England. It decimated the population, killing a third of England's inhabitants, laying the countryside to waste and leaving manorial crops unharvested. This tragedy resulted in a new system of tenancy that eventually made cottage gardens possible. Suddenly, lords were forced to rent their land to tenants as a source of income and to ensure the land was sown and harvested. Landlords came into being and simultaneously, the cottager appeared in the English landscape and social system. Each cottage, no matter how humble, had a meager yard, and so cottage gardens were born.

The cottage garden's primary function was as a place where food for the table could be grown. A poor countryman's primary sources of sustenance were vegetables, berries and fruits, (with an occasional rabbit poached at some risk from the landowner's forest). Cottage gardens were rooted firmly in survival; floral refine-ments and adornments came after the provision of food and healing herbs.

A cottage garden today

Close your eyes and imagine a cottage garden, and you'll probably conjure up a vision not far removed from the voluptuous landscape that wraps around Tasha Tudor's Corgi Cottage in northern New England. There, a complex labyrinth of paths so slender that you must walk single file (and often snag your hem nevertheless) wind up a breakneck hill. There, chimney bellflowers, 17th century dianthus, poppies that came from Tasha's Scottish nanny and roses that remain nameless but have traveled with Tasha from home to home throughout her long life surround a cottage in a cloud of bloom during New England's brief but dramatic growing season. The gardens are retrospective. And similarly, the cottage seems to harken back in time. Corgi Cottage was built less than thirty years ago, but the house was constructed purposely to look as if it had weathered that site for two hundred years or more. Vines climb up arbors curved over the walkways, vines encase little thickets hiding a table and chairs where tea is served when Tasha takes the time to carry the Canton china gingerly down the hill.

Vines scamper the walls of the house and snare your curls as you wander amidst beds dense with poet's narcissus, tulips, Johnny-jump-ups, forget-me-nots, crown imperials, single hollyhocks, fragrant iris and bicolored sweet peas. The season is short, to be sure, but even the porch is bedecked with potted bulbs and lilies forced to open before they would normally burst from the ground.

A children's illustrator by profession and inclination (and a rather well-known one at that), Tasha's flowers serve a practical function — acting as models for her work. But really, that's just an excuse. The profusion of flowers has been amassed because Tasha is first and foremost a collector. She collects old garden tools, rickety wheelbarrows, Belgian pots by the stackload, lusterware, crockery and handwoven baskets. Inside the cottage, vintage-style apparel crowds her closet, antique textiles fill the drawers. Tasha accumulates profusion in every avenue of her life.

And she collects plants with the same compulsion that drives her to acquire all things old and wonderful. So it's no surprise that scarcely a square foot around Corgi Cottage is left unplanted. But it's not a hodgepodge. Instead, she has created a place of rhapsody in melodious colors, with balanced hues and graduated tones. There are no strident shades, everything harmonizes, and it keeps right on harmonizing as the season wears on.

You can walk out of her back door at any moment between May and September to find a splendid display spread before you. It's all seamlessly executed. However, Tasha Tudor has a ready response for anyone with the effrontery to ask to see the plans for the cottage garden surrounding her New England home. "I never designed the garden," she insists, "it just grew like Topsy."

Tasha admits that the stone walls were drawn out on paper. "And if I had those walls built today, I wouldn't let Mr. Herrick waiver from my plan one inch," she'll proclaim. "I told him to bend the wall inward with pockets to tuck in pinks and whatnot. Instead, he built her straight and now she's beginning to lean out. I wouldn't let it happen today, I can promise you. I've grown savage in my old age."

As for the plantings, they increased over the years, by whim and will. Some seeded themselves shamelessly, to be sure. Others were invited to increase, but not necessarily through a great expenditure invested in rootstock. Whenever Tasha buys plants, she purchases them in quantities of three, which might lead you to believe that some guidelines are being followed. But there's no master plan. "I buy three and put each in a different situation. I watch, I see if one thrives, and then I move the others to that same sort of place."

When Tasha feels as though she's failing with a plant, she takes immediate action. Books are pulled off the shelf and consulted, professors at northern universities are called upon, letters are written to experts in the field. Nothing is planted and then forgotten. Tasha is a model steward. Corgi Cottage might not have a master plan, but a great deal of caring and nurturing is invested in each flowerbed.

The prototypical cottage garden wasn't an elaborate affair, by any means. There was just enough room for vegetables and salad herbs to nestle cheek to jowl, planted for harvest as needed during the growing season, with a carefully calculated surplus for storage through the winter. Beans, ground for flour as the main staple of the diet, were required in such large quantities that they generally grew in a field devoted solely to that one crop. When grains took the place of beans, they were also given a field of their own. When potatoes eventually hit the cottage garden scene, in the 17th century, they were similarly grown in a separate plot. By current definitions, the original cottage yard could hardly be classified as a garden. It was a place where a little of this and a handful of that could be grown. If there were rows, they were brief. Cabbages (worts) were universal, and other staples included various other brassicas, roots, onions, leeks, and herbs for the pot.

When Chaucer wrote his Canterbury Tales between 1386-1387, his pilgrims passed a series of humble cottages as they journeyed. And the yard that he documented was a rather rude affair. Although it was undeniably replete with vegetables and herbs, it also served domestic functions that weren't solely horticultural: there is something rather un-gardenesque about a tightly cramped place where refuse from the house was discarded and the movable "private house" was positioned. Children played in the same yard that hosted the livestock. Chickens pecked seedlings, kept weeds at bay, controlled insects and fertilized the crops with very fresh manure. It was a simple, and not unattractive scene, but it wasn't necessarily the type of garden we would strive to recapture today.

When you think of an early cottage garden, don't imagine an entirely functional scene devoid of any ornamental features. Every gardener – from the lord to the peasant – will try to the best of his ability to create a pleasing scene when working with the surrounding landscape. So the cottage garden did not solely confine itself to plants that we now classify as vegetables. Even in the 14th century some cottage gardens probably boasted madonna lilies and other flowers gleaned from monastic and manorial gardens, just as useful herbs and wildflowers were sown or planted in the earliest gardens. Violets and primroses were pretty as well as useful salad herbs, and it was not uncommon to see beds edged with aromatic lavender and other low growing herbs. As early as the 15th century most of the humblest gardens already had a scented rose or two, such as *Rosa gallica* or *R x alba*.

Gradually, more and more flowers that were beautiful as well as good for some purpose or other slipped into the beds. Even if they weren't actually "essential", some excuse was found for inviting ornamentals into the cottage yard. Given a little ingenuity, an application could be found for everything. By the 1500s, decorative yarrow (used to reduce a fever), lady's mantle (employed to stay bleeding), chives (added to season salads), columbine (used as a lotion for sore throats), corydalis (used as a diuretic), borage (availed to dispel melancholy) and bellflower (applied for complaints of the throat) – native to and readily available for the digging in Great Britain – all took their place in the cottage garden. Pennyroyal was grown for flavoring water, germander for cough syrup; tansy and wormwood, betony and mullein were all among the prototypical cottage garden flowers. Cranesbill, foxglove, centaury, campions and monkshood all appeared early on. Those flowers were gaily interplanted with the vegetables, giving the cottage garden the informality that has served as its hallmark throughout the ages.

By 1557, Thomas Tusser recorded that the average small farmer had an orchard as well as a garden surrounding his cottage. And he also observed that the cottage garden was typically

Believed to date from the 1700s, *Aquilegia vulgaris* 'Nora Barlow' is still available, and tends to come true from seed

Commonly called "bachelor's buttons", cornflowers *Centaurea cyanus* have graced cottage gardens and arable fields for centuries

cared for by the wife in her "spare time". It was a nod toward frivolity, but still mandated by the necessity of keeping the family fed and doctored. In addition to the herbs that already made the cottage garden their home, the first flowers that greeted Thomas Tusser were wild-flowers that had become so essential and frequently employed that common folks felt compelled to keep them conveniently close by.

During the 16th and 17th centuries increasing numbers of green immigrants also entered the scene. Fritillaries arrived from Turkey, gladioli from the Mediterranean, lychnis was imported from Russia, the daylily traveled from China and jasmine ventured over from the Himalayas. When they first arrived, those rarities were certainly not the property of the peasants but were cosseted by the nobility in gardens that were both grand and formal. But, forbidden or not, cuttings were too easily snipped by covetous garden boys and seed was too simply collected by servants. Once exotic, these flowers became just as much a part of the folk culture as the native wildflowers that preceded them.

Jasmines, clematis, and (of great importance later on) the scarlet runner bean could all be found growing in cottage gardens at the end of the 16th century, along with auriculas from Flanders, Turk's cap lilies from Asia as well as wallflowers, stocks, tulips, narcissus and hyacinths. All became part of the melting pot that was the cottage garden.

As erstwhile rarities became common they were banished from the great gardens by new introductions, and cottage gardens came to preserve these old plants – particularly old species and cultivars of dianthus, as well as polyanthus, ranunculus and shrub roses. The cottage garden took plants as they were provided, and hung on to them if they were pleasing. In the cottage garden, today's novelties have always sat comfortably beside yesterday's heirlooms.

HEIRLOOM BULBS

Like many plant preservationists, Scott Kunst realized a penchant for heirlooms in his youth. "I always gardened," he recalls. "I hated history as a subject in high school, it always seemed so dry and remote, but I was fascinated by old gardens." Scott met his first single peony when he bought an old house in Michigan, and that's when he was introduced to his initial tiger lily and privet hedge. Those plants kindled his interest, sent him researching historic gardens and inspired him to return to school, earning his Masters degree in Historic Preservation. But it wasn't until Scott Kunst's favorite tulip, 'Prince of Austria', disappeared from the market that he began to ponder the possibilities of selling heirloom bulbs.

That was when Old House Gardens of Ann Arbor, Michigan, was born (see page 182). Scott began collecting vintage bulbs, linking with other kindred spirits, selling the surplus and finally published a catalog in 1993, the first of its kind devoted solely to heirloom bulbs. The business has become a full time job, and wonderful things have happened: in addition to preserving 'Prince of Austria', Scott has put 'White Aster' dahlia, a pompom type from 1879, back in circulation. Thanks to his efforts, the flamed tulips 'Lac van Rijn' and 'Zomerschoon' (both c.1620) from the Dutch national bulb museum, Hortus Bulborum, are readily available.

Writing for many magazines, speaking at symposia and sparking the interest of kindred spirits in the Netherlands and Britain, Scott Kunst has roused interest in heirloom bulbs and changed the face of gardens. Deep in the trenches of horticulture rather than working on a design level, he prefers to call himself a horticulturist rather than a historian. As Scott puts it, "To me, plants are the heart of the garden."

COTTAGE GARDEN ELEMENTS

Cottage gardens all shared one universal trait. By necessity, they were all surrounded by a hedge or fence of one sort or another. After all, roaming livestock had to be kept at bay during a period of history when animals were driven down the lane regularly on their way to the common pasture. To prevent the inroads of nibbling passersby, the cottage garden fence was necessarily sturdy and well-maintained, and hedges were often encouraged to reach barricade proportions.

If there was a formal element to the cottage garden, it surfaced in the meticulously clipped topiary shrubs that often resided within the cottage realm. Most ga rdens had sturdy hedges, usually of privet, later of yew or box, and man loves to make patterns. The art of topiary was borrowed from the gardens of the great estates – often brought back by undergardeners – and embraced with little concern as to whether it fitted with the cottage garden scene. The hedge had to be kept within bounds, and it was more interesting and challenging, as well as making an individual statement, to clip it into some fanciful shape. Shrubs were also sometimes sheared to shape – apparently rosemary, grown for medicinal, culinary and housecleaning purposes, was frequently clipped into whimsical shapes, but as early as the 16th century this plant was strictly left for the women to clip, while hedges were the man's domain.

Arbors were rarely a feature of the poorest gardens, but became popular in yeomen's gardens from the 15th century onward, providing a foothold for vines and welcome shade under which to perform some of the household tasks such as scrubbing the laundry or shelling the beans. Ironically, arbors have become one of the most popular features of later, retrospective cottage gardens, surviving into modern times along with the heirlooms they nurtured.

Vines were usually encouraged to clamber up whatever was at hand. The chicken coop and outhouse provided vertical walls for some, while others were supported up columns or wigwams of hazel sticks. Apart from the space-saving advantage of vertically-growing productive plants, fragrant vines served important functions in the yard where the family most often congregated in summer. Their scent, beautiful in its own right, also conveniently masked the smells of the privy, and vines often clambered around its walls. The hop vine became a common character in latter day cottage gardens, though they were forbidden in Britain by Henry VI and weren't widespread in cottage gardens before the 18th century.

The hedge or fence defined and protected the outer boundaries of a cottage garden, within which the garden was laid out in the simple design of straight rectangular beds, sometimes raised but more often laid simply side by side with flowers scattered between the brief rows of herbs and food crops, and straight brick or stone paths dividing beds. Although the cottage garden appeared to be a confusion of cabbages and cornflowers, larkspur and lettuces when in full swing, the sense of profusion was created by the plants rather than the design.

Old-fashioned flowers often seemed unkempt because of their dimensions. Most cottage garden plants were initially tall and lanky. If things tumbled one into the next, it was partly because they all bore long stems balancing a few blossoms on top before breeders took them in hand in the 19th century and evened out the ratio. Thereafter the cottage garden was not easy to recreate. Tidy new annuals just don't do the trick. Long stems, subtle colors, and long-tarrying bloomers created the look.

Certain plants have always worked well within the cottage garden venue. Contenders have to be capable of enduring without complaint all the changes in climate typical of an average year

LEFT TO RIGHT: Cottage garden favorites: Larkspur *Consolida ambigua* and lupines *Lupinus perennis*

as well as an occasional severe season. And they tend to be noteworthy – little nondescript plants that can't compete favorably with their neighbors have rarely been introduced, nor botanical bullies other than those early wildflowers originally invited in for medicinal purposes. By the 18th century most of what we consider to be common cottage garden flowers had arrived. Spired bloomers such as foxgloves, larkspur, aconites, delphiniums, hyacinths and lupines were prevalent. Scabious, alliums, stocks, wallflowers, anemones and ranunculus grew alongside peonies and hollyhocks. Fragrance was especially coveted and could be found in pinks, roses, primroses, daffodils, lavender and nepeta. But any plant that would cheerfully perform and had an endearing character was invited to commune. If that plant could hold its own, it stayed.

One important function of a cottage garden, in today's terms, is as a repository of old-fashioned flowers and knowledge. Some of these gardens are gene pools preserving genetic information that would otherwise be lost. There are stories of, for example, a particular strain of stocks preserved in the cottage gardens of a small Scottish neighborhood for 350 years. And of a particular nutmeg clove pink preserved in one garden since 1652.

Curiously, some of the plants we consider cottage garden mainstays are relatively recent: bleeding-heart *Dicentra* is only a century old, the lupines you see in most gardens for example were only bred this century, and the bearded iris so popular today are also 20th century developments. Moreover, cottage gardens also sported fruit trees – an apple and a plum tree at least – and soft fruit bushes alongside the vegetables. Raspberries were grown from the 16th century onward in northern Europe, and gooseberries made their way into gardens even earlier, although German gardeners did not bring them in from the wild until the 1800s.

COTTAGE GARDENS REVISITED

The cottage garden landscape remained the province of peasants, small farmers, artisans and tradespeople for centuries. Moneyed gardeners kept their landscapes clipped and current with the trends. The slightly scruffy, rather dirty-behind-the-ears cottage garden seemed inferior to people who had the sophistication to follow fashion and keep abreast of the newest foreign introductions. When a plant was deemed too "common" by fashionable gardeners it was summarily abandoned in favor of something new and fashionable. But from the 14th to the 19th centuries the cottage garden remained oblivious to such trends; changes in garden style and art made little impact.

But all that changed in the late 19th century . Mary Russell Mitford began the rhapsodies about country gardens and traditional plants in the middle of the 19th century. She made the rural realm – complete with primrose outings and violet nosegays – seem fashionable rather than feeble, and she set the stage for later writers who were boisterously vehement about the importance of returning to rurality. The cottage garden became the source of ideas for larger gardens, and the heirlooms it nurtured were suddenly sought after and given a hero's welcome by gardeners who could afford to buy whatever they desired. Suddenly, cottage gardens were in the forefront of fashion.

Prominent horticultural commentators Gertrude Jekyll (1843-1932) and William Robinson (1838-1935) were particularly forceful in their praise of cottage gardens. They lived in an age of gardening excess. Wealthy garden owners encouraged incredibly wasteful planting schemes of labor-intensive annual exotics, pulled out when their moment of splendor was past and replanted. But those influential writers proposed a return to the past. They recognized a beauty in the old-fashioned cottage garden with its permanence and waves of seasonal glory. They sought to recapture that mood. And the world listened.

Those writers succeeded in imbuing the cottage garden with a dewy-eyed sentimentality that tugged at the heartstrings of a public in desperate need of deep roots. The romanticism of the cottage garden appealed to a class that certainly need not dwell in a hut. Suddenly, people who commanded many hundred acres and could afford the salaries of several full time gardeners to clip formal plantings, installed little thatched cottages somewhere in their domain. Most importantly, they surrounded those quaint little cottages with plantings. The turn of events was a stroke of luck for heirloom flowers, especially hybrids, many of which might have been lost and forgotten if they weren't revived at just that crucial juncture.

Gertrude Jekyll was especially keen on reviving a lifestyle that she saw as endangered. She was chauffered around the countryside, stopping at cottage gardens to chat with the cottagers and extract their secrets. She noted the resident flora and requested cuttings or seeds if the plant happened to strike her fancy. The flowers that she found in those landscapes provided grist for her garden designs and subjects to be profiled in her writings. She railed against pelargoniums, she decried strident colors and suggested a billowing garden less chromatically riotous than the currently fashionable fancy annual borders. She transformed formal landscapes into places where Lady's mantle and nepeta spilled beyond the edges of the borders. She urged people to invite violas and their ilk into the landscape. She designed brief seasonal displays – spring gardens, summer gardens, autumn gardens – that were glorious during their moment and then were clipped severely back. William Robinson also came to the aid of natives in no uncertain terms, writing venomously about annual bedding schemes and lovingly about the cottage style.

HEIRLOOM ROSES

Speak about heirloom roses for long, and Reverend Douglas Seidel's name always seems to slip into the conversation. He has labored long and hard to bring roses that have slipped into obscurity back into the fold. Take 'Champneys' Pink Cluster', for example, introduced in 1802. Founding the Noisette group, it was the first hybrid between a white musk and pink China raised in North America. Somehow that pink bloomer disappeared from cultivation in the 1950s until Reverend Seidel discovered the shrub growing in Bermuda and brought a cutting home. In an old cemetery in eastern Pennsylvania, not far from his home, old roses, peonies and daylilies were planted on every grave. That's where he discovered 'Little White Pet', a Polyantha from 1879. That dwarf mutant from 'Félicité et Perpétue' had slipped into obscurity until he took cuttings and reintroduced the plant.

Rev. Seidel is particularly keen on preserving the Noisettes. "The Bourbons and the Noisettes were once the mainstays from Zone 6 downwards," Rev. Seidel explains. "Mostly stemming from the 1820s and 1830s, the Noisettes are the earliest crosses between the Musks and the China roses. They were very hardy, they blossomed lavishly, but they bloomed only once a season." For that fault they eventually slipped away. Not only were they rarely sold, but the lingering bushes, traditionally planted as memorials, perished when cemeteries began to use herbicides.

Rev. Seidel is currently planting a Noisette garden at Monticello. "We've got to preserve these plants. They're hardier and more fragrant than many modern roses, and they're a good repository for genetic material."

Fences provide vertical climbing space for scented jasmine *Jasminum officinale* or a backdrop to the spindly *Verbena bonariensis*

ROMANTICIZED VISIONS

The neo-cottage garden of the 19th century was a scrubbed-up, pared-down version of the original, to be sure, but it had many of the same elements. Most notably, this time around, the vegetables were all but nosed out in favor of flowers. Meanwhile, the flowers were often slightly altered by the hands of hybridizers. Campanulas, larkspur, roses, poppies, peonies, cosmos, cleome, dianthus and lupines were all *de rigueur* as they had never been before. New colors were created and new growth habits were encouraged, making the new cottage garden a cleaner affair that it ever dreamed of being when it was born in the 1300s.

The romanticized cottage garden employed and elaborated on many of the same structures as its predecessors. A beeskep had been utilitarian in gardens since the earliest medieval examples when honey was an important sweetener; it was suddenly transformed to provide a quaint focal point. Wellheads were fancified as they had never been before, and the yeoman's arbor metamorphosed into the gazebo or – even more elaborately – the summerhouse. Dovecotes became fashionable garden features, with bird houses for fowl both common and exotic. Peacocks could sometimes be found strutting the cottage paths as well as other rare birds of every feather.

Containers, previously purely functional to coddle tender valuables such as precious calceolarias and dahlias, became widespread and increasingly decorative. Other ornamental elements filtered in. Sundials and rustic furniture of all descriptions were added as focal points or resting areas in the midst of a place where profusion demanded a respite. Fountains, statues and other features trickled in from more formal gardens. The cottage garden had strayed from its roots, but the forum that had nurtured the earliest heirloom flowers was preserved.

AMERICAN COTTAGE GARDENS

Just as the British working class had simple gardens, the earliest colonial gardens in America were also hardworking affairs. The modern interpretation of a proper Pilgrim garden is a series of neatly clipped, boxwood edged herb beds. However, that landscape was more accurately the garden of a wealthy landowner. The rank and file tended the same sort of cottage gardens as they had grown in Britain, with a stronger focus on survival in a new land. Topiary wasn't as frequently a feature, and some of the other extraneous frills only entered later in the cottage garden's metamorphosis. The early American cottage gardeners had all the billowing blossoms and well-manured cabbages that they had previously cultivated in their homeland.

The mood of the American cottage garden was the same slap-happy affair as its European predecessors, but the inventory was slightly different. John Josselyn chronicled his successes and failures with Old World plants in his 1672 treatise, *New England's Rarities Discovered*. He enjoyed success with spearmint, feverfew, santolina, pennyroyal, ground ivy, house leek, hollyhocks, comfrey, coriander, dill, anise, asparagus, sorrel, sweet briar, roses, tansy and peppermint – all plants with medicinal uses. However, despite his most concerted efforts, celandine grew slowly, bloodwort sorrily, clary sage lasted only a summer and fennel had to be kept in a warm cellar for winter. Furthermore, southernwood was no plant for this country, nor rosemary, nor bay. Rue would hardly grow.

Interestingly, the Pilgrims weren't as eager to welcome American wildflowers into their gardens as their British ancestors had been to adopt the native flora into the cultivated landscape. With a vast wilderness to tame and a relatively meager plot under cultivation, they stuck fairly faithfully to fillers that were considered garden plants. Natives have only recently earned a place in the garden.

The cottage garden didn't return to America when the British revisited that mode of planting. Perhaps it could be blamed on the fact that Americans had larger tracts of land at their disposal, or perhaps the reason lay in the fact that suburban homes rarely featured fences. Americans preferred a wide open vista with a few foundation shrubs hugging the ankles of their houses. They were unlikely to confuse the view of their proud abode with a crowd of flowers between the front door and the drive. Furthermore, the focus of activities was toward the backyard which afforded privacy in lieu of a fence. For many reasons, the closely snuggled cottage scene was not the American aesthetic.

No one knew what their neighbors would think if they suddenly plowed up the front lawn and planted delphiniums, foxgloves, salvias and Lady's mantle. Only a few brave souls have attempted the feat. Quite suddenly and wonderfully, cottage gardens are being revived, especially in America. Often generically labeled as "romantic gardens", these latter day landscapes have the same profusion, informality and plant palette that predominated the cottage landscapes of long ago. Not only are these new cottage gardens of interest from a design perspective, they also serve to sharpen public awareness of heirlooms when many are in serious danger of being lost.

But a cottage scene isn't crucial to the cultivation of heirlooms. Heirlooms can be grown anywhere. No matter if you grow flowers in a front cottage garden, in your backyard or on a 50 acre field, preserving the old varieties is the most important issue. Snapdragons look as impressive in front of a post-modern contemporary abode as they do facing a cottage. Anyone who grows heirlooms is a cottage gardener. Anyone who shares seeds, stories or cuttings of those plants is a steward, saving the past.

Although morning glories weren't a major factor in the earliest cottage gardens, they certainly played a major role in the revival, especially in America. Nearing her 90th year, Thelma Crawford collects many plants, but is best known for her work with morning glories. Look in the Flower and Herb Exchange, and you'll find Thelma mentioned for Ipomoea nil 'Blue Boy', 'Carnaby Red', 'Christensen Factory', 'Clark's Heavenly Blue' and 'Robe'. Thelma's goal is to get her heirlooms out to the public.

Thelma wasn't eager to sit down and chat about her all-consuming hobby. "Find someone younger to talk with," she suggested, "I'm too busy packaging seeds." When you receive a packet of morning glories from Thelma, she chronicles every tidbit of information that might be germane, scribbled in longhand on the meticulously folded envelope, no wonder she has little spare time to chat.

Fortunately, Thelma has caught the interest of a younger generation of morning glory collectors, and Adrian Kencik is foremost among them. Although propagation isn't easily accomplished in her garden in cold Williamsville, New York, (see page 184) she brings the seedpods indoors to mature in a warm, dry place.

One of Adrian's proudest acquisitions is 'Cornell', a flaming red flowering morning glory stemming from the 1950s. She is one of four gardeners in the country growing 'Cornell'. And she was delighted when her plant boasted 200 flowers last summer. Unfortunately, only 5 seeds resulted from those blossoms. A true seedsaver, she shared that meager harvest, sending some seed to Florida. Her generosity paid off – her seed has refused to sprout, while three plants are thriving down South.

Cosmos was greatly developed in the early 20th century, producing forms such as this 'Seashells'

Old-fashioned outhouse hollyhocks *Alcea rosea* have been grown in cottage gardens for centuries

Cottage gardens as collections

As the former editor of *The American Cottage Gardener* you could call Nancy McDonald a crusader of sorts, urging folks to adopt the dianthus, peonies, iris and foxglove that typify the cottage garden style. She spends the bulk of her time lecturing and writing, reintroducing people to plants that were once familiar faces. She dearly loves old fashioned plants, their physical characteristics, their quirks and the lore associated with them. And she could bend your ear about any given heirloom flower long into the wee hours of the night. But don't ask Nancy to describe a typical cottage garden. "There is no definition," she'll insist. And then she'll go on to say that the beauty of the cottage gardening style lies in its total lack of any rules whatsoever – except an acknowledgement of their informality They look blowsy and rough around the edges perhaps, as opposed to appearing meticulously groomed and clipped. But that's where the rules end.

Nancy McDonald insists that modern cottage gardens are usually not, nor should they be, confined to heirloom plants. "I grow anything under the sun in my own cottage garden. I've planted the costmary, old double feverfew and daylily given to us by my husband's grandmother right beside the latest introduction from Tibet," she'll explain, adding, "It's a cottage garden, I don't have to contain myself."

Although there are no limitations and few generalizations, Nancy has made one observation concerning cottage gardens. They are often collector's gardens rather than "designer" gardens. Instead of featuring a long chain of one plant edging a walkway, they tend to crowd several dozen different species in a very small space.

Not limited to plants that are actually heirlooms, Nancy mingles old and new. When consulted for advice, she suggests growing "what you love and what you have time for, the two are not necessarily the same." She urges cottage gardeners to seek out plants that will thrive in their climate, rather than troubling with fussy plants that sulk or tend to fail. She also counsels a relaxed outlook on planting: "Go for the jungly look," she coaches, "rather than being absolutely faithful to the actual plants of yesterday." The formula for the "look" for which she strives is simple - there's always room for more. The trick is to nestle as many plants as possible into a small space, tucking them cheek to jowl, utilizing vertical area as well as ground surface. So she has *Rosa rugosa* 'Alba' intertwining with deep red *Clematis macropetala* 'Madame Julia Correvon' while *Campanula persicifolia alba* (the white peachleaf bellflower) and stray nicotiana seedlings wade around the vines' ankles.

Even the size is negotiable. Nancy's own garden has grown to include arbors far removed from the front yard of her northern Michigan cottage. But despite expansion, the garden still remains essentially cottagey in feeling. Filled with a glorious medley of favorite "finds", her garden is lush, exuberant and jam-packed with plants – and that is, in Nancy's book, a prime requisite for a cottage garden. "They're not self-conscious places, they look like you scooped a scene from nature," is Nancy's favorite way of putting it.

Nancy McDonald is well-traveled. And wherever she roams, she keeps an eye out for cottage gardens. To her surprise, she's found them scattered throughout the world – in places as far flung as Hawaii and New Zealand. "Although we think of cottage gardens as being English, every culture had their version, and you find the remnants still lingering in small towns everywhere." Cottage gardens are the landscapes of the rank and file.

Searching for scents of the past

Denis Garrett readily admits that she harbors a weak spot for fragrance. An avid cottage gardener, she has devoted her life to finding seemingly unobtainable plants. From her Tennessee home, she counsels others suffering from the same habit. To help with their addiction, she searches through catalogs and plant lists, trying to locate obscurities past and present.

At the moment, Denis's "Holy Grail" is the double rocket, *Hesperis matronalis* 'Alba Plena'. She's familiar with all the available colors of single sweet rocket, but it's the doubles she lusts after. She has never seen the white double in the flesh, but it was love at first sight based on a black and white picture in Margery Fish's *Cottage Garden Flowers*. It all began in the 1970s, and she's still looking.

Apparently, double flowered rocket was extremely popular before World War II, acting as a bedding plant at Kew Gardens and in London parks, but it slipped away in the 1950s, although apparently it can still be found in a few places in Britain..

When she couldn't find the object of her desires available through any North American source, she turned to Britain. "I thought at first that surely the double rocket was available by seed," Denis explains, "but I was wrong. The double form has to be vegetatively propagated." And importing live plants from overseas is not easy. While in the process of hunting up the double rocket, she found other family members to whet her appetite. For example, she read descriptions of a double purple rocket with white blotches. But so far, only singles are prevalent.

Not only has the exercise been exasperating as a gardener, but Denis found the experience to be eye-opening from a consumer standpoint. "I always imagine that you can buy anything. After all, we live in the land of opportunity. But this flower has totally eluded all my efforts," she echoes the common refrain of people who seek out heirlooms.

As for finding the double rocket, Denis hasn't given up yet. She has hopes of importing it through a traveling friend someday. As she often says, "Either my enthusiasm will wax, or I'll find the plant." Other searches have left her exhausted after a few decades, but she's still hot on the path of the double rocket.

To say that Rand B. Lee is smitten with dianthus is to understate his affliction considerably. If ever you need to speak about sops-in-wine with someone, ring up Rand in Sante Fe, New Mexico and he'll talk long and passionately about pinks, Sweet Swivelsfield, gillyflowers, carnations and all their many kin. Editor for *The Gilliflower Times*, Rand traces his infatuation back to the earliest stirrings of his youth. It all started with sweet Williams, obtained by rather ignoble means.

Apparently Rand's maternal grandmother once swiped sweet William seeds from plants growing at Mount Vernon. Even though it was nothing more serious than a seedhead that his grandmother snitched from the former garden of the country's Founding Father, Rand has always been a little sheepish about his horticultural roots.

Rand's mother grew the seeds at the Lee's home in Connecticut, which, coincidentally, iis just down the street from my house, and I can say with a high degree of certainty that no sweet Williams remain. "I remember those sweet Williams very well," Rand recalls. "They were deep maroon with white edging, like the newer variety 'Homeland', but they also had a very strong clove fragrance. I was fascinated by them, and I've never found anything similar."

Sweet Williams seem to have lost and regained their fragrance repeatedly through the centuries. In Elizabethan times, they were selected for fragrance. From that point they were crossed with *Dianthus chinensis*, a tender dianthus introduced into England from Manchuria prior to 1749, usually grown as an annual and with diminished perfume. The result was a riotous bedding plant. But, as Rand puts it, "the scent was seriously diluted." He searches for the sweet Williams of his youth. So far, his efforts have proved fruitless.

4

Where have all the heirlooms gone?

The original cottage gardeners had no reason to search far or spend their hard-earned wages on blossoms to uplift their gardens. Flowers – and vegetables – were passed along freely from one gardener to the next, shared from cottage to cottage, sometimes acquired from undergardeners on big estates. Heirlooms were horticultural hand-me-downs. Anyway, the working repertoire wasn't vast. Cottage gardens owed their heart and soul to a few favorite bloomers found again and again. Inveterate performers such as columbine, holly-hock, calendula, borage, lavender, lilies and iris were repeated in the cottage garden down the lane as well as in the neighboring village, if the growing conditions were similar. In fact, cottage garden stand-bys were so commonly planted that sophisticated gardeners – people following gardening fashions – refused them space in their grander gardens, and accused the most commonly planted flowers of being botanical clichés. Heirlooms were not much sought after commodities until recently.

The seed and nursery business grew up several hundred years after the birth and blossoming of cottage gardens. When the plant trade began to flourish, seedsmen and plantsmen dealt primarily in novelties, selling not to cottage gardeners but to peole of wealth and status.

In the 1700s the seed business truly took off. Prior to that time nursery-gardening was most likely to be a gentleman's part-time occupation, and as late as 1688 only three major seedsmen could be found operating in London, with trade in flowers rare although the fruit trade was already established. One of the first examples of selling flowering plants was recorded in 1667, when George Ricketts, nurseryman of Hoxton, near London, sent a list of fruit trees for sale to Sir Thomas Hanmer. The list also included 23 varieties of gilliflowers (*dianthus*). In 1670 Hanmer's journals mentioned also receiving anemones and auricula primroses from George Ricketts. Although there were few official seedsellers, horticulture was beginning to gather steam.

ABOVE: Shirley poppies *Papaver rhoeas* were first selected and developed by the Reverend William Wilks in 1880

LEFT: Clematis 'Belle of Woking' is a hybrid developed at George Jackman's famous 19th century English clematis nursery

Thomas Jefferson's Heritage

For as long as she can remember, Peggy Newcomb has always saved seeds. When she was growing up in Kentucky, her mother saved the type of pole beans that melt like butter in your mouth. "You can't get them commercially, the crop is just too labor-intensive to be economically worthwhile," Peggy explains, "but they were really delicious. Even the pods were good; they don't get tough. They're a main course, rather than just a side dish."

So it should come as no surprise that Peggy Newcomb developed "a real affinity for seed savers". And fortunately, she's found the perfect place to make her predilection benefit a large number of people. Peggy Newcomb is Director of the Thomas Jefferson Center for Historic Plants, an appendage of Monticello in Charlottesville, Virginia.

Not only does the center study Jefferson's plants, but they ferret out and stewart heirloom varieties tottering on the verge of extinction. Before most heirloom specialists caught wind of the trend, the Center for Historic Plants was taking steps to get heirlooms in the hands of modern gardeners, postulating that the more broadly a flower is distributed, the less likely it is to slip away. And that was the motivation for the Center for Historic Plants' catalog listing such treasures as Thomas Jefferson's wine-red species snapdragon, the China aster (*Callistephus chinensis*) grown in 1750, Jefferson's scarlet pentapetes (*Pentapetes phoenicia*) and the original single-flowering Mexican zinnia species (*Zinnia pauciflora*) are offered in addition to more common heirlooms such as hollyhocks, flowering tobacco, French mallow and cockscomb.

First published in 1988, many (but not all) of the heirlooms featured in *Twinleaf* (which is the name the Center chose for its catalog, inspired by the common nickname for *Jeffersonia diphylla*) were once grown at Monticello. A gardener far ahead of his times, Jefferson sent requests for plants to all parts of the globe, acquiring flowers that weren't readily in cultivation, increasing the scope of horticulture in America. By sharing his novelties with contemporaries, Jefferson became a horticultural as well as diplomatic patriarch. Using Jefferson's plans, written in 1807, his correspondence and his Garden Book, historians have an excellent idea of the horticultural inventory thriving at Jefferson's Virginia home. Recently restored, Monticello's gardens again feature those plants in all their original exuberant majesty. And many of the flowers are permitted to go to seed. Rather than purchasing stock wholesale, whenever possible, the Center saves its own harvest. "Monticello seeds are cleaned and packaged by gardeners," Peggy says proudly.

Admittedly, they were mavericks at first... But, suddenly, the Thomas Jefferson Center for Historic Plants finds itself riding the cusp of the wave in fashion. "At the moment, heirloom plants are becoming mainstream. When one of the largest seed companies starts offering the pinwheel marigold and quoting Curtis' Botanical Magazine of 1791 in their glossy, full color catalog, you know that heirlooms are surely becoming an important economic factor," Peggy concedes. "But in a few years when the fashion cools, we intend to continue preserving these plants. We preserve because these plants are historically important. That's sufficient reason."

One of the best known early nurseries was "the great Nursery between Spittle-fields and White-chappel" established in 1643 by Captain Leonard Gurle who later became King Charles II's royal gardener. Gurle was one of the first seedsmen, but the first giant step in that direction came in 1677 when William Lucas, a member of the London Society of Florists who described himself as a milliner by trade, published the first plant list truly dedicated to seedselling. Operating at "The Naked Boy", he offered a comprehensive roster of salad seeds, potherb seeds, sweet herb seeds, medicinal herb seeds, flowering trees and beans as well as flower roots and flower seeds. Snapdragons, French honeysuckle, scabious, larkspur, columbines, sweet sultan, lychnis, impatiens, nasturtium, Canterbury bells, foxgloves, amaranths, aconites, convolvulus, poppies, wall-flowers and gilliflowers were among the seeds he listed for sale. He provided both French marigolds, *Tagetes patula* and African ones, *Tagetes erecta*. He sold rooted ranunculus ("all sorts"), anemones, crocus, cyclamen, lilies, jas-mines, hellebores, fritillarias, peonies (black, red, purple and striped), crown imperials (yellow, double and single) as well as double, striped and plain auricula primroses. Over 140 flowers were offered, not to mention the herbs that were sold under a different category. The list provides a thumbnail sketch of heirlooms in their heyday.

Obviously, the climate was favorable, because other merchants dove in and joined Lucas in the endeavor. In fact, the same list was published in 1688 in the appendix of J. Woolridge's book, *Systema horti-culturae*, and attributed to three different London merchants, namely Edward Fuller who succeeded Lucas as the proprietor of the Naked Boy, Theophilus Stacy at the Rose and Crown, and Charles Blackwell of the King's Head. By 1760, the number of nurseries – selling seeds, plants and trees – had swelled to approximately 100 firms operating in Britain.

FLORISTS AND NURSERYMEN

Confusion surrounds some aspects of the early plant trade. Most early growers were known as florists. During the 17th and 18th centuries, a florist was not a flower seller, as today, but a specialist breeder and grower. The first florists were rich country gentlemen with estates, often buying their original stocks from abroad. When numbers of new plants began to arrive in Britain from America and elsewhere during the 1700s, some florists turned their energies toward becoming collectors, a few became professional nurserymen.

Then a new race of florists arose, poor men, factory workers, artisans, petty tradesmen and miners who developed the flowers often referred to as "florists flowers": tulips, primroses, ranunculus, auriculas, polyanthus, pinks, hyacinths and carnations. Many popular heirlooms were created during this period.

Honeysuckle *Lonicera periclymenum* may be a rampant weed in some parts of the United States but it is still a temptingly fragrant climber

(black, red, purple and striped), hellebores, and double, striped and plain auricula primroses. Over 140 flowers were offered, with herbs sold under a different category. The list provides a sketch of popular early flowers.

Obviously, the climate was favourable, because other merchants followed Lucas' lead. The same list was published in 1688 in the appendix of J. Woolridge's book, *Systema horti-culturae*, and attributed to three different London merchants, namely Edward Fuller who succeeded Lucas as the proprietor of The Naked Boy, Theophilus Stacy at The Rose and Crown, and Charles Blackwell of The King's Head. By 1760, the number of nurseries selling seeds, plants and trees had swelled to approximately 100 firms operating in Britain.

London was the centre of British trade, but the early merchants were not solely dependent on domestic customers. This was an expansionary period for the United Kingdom and the colonies proved an eager audience. In particular, pioneers in the newly settled wilderness of America were keen on establishing a home-away-from-home and receiving the necessary seeds of their former flowering favourites to realise that goal.

Trade with North America was established early on, initiated in 1631 by John Winthrop, Jr, son of the Governor of the colony of Massachusetts. He applied to Robert Hill, grocer of a shop called The Three Angels in London's Lombard Street, for a supply of garden seeds which he took with him to America. These included a few recent introductions but the bulk were European natives, including columbines, clary sage, marigolds, hollyhocks, monkshood, poppies, sweet rocket, stock-gilliflowers *Matthiola incana*, tansy and wallflowers, as well as some favourite roses. There was nothing too exotic to begin with as the early colonials' lives were too busy for too much pleasure gardening. But it was the start of a

healthy exchange between the two continents. The colonists sought seeds of favourite plants unavailable in the New World, and many also struggled to remain abreast of the latest introductions from newly explored lands. Novelties were arriving in Europe at a brisk pace from explorations funded by wealthy aristocrats and enterprising nurserymen. Those plants were then duly distributed. As early as 1655 Dutch settlers in New Holland and New Amsterdam were growing fine tulips, crown imperials and several kinds of lilies as well as old favourites such as violets, anemones, and red and white roses.

The relationship worked both ways; distinguished London-based nurserymen such as James Lee and Conrad Loddiges fell over each other to offer European clients rarities obtained from the New World. But North America was not the only destination for plant hunters, nor was it the only country to feed the hunger for new plants. A vigorous market clamoured for anything foreign and novel. In the latter quarter of the 1700s, James Lee's nursery alone introduced some 135 exotics from Siberia, South Africa, Chile, Madeira, China, Australia, Mexico, Guinea and the West Indies, in addition to the plants that came from North America. Many of the latter were culled from North America's vast native flora, much greater than that in Europe, and became essential perennials for gardens great and small.

Traditional plants from one continent became fixtures in gardens farther afield, and trading in seeds and plants was a vigorous business. By 1840, over 150 nurserymen were engaged in brisk business in Britain, with 30 principal firms plus a number of smaller ones in London, the rest scattered throughout England. Individual nurserymen played an important role in the development of gardening,

North Americans were relatively slow to adopt the business of selling plants. John

THE PELARGONIUM STORY

In the 18th century the first pelargoniums, native to the Cape of Good Hope, infiltrated North America. They were novelties at first, but fast became omnipresent, carried across the continent in the covered wagons of pioneers and becoming almost a symbol of the new country.

Pelargoniums were first recorded being offered for sale by the Parisian nurseryman Rene Morin in 1621, but were not seen in London until the beginning of the 18th century. They were sent to John Bartram in the United States by his British friend Peter Collinson in 1760, and thereafter pelargoniums became hot commodities on the market.

Rembrandt Peale found the pelargonium so appealing that he positioned a blooming plant proudly beside his brother, Rubens, in the portrait that he painted in 1801, inferring that it was among the rarest treasures in the family's collection of accrued wealth. Bernard McMahon – the Philadelphia merchant who received the horticultural collections from the Lewis and Clark Expedition – mentioned pelargoniums repeatedly in his 1806 publication, American Gardener's Calendar. Americans could read about pelargoniums and, with the help of Grant Thorburn, Bernard McMahon and other like-minded merchants, they could acquire this fascinating flowering foreigner.

added 30 acres of cropland to supply the demand for his seed. Landreth featured some old faithfuls, but he was most proud of his inventory of exotics such as camellias, rhododendrons, hyacinth, citrus, bananas and the Bird of Paradise *Strelitzia reginae*. Other Philadelphians noticed that Landreth was thriving and opened similar botanical establishments, including John Mackejohn in 1792, William Leeson in 1794 and Bernard McMahon in 1800. In 1802, Grant Thorburn introduced the trend into New York City. Grant Thorburn's tale not only illustrates how an early layman fell into the plant business, it also speaks of the avenues that plants traveled to become widely dispersed. Scottish born Thorburn was originally trained as a wrought-nail worker but found the grocery trade more seductive when he arrived as a youth in New York. Innovative, and fond of a female clientele, he noted the popularity of horticultural supplies elsewhere, added flowerpots to his inventory, and painted those pots green, just to further confound the competition. One day, while visiting the Fly Market, Thorburn found a scented-leaf geranium, probably the rose-scented *Pelargonium capitatum,* and thought it might make a suitable companion for his green painted pot. So began a partnership with a grower in Brooklyn who provided a ready supply of pelargoniums. The Brooklyn farmer eventually went into business solely for Thorburn, producing not only scented geraniums, but growing seed wholesale to be sold in the city shop.

Heirlooming is an on-going process; most plants were novelties at first, buyers scrambling to purchase them and remain one step ahead of their neighbors. If the plant was worthy, it became widely disseminated. Eventually, the novelty wore thin. For a while the plant was commonplace. And then, after time had marched on, it became an heirloom. What is old today was once new.

Johnny-jump-ups, *Viola tricolor,* also known as heartsease, were grown by the Elizabethans

Grandpa Ott's morning glory inspired the foundation of Seed Savers Exchange and the Flower and Herb Exchange

FLOWERS GAIN IMPORTANCE

From the 1700s onward, nurseries and seedsmen have proved an important link in making flowers available to the people. But flowers weren't always in the horticultural mainstream. Although William Lucas' catalog featured many flowers, edibles were far more prominent in commerce for many years. Most early British catalogs focused primarily on vegetables or fruit trees with a few flowers thrown in. In North America, vegetables totally predominated until the 1800s with a smattering of flowers included for good measure. Flowers didn't step into the fore until the middle of the 19th century when the living was easier in the New World.

The cityward shift had something to do with the change in focus. With the creation of suburban communities, gardening moved from a hard-and-scrabble agricultural subsistence to a more enjoyable endeavor, and so flowers were more apt to be given play. Although Americans had a penchant toward utilitarianism, they had always invited flowers into the fringes of their gardens. This encouragement of flowers became more pronounced as technology and the transportation of goods improved. In the early 19th century, as the average citizen gradually began to purchase an increasing proportion of his staples from merchants rather than producing them all himself, plants were enjoyed not only for their uses, but for their beauty as well. Prior to this time, the scented pelargoniums that were brought across the country in covered wagons were doubtlessly appreciated for their handsome flowers, but they were also valued for their role in cooking; toward the beginning of the 19th century, zonal pelargoniums also came into prominence, appreciated solely for their ornamental flowers with no ulterior motive.

FASHION COMES INTO PLAY

Any industry waltzes to the tune of supply and demand. If the public turns up its nose and refuses to buy 10 different heliotropes, then seedsmen and nurseries quite naturally whittle down their inventory to the one heliotrope that has proved the most popular. Or if their audience crave morning glories and purchase every *ipomoea* vine that they can lay their hands on, seedsmen and garden centers clamor to find further morning glory varieties.

"Old-fashioned" varieties have only recently been marketed with their history as a drawing point. The term has more often had rather negative connotations. Plant buyers demanded the latest sweet peas and begged for new giant everblooming carnations. And could you blame them? If wilt-resistant double asters were to be had, then the public beat a path to the door of any company capable of fulfilling the promise. Who wouldn't seek out rust-resistant snapdragons? Who wouldn't be curious to try improved double nasturtiums or dahlia-flowered zinnias? Often, newer varieties exhibited sought-after traits. If cosmos could be coaxed to bloom earlier in the season rather than flowering only briefly before being smitten by frost in autumn, who can blame tradesmen for rushing to carry the better product? However, as the newest and the latest was offered, old faithful species and varieties went into decline.

Plants are living things and sometimes a certain sport is a freak of nature unlikely to happen again, and should be guarded. It is a pity when flowers such as the intensely fragrant sweet peas disappear, upstaged by varieties that boast more blossoms and larger flowers on longer spires. But merchants can't be expected to steward heirlooms. That responsibility should fall primarily on the shoulders of devoted gardeners.

FLOWERS OF YESTERDAY

The definition of how the perfect flower should appear has changed with time. Most dramatically, the height has decreased. From tall blowsy plants that tower over their modern counterparts, ideal bloomers gradually became waist high or shorter. In America the lawnmower's arrival in the middle of the 19th century probably had something to do with it – clearly circumscribed beds allowed flowers to be seen to great advantage, and the trend toward dwarfing really took off during the Victorian era, with its ribbon borders and bedding schemes.

Modern varieties tend to be bred with more blossoms per stalk, and to be self-branching whereas their older counterparts were apt to shoot obstinately straight up. Colors are more intense than they were a few hundred years ago. And the visual element became a greater factor when catalogs began displaying their wares in color. Compared to the modern garden, the heirloom bed was relatively drab.

Another trait that has proliferated over the centuries is doubleness. Most heirloom flowers are single – they are open-faced, like the single hollyhock, rather than featuring a nest of many petals like the double zonal pelargoniums that have gained supremacy, nudging their single counterparts off the market. One problem with double flowers is that they tend to be sterile – the reproductive organs fail to develop, resembling petals instead. By and large, double flowers cannot be reproduced except by vegetative means. There are exceptions. If only the stamens are transformed into petals then they can be fertilized, although insects are usually unattracted, making hand-pollination necessary. Some flowers, such as primroses, stocks, peonies and poppies, are genetically prone to slipping into doubleness. Peonies have displayed double forms for a good two thousand years.

So there are double heirlooms. But the first zinnias and marigolds were single and some people treasure the simple single flower as the pure state. To each gardener, his own fancies. The only problem lies when single philadelphus disappear from the market, superseded by their doubles, to the dismay of those who find the single version more fragrant.

Many gardeners miss fragrance most of all. Florists are the culprits most frequently accused of taking the perfume from blossoms. Whenever flowers have been bred for the long stems that florists' crave, they lose their scent. It happened with roses, sweet peas and dianthus. Even nosegay flowers such as violets became relatively unaromatic when florists began selecting for bigger blossoms and longer stems.

Some people suspect that fragrance has been intentionally deleted. Not everyone likes the musky smell of jasmine, not everyone luxuriates in the pungence of marigolds. Breeders could be trying to eliminate a wild card that they can't easily promise as being positive. Or perhaps breeders strive toward other, conflicting goals. When they work with flowering tobacco, they go for a dwarf plant producing many showy flowers with interesting colors. When they work with freesias, they want to add blues and pinks to the color spectrum. Unfortunately, when breeders strive for a visual bombast, they gain eye appeal but they very often forfeit fragrance.

The fashion at the moment has taken a retrospective turn. Cottage gardens are again popular, herbaceous borders are in vogue and the climate is so right for heirlooms that several major catalogs have been inspired to mention the history of the plants that they offer. Many merchants, especially companies that have remained in business for a century or more, have published specific catalogs of the heirlooms that they still carry. Old-fashioned is no longer a negative term.

This old Austrian copper rose would grace any garden

Colorful daylilies and blue-toned delphiniums form an attractive combination

Saving the day – Heirloom specialists

Marilyn Barlow of Select Seeds traces her affection for heirlooms to fragrance. After all, she grew up amid a landscape dense with lily-of-the-valley, pineapple bush and sweeping iris beds that her grandfather planted in his spare time during the Depression. So her childhood memories are steeped in scent. And perfume is what Marilyn missed most when she married and moved into an 1830s farmhouse. "Although there was a pheasant's eye narcissus in evidence when we arrived, there wasn't much else," she recalls. Her solution was to travel around New England, checking out abandoned cellar holes. "I didn't deplete anything, but I took a piece of iris from here and a daylily division from there."

It was curiosity about those abandoned plants that provoked Marilyn to frequent the library at Old Sturbridge Village in Sturbridge, Massachusetts, a restoration that focuses back on the 1830s, which coincided perfectly with the vintage of her home. Meanwhile, she spent winter days in periodical basements of libraries perusing old seed catalogs and magazines.

The more she read, the more she yearned to grow the plants mentioned in 19th century books and that's when she began writing to people throughout the country in search of heirlooms. They sent her seeds and she shared the surplus from her supply. "I met wonderful people. Strangers signed their letters 'Your Flower Friend', it was really very nice," Marilyn says. In 1988, she began Select Seeds, packaging seed on the kitchen table of her Union, Connecticut home.

Marilyn and I met over sweet peas. The seedswoman happened to visit the greenhouse where I was working and caught wind, literally, of the sweet peas in the backyard. Those sweet peas originally came from Peter Grayson, one of the most boisterous members of Great Britain's National Sweet Pea Society, a collector of pre-Spencer sweet peas and a hybridizer who is working to restore heady fragrance to sweet peas. Not only does he hybridize sweet peas and grow those flowers to exhibition quality, but he sells sweet peas wholesale, and that's how we began corresponding.

When my heirloom sweet peas came into blossom, everyone from the mailman to greenhouse customers were coaxed to come take a whiff of a scent that rivaled any aroma I'd experienced before. And Marilyn agreed.

By the early 1990s, Marilyn became the sole source of Peter Grayson's antique sweet peas in North America. Not only did she make available to American audiences the best of the British sweet peas (many hybridized by Henry Eckford in the 1890s). But she concentrated on reintroducing early American sweet peas into this country, especially pink and white flowering 'Blanche Ferry' (introductory date unknown), the first sweet pea hybrid created by an American seedhouse. Due to her efforts, 'America' (1896), a cherry red with white striping, twines again around fences throughout the country. While 'Janet Scott' (1903) and 'Flora Norton' (1904) again wend their way around cottage gardens, perfuming the air. Many people complain that the scents of their youth have vanished, but Marilyn has taken action to restore the perfume of her childhood.

Ed Rasmussen of The Fragrant Path is the consummate small seedsmen. Not only does he research and write his catalog with an emphasis on "fragrant, rare and old-fashioned plants", but he grows most of the seed offered in its pages on his Fort Calhoun, Nebraska farm. Furthermore, he aggressively seeks heirlooms – no need to look far, he's found many older varieties in the 'Little Italy' neighborhood of Omaha. Warming to his subject and setting the stage, Ed explains, "It's called 'Little Italy', but it isn't solely the Italian section.... People from every background came there to work in the packing plants." And it's proved fertile ground for ferreting out heirlooms, "Lots are tiny in 'Little Italy', houses are small and people live there forever. It's the ideal climate to find heirlooms. You can still find the old, small flowered German iris and the ancient peonies in 'Little Italy'."

Ed is preoccupied with perfume. Although he readily admits to a predilection for vines, any fragrant flower catches his eye... and nose. A connoisseur of scent, he watched as that trait was downplayed, "For a while, it wasn't even mentioned in catalogs, they just ignored that attribute," he observes. And he feels strongly that breeders responded by deleting that virtue. Rather than a simple genetic slip that occurred when florists' strove toward long stems, he feels that the fragrance was intentionally edited out.

Ed Rasmussen theorizes that the move away from fragrance coincided with the suburban exodus. People had yards, the yards were in close proximity to the backyard next door, and Ed surmises that they didn't want to risk mingling possibly conflicting scents. "They didn't want to mix strong scents such as fermented cinnamon rolls with the cucumbers and pumpkin

pies." Ed, on the other hand, indulges his nose on every possible occasion. And he shares his olfactory odyssey with anyone who meanders into the pages of his catalog. Flowers you never really thought of as fragrant are rated on the perfume scale. The leaves of *Caryopteris x clandonensis* are reminiscent of lavender and resin. The flowers of *Coreopsis lanceolata* have a "warm sweet fragrance". Intimacy has led to some intriguing olfactory revelations. Not even seeds escape Ed's discriminating nostrils. The seed of *Nigella damascena* smells "like grape soda-pop" when rolled between the fingers. On the other hand, *Centranthus ruber*, a plant once described as bearing "the unpleasant smell of perspiration," is scent-free according to Ed Rasmussen. Whatever your olfactory opinions, all gardeners are fortunate to have this small specialty seedsman hunting to find and preserve the most aromatic flowers.

Renee Shepherd of Shepherd's Gardens in Felton, California feels very positive about the seed situation at present. "It's market driven, there is no conspiracy," she insists. "It's not simplistic and I can't make a David and Goliath analogy here." Things have changed, she'll agree. "I can't always buy what I want from the big seed houses. Some of those houses originally carried 120 different plants. Now they have 40. They don't produce the diversity anymore, it's true, but small producers pick up the slack. The sky is not falling."

Renee's Garden functions on a thoroughly modern level selling its seed line on seed racks and through the internet. Renee issues no mail-order catalog. The approach is novel, but the line has a retrospective – but not exclusively historic – slant. Renee's Garden features both heirlooms and novelties, and Renee Shepherd feels strongly about offering the mix. "New and improved varieties are worthy of a second look," she opines, "seeds have a product cycle. Varieties that disappeared left because they didn't sell." Among the heirlooms that she offers

are 'Empress of India' nasturtium, Thomas Jefferson's purple hyacinth bean, and a ferny-leaved version of the cypress vine *Ipomoea quamoclit* that she calls 'Hearts and Honey'.She convinced a South American grower to produce the seed specially for her. Renee lists the 'Persian Carpet' zinnia, a variety that is closely akin to the species, *Zinnia haageana*, grown in the 19th century – but, to be perfectly democratic, she also carries a new early flowering and disease-resistant zinnia called 'Blue Point Bouquet'.

5

Spreading the word – propagation

Other kids had bureau drawers full of sweaters and blouses, but mine were stuffed with marigold seeds. It all started with a packet of seed of mixed crested marigolds from the supermarket and a Brownie project. My goal was nothing more ambitious than to fill the backyard with marigolds, much to my parents' chagrin.

Being a kid and otherwise preoccupied, I neglected to deadhead as often as necessary. This led me to discover that, if left to their own devices, the dried flowerheads contained a sheaf of seeds, and these looked suspiciously similar to the seeds in the super-market seed packet. Dust to dust and seed to seed. This appealed to my frugal nature.

The marigold project continued year after year, leaving my bureau drawers with less and less room for sweaters and blouses. And gradually the backyard scene also began to alter. After a while I didn't care so much for the bright orangish-yellow marigolds. Instead, I favored the deep brick-colored version

– preferably with a tiny band of yellow hemming the edge of each petal and a crest in the center. So began a very unscientific selection process.

I've moved beyond marigolds. Nowadays, sweet peas vie for room in the bureau drawers. But there's a safeguard with sweet peas – they only remain reliably viable for one year. On the one hand, I have the responsibility of harvesting enough seed for myself and friends annually. But after that season, I can toss out the leftovers in the bureau with a clean conscience.

The only way to be certain of keeping any heirloom flower in the fold is to share it with fellow gardeners. That's how the original cottage gardeners kept their strains alive for so many years, and the same is true today. Throughout the centuries, gardeners have sent friends and fellow gardeners home with a handful of seeds or a cutting from their garden. Not only does their generosity render them popular among the neighbors, it also assures that heirlooms won't slip away.

ABOVE: Shining white old-fashioned 'Crystal white' single zinnias are much sought by seed savers

LEFT: Many favorite heirloom flowers are as popular with bees and other insect pollinators as they are with gardeners

Southern Exposure Seed Exchange

Jeff McCormack never planned to start a seed catalog. But heirlooms sort of drew him into it. His background isn't far off the mark – he has a Ph.D. in botany with a special interest in regulatory biology, pollination techniques, pharmacology and organic chemistry. And at the beginning of his professional career, he taught courses in alternative energy and agriculture. Then he happened to visit Old Sturbridge Village in Massachusetts, a recreated village from the 1830's, and was intrigued by the heirloom vegetables he encountered there. He moved to Virginia, continued to teach at college and joined the Blue Ridge Seed Savers, where he discovered multiplier onions. "They're called potato onions and they have many offsets. They were wildly popular around 1900, but by 1930 they had disappeared from commerce. I couldn't understand why they weren't in catalogs." So Jeff decided to remedy the situation.

In 1982, after an article attracted fervent correspondence from kindred potato onion enthusiasts, he wrote and published a catalog in three months. "I didn't have a clue what I was doing," he admits, "I had a closet full of seeds, a weighing balance and 40 hand-dug raised beds. In 1986, after I realized a net profit of $50.00, I went into business full-time."

Southern Exposure is a seed supplier and seed exchange. Jeff encourages gardeners to save seed by offering a gift certificate in exchange for shared varieties. He asks his customers to contact him about the variety's origins. How long was it saved? Who was it saved by? He loves to hear stories. Vegetables are his main forte, but he lists heirloom flowers such as bachelors buttons, cleome, cosmos, Johnny-jump-ups, larkspurs, hollyhocks and four o'clocks. And he has succeeded in rendering several family heirlooms readily available to the public.

Jeff likes to pass along the stories with the plants. For example, there's 'Tina James' Magic' evening primrose. Tina James is a garden writer who found a rarely grown species of evening primrose blooming in Maryland. She took plants to a taxonomist and had them keyed out as *Oenothera glazioviana,* whereas the more common evening primrose on the market is *O. macrocarpa* (formerly *O. missourensis).* The beauty of the plant is its drama. "It's like a time-lapse movie," Jeff explains, "the flowers open that fast." And it's floriferous. "Tina's three foot square stand of the flower is on a jogging path and people stop to watch it open. She put up a score board so the joggers could record the bloom count. One night, someone counted 1,500 blooms."

Many of the heirloom varieties can be traced to people with strong ethnic roots. "When we lose our cultural diversity," Jeff's fond of saying, "we lose our biological diversity as well." About assimilation he comments, "Something is gained, but something is always lost as well ...I like to hear about the traditions and learn what these seeds meant to people," Jeff explains. Many had a deep meaning, especially to people who had traveled from their homelands. The 'Don Pedros' four o'clock in the Southern Exposure Seed Exchange catalog was just such an immigrant, coming to America with a transplanted gardener. Unlike most *Mirabilis* commonly available, its blossoms have magenta streaks, stripes and spots. It came from a neighbor who brought it from her mother's home town in Spain.

Of all the heirloom flowers, Jeff has the strongest personal bond with 'Mona's Orange' cosmos, a family heirloom from southern California with single-flowering, radiant orange blossoms. He noticed that 10% of the blooms bore a red border on the petals which prompted him to begin a selection project that spanned seven years. In 1991, he found one or two plants with more red coloration on their petals, he marked them with tape and saved the seed. The next year, he found 2-3 plants out of 50 strongly showed the characteristic and continued to select those plants until he had plants that were predominantly red. The project took time, but it wasn't difficult. "I took the easy, lazy way to do it," he confesses. "And I could have taken it further, but I liked the bit of orange remaining." He called his selection 'Memories of Mona'.

The freedom that an independent hybridizer can exercise is part of the beauty of breeding for Jeff McCormack. "You can tailor the plant to your own fancies," Jeff says. He's found that other gardeners who have worked with their family strains develop a special relationship with the plant. He can only explain it as, "They transform the seed, but the seed changes them."

FIRST CHOICE – PROPAGATION

Plant propagation needn't be confined to professionals. Anyone can perform the feat. For tools, you need nothing more complicated than a shovel if you plan to divide your plant or an envelope if you're collecting seed. And it isn't a particularly complex skill. Plant propagating isn't a difficult science, but timing is everything when seedsaving.

When you find a plant that might possibly be an heirloom growing in an abandoned foundation or an old estate, propagate it rather than digging the original plant. The same applies to wildflowers. Unless the plant is doomed to certain destruction through habitat alteration, leave the original plant unharmed. No matter how good a steward you are, relocating can be traumatic to a plant. If it has survived for several generations in its current location, chances are that, however it appears, the location has proved a happy home for the heirloom. Overzealous collection has proved the ruination of many heirlooms. For more information about the proper methods of collecting plants, contact the United Plant Savers (see *Resources page 186*).

BASIC PLANT PROPAGATION

Much has been written about different propagation methods. It's not a cut and dry science – every plant has its own eccentricities. But that shouldn't stop you from attempting the feat. If the basic method fails, experiment. Try again at a different time of year or under different weather conditions. If a stem cutting doesn't work, try rooting a side shoot taken at its juncture. Give the cutting more or less sun, increase or decrease the humidity.

ANNUALS

The first factor to consider when sharing plants is whether you're dealing with an annual, biennial or perennial. Annuals survive only one growing season. In fact, in some cases – in severe desert climates, for example – annuals are ephemerals which sprout, grow, blossom, set seed and die in a few brief months. However, the lion's share of annuals commonly on the market for garden purposes linger throughout most of the growing season. Some of the best known examples of heirloom annuals are marigolds, sunflowers, snapdragons, morning glories and cosmos. Most annuals are best propagated by seed. Their seed occasionally proves hardy (especially during mild winters) and seed scattered by the winds will germinate the following season. Flowering tobacco, love-in-a-mist and morning glories, for example, usually self-seed, but their reappearance is not reliable. Annual heirlooms are usually the first to slip into extinction.

That's where you come in. Gardeners keep annuals alive. In some cases, properly stored seed can endure for several decades with only slightly diminished germination rates – for example the sacred lotus *Nelumbo nucifera* is reputed to remain viable for 1,000 years, although proof is understandably limited! In fact, landscape historians often turn over the soil of an historic garden such as Mount Vernon or Monticello to encourage latent, deeply buried seed to germinate, helping them to find out what was grown in the garden centuries ago. Morning glory seeds from forty-year-old packets have been successfully sprouted. However, seed of certain annuals, such as sweet peas and other members of the legume family, go stale rapidly and the percentage of viable seed in a packet diminishes drastically after 18 months. Unless seed of those annuals is saved faithfully every year, the variety will slip away.

Old-fashioned sweet Williams *Dianthus barbatus* have much stronger fragrance than modern cultivars

PERENNIALS

Perennials survive as living rootstock from season to season. Some, including peonies, dianthus, daylilies, roses and phlox survive for hundreds of years as a testimony to past gardens and bygone trends. However, even perennials are not impervious to the traumas of time. Many lavenders and certain artemisias, for example, tend to be short-lived. Occasionally, a winter will prove so severe that a previously hale and hardy perennial suddenly perishes. Sharing perennials with fellow gardeners is a wise safeguard to make certain that they endure. Horticulture is an unpredictable science, which is why we hedge our bets.

Perennials are propagated by cuttings, divisions (if they form separate-rooted clumps as in the case of mints, phlox and asters), or seed. However, saving seed of perennials is not without caveats. When you allow a perennial to go to seed rather than deadheading it, this can weaken the plant and undermine its winter hardiness. The plant throws all its strength into its progeny rather than fortifying itself to survive. Also, if you allow a perennial to go to seed early in the season you are unlikely to get the benefits of a second, late-season blooming.

TENDER PERENNIALS

Tender perennials are usually treated as annuals because they are not winter hardy and perish with frost, though they will survive from year to year in a mild climate. They can be kept alive indoors throughout the year and some, such as pelargoniums, make wonderful indoor companions over the winter on windowsills or in a greenhouse. Many tender perennials can be propagated by seed, but if you want a heavily hybridized tender perennial to come true, and look like its parent, you will have to take cuttings and shelter them over the winter.

BIENNIALS

Biennials blossom during their second year and die back shortly after setting seed. However, their seed is often hardy and so a colony, once established, might continue in that spot year after year, although reappearance isn't as reliable as an established patch of a hardy perennial. Foxgloves, hollyhocks and angelica are biennial.

Biennials are shared by seed, seedlings or root divisions, and are rarely propagated by cuttings.

DIVIDING PLANTS

Dividing an heirloom is an easy, untraumatic method of propagating, especially useful for hybrids that might not come true from seed. Best done in the spring when the plants are small and upheaval will be minimal, and in cloudy weather when the plants will not be stressed, divisions can only be accomplished if several separate crowns of a plant have their own roots. Take a trowel or shovel, dig gently into the soil and pull apart a section of the plant keeping as many roots and as much soil intact as possible. At the same time, bring a jug of water to quench the donor plant after you've disturbed its roots. Also sprinkle the roots of the division with water while you transport it to its new location. Pot or replant the division immediately, watering it generously while the roots become re-established.

TAKING STEM CUTTINGS

This is not as difficult as you may have been led to believe! Known as taking stem cuttings or slips, vegetative propagation is the method of choice for producing progeny of complex hybrids that might not come true from seed. Unfortunately, it is usually only professionals who take cuttings, which explains why so many heirlooms slip away. Granted, there are a few plants that prove stubborn to propagate by cuttings, but many will take root without undue fuss or bother.

As a rule, take cuttings, or slips, when new growth has "hardened off", or when new shoots are firm and not so tender that they wilt easily. Early spring bloomers will produce new growth in summer after flowering, while cuttings from late season bloomers should be taken in spring before buds appear.

The length of the slip depends on the type of plant you choose: take a 3-4 inch long sprig of a thickly foliated herb such as box *Buxus sempervirens*. But if your target plant has several inches of bare stem between the leaves, cut off a longer stem with at least two leaves or sets of leaves.

Take cuttings on a cloudy day and water the plant at least an hour or two beforehand. Bring the cuttings into a cool, shady place immediately. If you can't pot them straight off, wrap their stems in a damp napkin and slip them into a plastic bag, keeping them moist – most slips will survive for several days.

Although some plants root easily in a glass of water, roots started in water may adapt poorly to life in soil so it's wisest to root directly in sand, rooting medium or soil. Remove the leaves from the bottom third of the stem. If you want to speed the process, you can dip the bottom third of the cutting into rooting hormone.

Fill a small pot with a light, friable soil or sand (sand is best for difficult-to-root or hardwooded cuttings such as rose sprigs) and insert the lower third of the cutting into the medium, making certain to firm the medium around the base of the stem, and water the cutting immediately. Put the cutting in a shady spot.

To raise the humidity and prevent wilting, enclose the pot and cutting in a plastic bag, under an overturned glass, bell jar or cloche. Keep the soil moist while the cutting is rooting. Depending upon the plant, roots should initiate in 2-4 weeks. Repot the plant if necessary.

SAVING SEEDS

If it's possible to save seed from a plant, this is by far the most efficient and time-honored method of propagation. It produces the most offspring and yields the most propagative material for sharing with gardeners near and far. Seed collection is rarely detrimental to the donor plant, but over-zealous collection can diminish a wild population, so be moderate.

POLLINATION

The first step in saving seeds is to make certain that the flower you're hoping to propagate is pollinated. A flower's stigma (female organ) must receive pollen from the anthers (male organ). If a species is self-pollinated, the pollen is transferred within the same flower and your chances of duplicating the plant precisely are excellent. Morning glories, for example, will usually come true from seed, even if your vine is within easy pollination distance of another morning glory. On the other hand, if a flower is fertilized by cross-pollination, like sunflowers, flowering tobacco *Nicotiana,* and petunias, pollen must come via the wind, insects, or with your help from another flower.

The characteristics of most heirlooms have stabilized over years. Even if you are working with a cultivar, a large percentage of seed will come true if you make certain that your flowers don't cross-pollinate with a nearby cultivar of a different shade. But there are important exceptions: columbines, pansies and members of the violet family cross-pollinate shamelessly. They will return in a range of different colors unless you take steps to keep a strain pure.

To prevent cross-pollination between two different species or cultivars, you can separate the plants by isolating them. Although there is little precise data about the distances necessary to prevent mingling, most seed savers feel that

Marigolds were popular plants in the 18th century, the old-fashioned scented leaf varieties are good companion plants

about 50 yards should do the trick. Physical obstacles such as solid fences, buildings and large shrubs also help in preventing contamination of your seed strain. Or you can affect the times at which some flowers bloom to make certain that opening days or nights don't coincide. Sow seed at intervals, pinch one variety to encourage a later blooming date or start one variety in a greenhouse and sow the other outdoors. These methods work best for flowers with a short blooming span. Any seed set when both flowers are blooming simultaneously could possibly be a mongrel between the two.

To be absolutely sure that a flower does not cross-pollinate, cover the flowers with a paper or mesh bag and hand-pollinate the flower yourself. If you have a sizeable plot and many flowers, you will need to cage the section with mesh screening to keep pollinators at bay. You'll have to pollinate the flowers personally, or you can let insects do the work by switching the caging on alternate days. Evening-scented and flowering plants such as tobacco plants and brugmansias are pollinated by night-flying creatures so keep their seed pure by barricading from dusk until dawn.

Grandpa Ott's Morning Glory

Diane Whealy's Grandpa Ott didn't have to replant seed of his royal purple morning glory each year, the vine just self-sowed and sprouted up with no encouragement whatsoever. But that didn't stop Grandpa Ott from collecting seed. He was famed for his generous hand sharing the morning glory he brought with him when he immigrated from Bavaria. "That was just his way," Diane Whealy remembers, "everyone who ever came to visit his little 40 acre farm in St. Lucas, Iowa went home with some of his morning glories. Before long, the entire community was sprouting with those unique flowers." Maybe it made him feel less lonely for his homeland, or maybe, as Diane suspects, he simply wanted to make certain that no one left the farm empty-handed. At any rate, Grandpa Ott was the one who initially inspired Diane to save seed. He planted the first seeds, so to speak, of what became a life-long passion.

It wasn't until Diane and Kent Whealy began the Seed Savers Exchange (SSE) in 1975 which branched out into the Flower and Herb Exchange in 1989, that she had to worry about harvesting her Grandpa Ott's morning glory with some degree of certainty. Other gardeners were depending on the SSE Heritage Farm for seed of the unique morning glory. Cross-pollination wasn't a problem as 'Grandpa Ott's' was the only morning glory that Diane grew. The main concern was harvesting seed before it shattered. "You have to keep an eye on the seed," she explains. "Morning glory seeds are held in little round buttons, they turn deep beige when they're ripe. And they shatter if you wait too long. I find myself picking every other day. When frost threatens, I lay a tarp on the ground, pull up the vine and haul the whole mess into a shed so the seed will spill onto the tarp if it shatters." Since she started the Flower and Herb

Exchange, Diane has been harvesting seed of other flowers as well, each with its own set of concerns. The old-fashioned vining petunia, for example, forms a sticky seed pod that shatters at the slightest touch, releasing an uncollectible dusting of seed as fine as sand. "The nice part of growing seed is you don't have to deadhead your flowers all the time. But still, you have to be vigilant," Diane warns.

She never made a fine science of saving flower seed until recently. But she soon discovered she instinctively knew how to do the deed. She feels that most gardeners are the same way. "Most gardeners are generous people," she's noticed, "they've often shared from their garden on a very informal basis." As any gardener knows, part of the joy of gardening lies in sharing your finds with friends near and far. This is how flowers are kept alive for generations.

COLLECTING SEED

Ideally, you should collect seed when it has fully ripened but its seed case hasn't yet shattered. Collecting seed too early isn't as irreparable as letting your seed scatter to the wind, you can often ripen seed after it's been plucked.

As a rule, whatever their shape or style, seed pods darken as they reach maturity, and cases usually begin to look dry and turn papery. The trick is to harvest before they split — it's wisest to harvest with a napkin or something else that the seed can spill into, just in case the seed falls free of the pod while you're collecting. Some seeds, such as *Impatiens noli-tangere,* are notoriously prone to popping and even legumes such as sweet peas will shatter if you pluck them vigorously. If there's any danger of frost before fleshy seed pods or berries are ripe, harvest them green and bring them indoors for the duration of the ripening process, then remove the seeds.

SAVING SEED

Store your seed carefully. First make quite certain it is absolutely dry. High temperatures and direct sun can be damaging — never try a "quick dry" method in a microwave or oven, as these can be lethal. Instead, spread the seed on a piece of paper or, ideally, on an elevated fine mesh screen in a cool, dry, airy (but not windy) place for a week or so, longer if the weather was damp or rainy when you harvested. This is especially crucial for seed that has been removed from a moist fruit or berry (such as brugmansia or roses). Shuffle the seed around while it's drying to expose all sides to the air.

Keeping seed free of extraneous matter isn't crucial for amateurs who aren't selling by weight, but plant parts can harbor insects that might contaminate your seed and effect its viability. So try and sift your seed through a medium mesh screen.

Label your seed, put it in a paper or glassine envelope, and store it in a cool, dry and dark place — an airtight canister is ideal.

SEED SOWING

Although most seed should be sown at the beginning of the next growing season, there are exceptions. Sweet cicely *Myrrhis odorata* seed, for example, must be sowed immediately after it is harvested. Gentians, saxifrages and sedums should be sown in autumn. Many biennials are best sown the autumn after the seed is harvested and kept in a cold frame over the winter.

Sowing methods vary drastically depending upon the plant. Some like it warm, some like it cold; some (most larger seeds) should be covered, others (such as snapdragons and fine seed) are scattered on the soil's surface. Don't be disheartened if your seed does not sprout immediately. Some seed is frustratingly lethargic, particularly monkshood *Aconitum,* bleeding heart *Dicentra,* gas plant *Dictamnus,* roses and Christmas roses *Helleborus.* They can take a year to germinate. Try shocking them with a sojourn in the refrigerator. But don't give up.

HEIRLOOMS: THE NEXT GENERATION

When a flower has been in a family for several generations, an intimacy is achieved. Seed savers are privy to a plant's needs and eccentricities, and usually very willing to share that knowledge. Most heirloom gardeners are proud of the heritage of their plants, and they are anxious to insure their future.

Do your part to continue the chain unbroken. Keep your heirlooms alive by propagating them, by whatever method, and sharing them with other gardeners. Make certain that the flowers of yesterday are also the flowers of tomorrow. Pass them along.

Part Two

The Directory
of Heirloom Flowers

The Directory – Introduction

Delving into the individual case histories of heirlooms is fascinating. Political intrigue, the life and death of kings, the conquest of lands and the economy of nations are all bound into the comings and goings of blossoms. That unassuming little violet growing in your garden was once grounds for arrest if it was found being worn on your person. The meek anemone that opens in spring once crowned the heads of Ancient Greek maids. Plants that are popular now were once avoided because of the superstitions that surrounded them; flowers that were once commonplace have now vanished without a trace. There's never a dull moment.

Many flowers have deep roots. As fashions came and went, as gardening styles slipped in and out of vogue, an ever-changing roster of plants became prominent and were prolific. The tall and lanky, small-petaled and drably colored flowers of yore, the "inferior" plants of the past, all had their moment in the sun. They were champions long before being rendered the sleek, compact, profuse-blooming plants of today with their knock 'em dead flower dimensions in retina-arresting colors.

The list of heirloom flowers is incredibly lengthy. There are so many historically important plants that their members would easily fill several thick volumes. We had to be selective when composing this directory. We chose only the key players, and it wasn't easy to winnow down the roster. For help with the task, we turned to the earliest known garden catalog, published in 1677 and issued by William Lucas of the Naked Boy, a shop near Strand Bridge, London. The plants included in that catalog formed the nexus for this directory of heirlooms. But Lucas's list formed the basis only, because our directory of historically important worthies grew to include plants that became popular long after the Naked Boy closed shop. Even heirlooms evolve.

Morning glories, for example, have been around since 1621. But due to their association with the rampant pest, bindweed, they weren't particularly popular until the 20th century. However, when they did step into the fore, they captured the hearts of cottage gardeners with a vengeance. From the early part of this century to the 1960s, morning glories were a crucial element of gardens. Then they fell from fashion again, leaving many wonderful varieties forgotten. At present, a closely knit group of preservationists are laboring to reintroduce morning glories that aren't technically antiques, but which have disappeared from cultivation. Morning glories are modern day heirlooms and warrant inclusion here.

Some histories delve further back than others. Every part of the world has its own history, flora and heirlooms. Peonies flourished in Oriental gardens long before Europeans were aware that they existed. When composing this directory, it was necessary to select a vantage point from which to follow the tide of flowers. Since the British have been excellent chroniclers of horticultural history, it seemed logical to take a European perspective. For the most part, the introductory dates mentioned in the directory that follows stem from the first record of that plant in Britain. For insights into when that happened, early herbals have traditionally been consulted. The herbalists were the naturalists of yore. Some of the earliest chroniclers of matters horticultural were the ancients such as Pliny the Elder, born in Verona during the 1st century AD, and author of *Natural History*, a 37 volume set. He perished watching Vesuvius erupt. And often quoted is Theophrastus, a Greek philosopher born in the 4th century BC and student of Plato and Aristotle as well as the author of *Enquiry into Plants*. Jules Charles de L'Ecluse (alias Clusius) who was born in Flanders (his life spanned from 1526 to 1609) designed the Botanic Garden at Leyden where he was a professor, but traveled broadly and wrote about what he found in *Rariorum Plantarum Historia* published in 1601.

However, we lean most heavily on John Gerard's *Herball or Historie of Plantes,* published in 1597, to keep us appraised of what was in cultivation during the Renaissance. John Gerard (1545–1612) was born in Cheshire and served as a gardener for others as well as creating his own little botanical collection in Holborn. And that explains why you'll find the date 1597 invoked in association with so many heirlooms in our directory. The plant in question may have entered earlier, but we are certain that it was being grown by Gerard's day.

Another milestone in early horticultural history is John Parkinson's *Paradisi in Sole, Paradisus Terrestris*, published in 1629. John Parkinson (1567–1650) was a British apothecary as well as the botanist to Charles I. His opus provides a wealth of plant descriptions in addition to giving a glimpse at the medical and culinary uses of yesterday's flowering plants. So Parkinson is often cited for this insight into early plants, their employment, whether double varieties existed and the color range of flowers in the 17th century. Another apothecary, Nicholas Culpeper (1616–1654) was even more keen on herbal healing, having authored 79 books upon his death at age 38.

As history moved closer to the present, more herbalists and gardeners recorded plants that they saw growing and novelties that were introduced. In North America, we paid keen attention to the lists of John Winthrop (1588–1649)), first Governor to Massachusetts, and Thomas Jefferson (1743–1826), both ardent early gardeners. We lean heavily on 19th century catalogs and encyclopedias, both British and American. And we rely on the scholarship of modern day historians such as Alice M. Coats, Mrs. M. Grieve (author of *A Modern Herbal*), Roy Genders, Scott Kunst (of Old House Gardens in Ann Arbor, Michigan), Marilyn Barlow (of Select Seeds in Union, Connecticut) and Rand B. Lee (of the American Dianthus Society in Santa Fe, New Mexico.

Since history is forever on the move, we hope that this directory will someday need updating. Most especially, we pray that many of the plants that are listed in these pages as vanished will soon be reclaimed.

Temperature Zoning System

The USDA (US Department of Agriculture) has created a guide for the adaptability of plants to different areas of the country based on the average minimum temperature in each area. This zoning system is used to describe the hardiness of each perennial. However, there are many other factors besides temperature which determine hardiness. Often the soil type in a garden and the snow cover during a specific winter will affect a plant's ability to survive. Furthermore, certain perennials fail to thrive where temperatures are too warm or humid during the summer. When cold hardiness is normally the only factor to influence a plant's survival, we mention the coldest zone in which that perennial will survive, though you may be lucky elsewhere. When a perennial often fails to thrive in very hot or humid areas, we provide the upper limit of its range as well.

ZONE NUMBER	CENTIGRADE	FAHRENHEIT
❶	below –45°C	below –50°F
❷	–45 to –40°C	–50 to –40°F
❸	–40 to –34°C	–40 to –30°F
❹	–34 to –29°C	–30 to –20°F
❺	–29 to –23°C	–20 to –10°F
❻	–23 to –17°C	–10 to 0°F
❼	–17 to –12°C	0 to 10°F
❽	–12 to –7°C	10 to 20°F
❾	–7 to –1°C	20 to 30°F
❿	–1 to 5°C	30 to 40°F

Contents

THE BIRDS AND BEES OF HEIRLOOMS

SPECIES

Many heirlooms are species, that is, they are the pure plant before birds, bees or humans start to meddle with them. They occur naturally in the wild, and occurred naturally wherever they were native several hundred years ago. Known or unbeknownst to man they existed before people started to corral plants into gardens, their tenure predated the advent of botany, but when taxonomists started naming plants, they affixed Latinized binomials such as Alchemilla mollis, Chrysanthemum parthenium and Dicentra spectabilis. They are the prototypical heirlooms. From a seed saving standpoint, their seed will come true when planted.

VARIETY

Some heirlooms are varieties, that is, they occur in nature, and they're similar to a species but they have some defining trait differing from the species – perhaps white flowers such as the white bleeding heart Dicentra spectabilis alba, or naturally occurring double flowers such as the double fragrant Viola odorata florepleno. Although they are occasionally weaker than the species itself, they will come true from seed if segregated from other species and varieties.

CULTIVAR

Here's where humans and other pollinators step in. A cultivar is a cross between two plants of the same species often performed intentionally by people, sometimes popping up by surprise, the work of insects or the wind. A good example is the scarlet morning glory

Ipomoea nil 'Scarlet O'Hara'. When sown, the seed will probably come true, especially if it is an heirloom and has been grown for many generations, but its purity is not guaranteed.

HYBRIDS

When plants from two different species or genera are crossed, a hybrid results. Seed from the resulting progeny usually does not come true. In fact, some of the seed is not fertile. Martha Washington pelargoniums (Pelargonium x domesticum) are a good example.

OPEN-POLLINATED PLANTS

When you collect seed of an open-pollinated plant, chances are good that it will come true to its origins – if you segregate that plant from other species, varieties or cultivars that might interbreed.

SELECTIONS

Many heirlooms came to us through the selection process. An excellent example is the work that the Vicar of Shirley, Reverend W. Wilks, performed with poppies. He happened to be hiking in a cornfield one day and noticed a scarlet poppy with a white edge to its petals. The Reverend returned when seed was ripe, collected it and sowed it. He continued along the same vein for several seasons, always confiscating any ordinary poppies that polluted his crop. The result was Shirley poppies which sport white rimmed petals with a fair amount of reliability. If you purchase a packet of Shirley poppies, you'll get by-and-large plants with the same traits that the Reverend Wilks fixed.

Perennials and Biennials

Aconitum napellus   ❻

RANUNCULACEAE

monkshood, wolf's bane, helmet flower, dumbledore's delight, cupid's car, chariot and horses, granny's nightcap, auld wife's hood, captain of the garden

Native to Europe, Asia and America but particularly common in Europe's damp woods and hedgerows, monkshood was listed as indispensible for 13th century physicians and must have furnished one of the more ornamental elements of monastery gardens. By the 16th century, the violet blooming, regal spired native species, *Aconitum napellus anglicum* was a fixture in cottage gardens, and by 1597, three other species, *A. anthora* (pale yellow flowered), *A. lycoctonum* (purple-lilac flowered) and *A. variegatum* (violet and white) were mentioned.

Reputed to have sprouted from the saliva of the frothing jaws of Cerberus, the three-headed guard dog of the Underworld, monkshood was once suspected of being an ingredient in the potion that helps witches to fly. The earliest Anglo-Saxons named the plant "thung" meaning "very poisonous", and cautionary words have invariably accompanied any mention of monkshood. Many early authors questioned the wisdom of recommending a plant that could wreak so much havoc after ingestion. To underscore the peril, Gerard described an Antwerp scenario in which an entire party perished when "ignorant persons" tossed monkshood into the dinner salad. Monkshood was apparently commonly mixed with bait to dispatch wolves and badgers – and was rumored to be occasionally employed to eradicate unwanted husbands and wives as well, but the handsome plant continues to be popular.

Monkshood bears delphinium-like spires of purplish blue blossoms on 2½ foot tall ferny-leaved stems. The white form of monkshood *A. napellum* 'Album' has also been grown in English gardens since the 16th century and remains a popular garden flower. The plant thrived in American gardens from an early date. For reasons that might have been medicinal (aconite was used for rheumatism, neuralgia and lumbago), monkshood appeared on John Winthrop's initial seed order from Robert Hill, the grocer at the Three Angels in 1631.

Monkshood prefers a soil that is fertile and retains moisture; plants thrive in both sun and partial shade, but the flowers linger longer when they aren't stressed by bright sunbeams. Monkshood can be propagated by division, transplanted in fall or early spring, or from seed planted as soon as it is mature. Wash your hands after handling the black poisonous roots. One of the flower's chief advantages over the rather similar looking delphiniums is that the stems are wispy and unlikely to snap in the wind, so staking is not necessary.

Alcea rosea

MALVACEAE

hollyhock

Hollyhocks were *Malva hortensis* to Gerard and *Althaea rosea* to more recent taxonomists, but are now designated as *Alcea rosea* stemming from the Greek word meaning "to cure". Probably originating in Turkey or Asia but introduced to Britain in 1573, one story suggests their common name derives from the application of their broad leaves to soothe swollen horses' heels, thus hollyhock, while *hoc* is the Saxon word for mallow and some associate their introduction with the Crusades, thus "holy hoc". Early physicians found the flowers useful for tuberculosis and bladder inflammations, and the flowers were once used as dyes.

If ever there was a flower that embodies the cottage garden, it is the hollyhock with its towering spires densely packed with sizeable blossoms, like single roses on a linear stem in the single-varieties, like fluffy pompoms in the double versions. Hollyhocks seem to stick in your memory and capture the imagination. Many youthful reminiscences are entwined with that flower that stands tall, seeds liberally and comes up in a smorgasbord of mostly pastel color combinations. Hollyhocks are among the most popular heirlooms; they're pass-along plants.

Heirloom gardeners often complain about double flowers overtaking the market to the exclusion of older, single varieties, but double hollyhocks have been around for centuries. William Lucas' first seed list of 1677 lists double hollyhocks (no colors specified) and Bernard McMahon's broadsheet published in Philadelphia in 1807 offers doubles, all colors.

In 1823, Thomas Hogg, the nurseryman of Paddington Green, listed no fewer than 80 named cultivars and varieties including the much-coveted striped sorts. However, their flirt with fame was brief because the fungal disease, hollyhock rust, rampaged through the family, rendering hollyhocks into biennials rather than perennials by the end of the century.

'Chater's Double' hollyhocks, created in the 1880s, are still readily available. And *A. ficifolia*, the fig-leaved hollyhock or Antwerp hollyhock, mentioned by Gerard, is also still on the market. 'Nigra', a chocolate burgundy version is a named variety that has been selected and remains true. Lesser grown but along the same theme, *Malva moschata*, the musk mallow, was native to Europe and quickly naturalized in North America. Very hardy, more compact and perennial rather than biennial, but with smaller blossoms, the musk mallow could be found in gardens both in the Old and New Worlds by the 17th century.

Leave plenty of room between hollyhock plants (at least 3 feet is advisable) – they tend to be broad at the base. Hollyhocks are thirsty plants and tend to wilt easily; a fertile soil is not essential, but it will encourage tall blossom spires. Staking may be necessary to keep the tall spires from snapping in a gust. Hollyhocks are magnets to deer. Removing the flower spikes the moment they have finished their performance keeps a hollyhock performing, but eliminates the chance of producing seedlings.

Alchemilla

ROSACEAE

Lady's mantle, lion's foot, bear's foot, nine hooks

Native to Europe, *Alchemilla vulgaris* was cultivated from the 14th century and valued as a cure for wounds. Jerome Bock, who wrote under the Latinized name of Tragus, coined the name Lady's mantle for a plant closely associated with the Virgin Mary. The name Alchemilla comes from alchemy – it was thought that the dew that collects on the serrated edges of the rounded leaves could turn metal into gold. Better still, it was also reputed to restore fading beauty. A leaf tucked under your pillow at night was said to guarantee sweet dreams.

Extremely hardy, often spending most of winter still fully clothed with those rounded, serrated-edged leaves, dew-drops clinging to alchemilla's serrated leaf-tips provide a pleasant picture. *A. mollis*, formerly known as *A. vulgaris*, came from Asia Minor in the 19th century: this is the commonest and some would say the best garden form. It blossoms through most of the summer, crowned with clouds of palest yellow blossoms, long-lasting in flower arrangements and equally suitable for drying. *A. erythropoda*, a dwarf form from the Carpathians, was introduced earlier this century.

Lady's mantle will grow in full sun as well as dense shade and rarely wilts, even during periods of drought. It forms the most impressive show when given plenty of elbow room between bedfellows and afforded rich, fertile but friable soil. Although dead-heading isn't essential, the plant will remain tidy if flower spikes are removed before they begin to brown. Lady's mantle makes a handsome foil for *Centaurea cyanea* or golden hostas. Poppies are displayed to good advantage when wading through (and later buried beneath) Lady's mantle foliage.

Aquilegia

RANUNCULACEAE

columbine, granny's bonnets, meeting houses

❸ (shade is required in the southern U.S.)

Prior to the long-spurred *Aquilegia canadensis*' arrival via John Tradescant the Younger in 1640, there were only the short-spurred columbines, derived from the European native *A. vulgaris*, to entertain British cottagers. Gerard compared the foliage to that of the greater celandine and the flowers were always likened to birds. Both the common and Latin names reflect the ornithological allusion: *columba* refers to the stylized resemblance of the flower spurs to a clutch of pigeons, *aquila* is Latin for eagle.

A. vulgaris and variations on that theme were the common columbines of cottage gardens. And there were plenty of variations to please the populace. Gerard documents an upside down columbine with spurs at the tips of the flowers rather than toward the pedicel. The oddity survived into the 18th century but is no longer known to exist. In the 1600s, striped columbines were all the rage, but they didn't survive into the 20th century. When *A. canadensis* (scarlet flowering), arrived in Europe from North America it revolutionized the look of columbines. William Lucas' Naked Boy catalog of 1677 mentions *Aquilegia vulgaris flore pleno*, and double columbines have existed at least since the 16th century, especially the "rose" or "degenerate" columbines. The double "rose" columbine 'Nora Barlow', with its many clustered petals, readily on the market, is reputed to have originated in the 1700s, but its name is of recent vintage. *A. formosa* (red flowering) was another relatively early arrival. But the influential *A. chrysantha* is a canary yellow species introduced into cultivation as recently as 1873 from the Rocky Mountains.

Known to cross-pollinate shamelessly and setting seed with little provocation, most columbines must be segregated to remain true. Division is

recommended as the only sure way to perpetuate columbines with any degree of certainty. Some seed, such as that of 'Nora Barlow' tends to come true. The seeds must be sown onto soil that stays continually moist until germination, which occasionally takes several months.

Columbines prefer partial shade and a light, sandy soil with good drainage. Although leaf miners and nibbling caterpillars love to eat their leaves, they usually rally the following year. Their beauty is especially dramatic combined with Siberian iris or lupines.

Armeria

PLUMBAGINACEAE

thrift, sea pink, ladies' cushion

Armeria maritima was a plant with a purpose – native to Europe, Asia Minor, North Africa and North America, it was embraced by Elizabethan gardeners specifically to enhance their tidy knot gardens. And no wonder. Sea thrift grows only a foot in height with grass-like tuffets crowned by little orb-shaped clusters of blossoms. The problem, as John Parkinson pointed out, was that the little mound tends to stretch along the ground with time - growing no taller, but ruining the clean cut of a knot garden's precise lines. For edging a border, however, armeria is ideal.

Although the species *A. maritima* blooms with pale pink blossoms, a white form ('Alba') was available in the 18th century. And different variations in the size of the mound and the subtle shades of pink in the flowers came and went. Nowadays there are several shades on the market, including a recommended rosy-pink with the tantalizing name of 'Vindictive'. L. H. Bailey mentioned a form with white leaves, no longer listed on the market.

Not only was armeria too expansive for Parkinson's tastes, he also complained that it couldn't be relied upon to survive the winter. Perhaps his problem was damp soil, because when bedded in a well-drained, gritty soil, armeria is quite hardy. In fact, in later 19th century books (where it is often listed under the name of *A. vulgaris* rather than *A. maritima*) sea thrift was often recommended for rock gardens, capable of withstanding drought without quibble but disliking wet weather (one 19th century reference cautioned against the drip of trees) and soggy underfootings.

The best idea when dealing with sea thrift is to divide the plant regularly, thus preventing the centers from dying out. And division (best done after blooming in spring) is the most common method of propagating the plant, although seed is readily set.

Aster

COMPOSITAE

Michaelmas daisy, starwort, frost flower

The first aster to arrive in Britain was *Aster amellus*, a purple-flowering species from Italy, described by Virgil and already firmly entrenched in gardens by 1596. Known as the blue Italian starwort, this aster wasn't a major player in either the garden or medicine, although it was sometimes invoked for mad dog bites (combined with old hog's grease and applied). Instead, it was the asters of the New World that truly made a splash in gardens. The first North American aster to arrive in Britain was *A. lateriflorus* (formerly *A. tradescantii*) brought from Virginia by the younger John Tradescant in 1633. Although it didn't have the impact that later starworts enjoyed, it was listed in catalogs and became naturalized throughout Europe. Of much greater import was *A. novi-belgiae*, the Michaelmas Daisy with violet-blue ray petals, introduced into Britain in 1710. It's fascinating to ponder the fact that *A. novi-belgiae* was named for New Netherlands or New Amsterdam – a place where asters probably once abounded – later renamed New York for James II. However, *A. novi-belgii* owes its popularity to Ernest Ballard, who has been called the George Russell (of lupine fame) of the Michaelmas daisy. In his garden in Colwall, Worcestershire, he honed a more compact, tidier plant than the ragged aster of New York. Although his first introduction, 'Beauty of Colwall' (1907) is no longer available, several of the ensuing hybrids are still on the market including 'Queen of Colwall', 'Marie Ballard' and 'Rachel Ballard'.

Also more popular in Britain than in its native North America was the deep purple blooming New England aster, *A. novi-angliae*, which arrived in Britain from North America in 1710 and became wildly popular a century later. This is the parent that gave us the omnipresent, 3 foot tall 'Alma Potschke' (originally 'Andenken an Alma Potschke') with magenta blossoms. Heirloom asters are difficult to find. 'Harrington's Pink', dating from the 1930s, is one of the oldest New England asters commonly available in the United States.

Asters provide a spark of color in autumn long after most other flowers have come and gone. They prefer full sun and well-drained soil, although asters will endure more moist conditions. To perform their best, asters should be lifted and divided every three years. Unfortunately, their lower leaves often shrivel before the flowers open, the best idea is to hide the unsightly lower extremities with artemisia or some other clump-forming plant crouching in front.

Bellis perennis

COMPOSITAE

English daisy, paquerette (in France),
daeyeseye, bonewort, bruisewort

Chaucer waxed poetic, writing, "Of all the flowers in the meade, Then love I most those floures white and redde, Such that men call daisies in our town..." He referred to *Bellis perennis* as daisy, but also by its Anglo-Saxon name, daeyes-eaye, or "the eye of the day." That European native has always been linked with rural life – no one really knows when it came into cultivation.

Although the single version was reputed to be in cultivation since time immemorial, by the late 16th century, double flowers in combinations of red and white could be found popping from the little rosettes of pale green, sorrel-like leaves. 'Alba Plena', a double white stemming from the 16th century, is still readily available. At the same time, another fascinating sport occurred: the hen-and-chickens version sported many tiny stalks sprouting from the base of a flower, dangling with tiny flowers. That form became known as *B. perennis* 'Prolifera' and it is still available today.

By the 17th century, streaked and speckled varieties were added to the roster. The 18th century brought the dwarf double pale pink 'Dresden China' and crested daisies also appeared. The 19th century brought a variegated version. 'Rob Roy' is a 19th century daisy still popular, boasting ruby red blossoms so fully double that no yellow eye exists.

Like many other Americans, Thomas Jefferson flirted with and was flouted by *Bellis perennis*. Inspired by the blooming British lawn, he planted daisies at Monticello, only to watch them perish under the hot Virginia sun. As the New York based Peter Henderson explained, they are "impatient of our hot summers."

In cooler climates, daisies blossom from spring through summer with scant attention and tolerate any soil, but prefer plenty of humus underfoot. They tend to be susceptible to red spider mite but frequent applications of cold water help to keep them free of the pests.

Camellia

THEACEAE

camellia, snow camellia

Not all plants arrived in Britain intentionally. The first *Camellia japonica* plants, for example, were a major disappointment when they were first imported in 1730. The East India Company was expecting a shipment of tea plants, *Camellia sinensis*, and the substitute was greeted with something less than complete enthusiasm. Named for an Austrian missionary, Georg Joseph Kamel, who studied plant until his death in 1706. The first camellia to blossom in Europe unfurled in the Essex greenhouse of Lord Petre in 1739, but it died within the year, a victim to the fits and starts of the heating systems of the times. Lord Petre himself also expired shortly thereafter.

Long before camellias set foot on European soil, they were grown and hybridized in the Orient. Records of *C. japonica*'s cultivation date back 1,200 years and its employment in Oriental gardens undoubtedly predates written reference.

Known in Japan as Tsubaki, the tree with shining leaves, camellias were worshipped in the Shinto religion as the residence inhabited by gods while in their earthly transfiguration. The tree was similarly revered in China. In addition to its shiny leaves, the woody shrub is blessed by an abundance of peony-like blossoms that open in midwinter in the greenhouse or unfurl in early spring outdoors. By the time *C. japonica* came to Europe, there were already doubles, singles and semi-doubles in all shades from white, through pink to red. Little wonder that the plant was embraced so whole-heartedly by wealthy gardeners (and camellias were most definitely estate heirlooms rather than cottage garden plants).

The railroad magnate, John Stevens of Hoboken, New Jersey was the first to import *C. japonica* into North America, importing a single red flowering hybrid in the 1790s. Although no one is certain of the identity of Stevens' first camellia, he immediately sent for a double white and received 'Alba Plena', still in cultivation. By 1822, William Prince's Linnaean Botanical Garden in Flushing, New York listed 17 cultivars in its catalog. It was not uncommon during the Victorian era for special greenhouses to be constructed solely to house a camellia collection on a grand estate.

As Lord Petre discovered, camellias can be peevish to grow. They require cool temperatures that don't go above 55 degrees fahrenheit while setting buds, an atmosphere that can prove difficult to furnish in the average home. They also detest a dry atmosphere. If hot and dry conditions don't kill a camellia outright, they usually lead to bud drop. Generous watering is

also required while the buds are in their developmental stages. Camellias are not reliably hardy outdoors and should be situated against a south-facing wall.

Campanula

CAMPANULACEAE

harebell, bluebell, bellflower, Canterbury bell, Venus' looking glass, corn violet, bats in the belfry

Campanula comes from the Latin, meaning a tower of bells, which is certainly an apt description for the blossoms that bedeck members of this family. There are so many campanulas (300 at last count) and such a large number are garden-worthy, that the family figures deeply in horticultural history. An age-old favorite is the harebell or bluebell, *Campanula rotundifolia* (not to be confused with *Hyacinthoides non-scripta*), native to the northern hemisphere and frequenting meadows in both the Old and New Worlds. Sir Walter Scott penned lines to that little heath-flower in Lady of the Lake and it was sufficiently common to be free for the plucking, precluding inclusion in the early plant lists, except perhaps in France and Italy where the harebell was cultivated as a vegetable for its fleshy roots. In addition, other campanulas were introduced as edible and granted garden space ostensibly for purposes of feeding the family. Most especially, peasants resorted to digging and boiling the roots (reputedly served with meat) of *C. persicifolia*, the peach-leaved bellflower, introduced into gardens about 1578. In fact, every part of the campanula was pressed into service. Cottagers gargled infusions of the leaves and flowers of several campanulas to combat sore throats and made lotions of all the vegetative parts to cleanse the skin.

The date when *C. rapunculoides*, the creeping bellflower, was introduced into Britain remains unknown. Known as rampions to cooks, *C. rapunculoides* is sometimes associated with the legend of Rapunzel – a peasant who yearned for the plant during her pregnancy sent her husband into a neighbor-

ing witch's garden to appease her craving. He was caught in the act, and only released with the promise that he'd give his daughter, Rapunzel, to the witch upon birth. Locking her in a tower seemed the only solution. Other important heirloom campanulas include *C. glomerata*, a European native grown by Elizabethan gardeners, *C. lactiflora*, introduced in 1814 from western Asia, and *C. latifolia*, a European native Elizabethan favorite.

C. medium or Canterbury bells is a favorite heirloom, hardy to Zone 8. Native to Southern Europe, and introduced into British gardens in 1597, *C. medium* (also known as *C. media*) has been a highly popular biennial for several hundred years. Much to the confusion of everyone, Canterbury bells were called Coventry bells in the 16th and 17th century when the native *C. trachelium* was called Canterbury bells. *C. medium* later took over the common name of Canterbury bells and *C. trachelium* was dubbed the nettle-leaved bellflower.

The stems of *C. medium* are 3-4 feet high, and thick with sizeable, inflated trumpets in shades of blue, rose, purpl, and red. The cup and saucer type, known as 'Calycanthema' with a trumpet configuration similar to daffodils, is currently more common than the true species. There is also a double, flower-within-a-flower (or hose-in-hose) version in pink, white and blue which Tilton's *Journal of Horticulture and Florist's Companion* of 1870 proclaimed more a curiosity than a thing of beauty, with flowers that could be likened "to a nest of tubs or boxes". Doubles featured in most 19th century catalogs, in

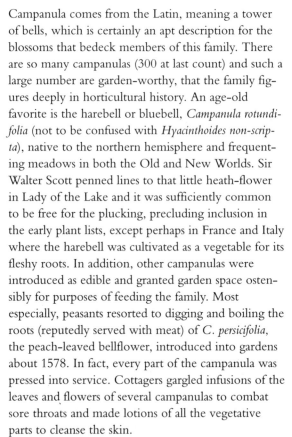

both blue and white, and are still available under the cultivar name of 'Flore Pleno'.

C. pyramidalis or the chimney bellflower is a southern European native, hardy to Zone 8. Introduced to England by 1596, it proved a poor garden plant, so became traditionally cultivated in containers; the pots were used annually as summer decorations for the fireplace when it was not being fired. Apparently, the custom of potting bellflowers continued from the 17th through the 19th century. There are few displays as impressive as the tall (sometimes upwards of five feet) pyramids of stunning blue blossoms. Needless to say, the spire needs staking. I have a friend in New England who keeps a chimney bellflower growing faithfully on her porch every summer, but generally it has been difficult to find these campanulas for over a century: according to an

1870 Tilton's *Journal of Horticulture*, "its popularity has long since passed away, to give place to other more fashionable flowers, which have, in their turn, also been succeeded by other rivals more beautiful. But, in Holland, it is said that the pyramidal bell-flower is still in fashion with the old-fashioned people."

Campanulas prefer a light soil (preferably chalky) and plenty of moisture, so need to be kept well watered to perform at their best – whether in a border or in a pot. Most campanulas look best when massed together, although they should be given 2-3 feet between plants. They transplant well and are easily divided in early fall. The flowers are weighty and their stems should be staked. They look handsome grouped together or combined with *Salvia officinalis* and its hybrids. Canterbury bells also make excellent and striking cut flowers.

Cardamine pratensis

CRUCIFERAE

Lady's smock, cuckoo flower, meadow cress, bitter cress

The name cardamine probably stems from the Greek, *kardia*, the heart (referring to its former use to strengthen that organ) paired with *damao*, meaning "I overpower". The overpowering allusion hints at the plant's former use to deaden pain. More often, the leaves were eaten in salad, serving the same purpose as watercress. As for the nicknames, Lady's smock connects the flower with the Virgin Mary, while cuckoo flower links the bloom with the time of year when the strange call of that bird can be heard. Native throughout Europe and widely distributed throughout the meadows of North America, Lady's smock is a spring bloomer with a rosette of leaves anchoring stalks of lilac flowers.

Beloved as a garland flower to welcome spring, Izaac Walton (author of *The Compleat Angler*, 1653) mentions that, in May, the meadows were rife with

young boys gathering the flowers for that purpose. Shakespeare also makes frequent mention of the Lady's smocks he found growing on river banks. However, the flower was more admired in the wild than as part of the garden, especially in North America. Described politely as a plant of "mild merit" by Thomas Everett of the New York Botanical Garden, the single form is not as often invoked as its double counterpart. And the double version seems to proliferate unbidden in the wild.

Although Lady's smock is easily found in British nurseries, it is not commonly found commercially in the US. The plant prefers a moist soil underfoot, and can be propagated by seed or division. But a more entertaining method of increasing the stock is to pull off leaves, bury their petioles in the soil and watch plantlets emerge.

Convallaria

LILIACEAE

lily-of-the-valley, wood lily, may lily, muguet, our Lady's tears

Incredibly hardy and native to Asia, Europe and naturalized in parts of North America, *Convallaria majalis* has won a place in cultivation from at least 1000BC onward. In the 17th century, lily-of-the valley was known to be used for gout and heartburn, and the dried flowers and roots were sniffed like snuff, to clear the head and restore memory. It is now used by herbalists for treating heart conditions.

Best known for the small white glistening bells that line the slender, 6–10 inch long, arching stems, the funneled, pointed leaves are also attractive. A pale pink form existed early, mentioned in the 16th century. A red version was available by the mid-18th century, known as 'Rubra', as well as a striped flowering sort and even a double striped and double white form in the 19th century (described as "not worth cultivating" by George Nicholson of the Royal Botanic Gardens at Kew in 1887). A giant version known as 'Major' was available in 1887 as well as a fragile golden variegated sort, which is now being touted as a novelty.

Lily-of-the-valley thrives in the shade and once the rhizomes are planted, they cover ground vigorously, forming a carpet so dense that even poison ivy can't compete. A fluffy woodland soil is best, with dense humus and plenty of leaf mould. Although it prefers ample moisture lily-of-the-valley will not usually complain unless a drought is severe. The flowers last well in bouquets but don't ship successfully. Propagate lily-of-the-valley by division at any time of year.

Delphinium

RANUNCULACEAE

delphinium

Another classic cottage garden plant, the delphinium hybrids we grow today are in fact comparatively recent garden introductions. *Delphinium elatum* was introduced in 1597 and is native from France to Siberia. Although its flowers are not semi-double, it was one of the primary players in the modern-day delphiniums. Hybridization on delphiniums began in 1859, with the named varieties available by 1881. You can now find plants producing their distinctive tightly packed flower spikes in a wide range of colors. *D. delavayi* was collected from China by the Catholic missionary and plant hunter Delavay in the 19th century. Growing to about 4 feet tall, it produces narrow spikes of rich blue flowers toward the end of summer. *D.* 'Alice Artindale' is another old variety which is now rare. Smaller than many modern delphiniums, growing no more than 3½ feet, it produces tightly packed spires of double lavender blue flowers.

Some of the early cultivars will seed, although many can only be kept true by division. They thrive best in sheltered locations, or well protected by other plants, in sunny spots in well-fed soil. Not only are they prone to viruses, delphiniums also require staking, but this is a small price to pay for such a striking flower.

If delphiniums are planted in a sunny sheltered position and flowers are cut back immediately after flowering, many cultivars will reflower, sometimes three times in one year with the first blossoms appearing in late spring and the final blooming in fall.

Dianthus

❸-❽

CARYOPHYLLACEAE

gillyflower, gillimaufries, Julyflower, divine flower, sweet William, sweet John, sweet Swivelsfield, pink, grass pink, clove pink, carnation, sops-in-wine

The history of dianthus is a long and convoluted affair spanning at least 2000 years, beginning with the moment that the Athenians dubbed the plant Dianthos, Flower of Jove. Since that time there has been much mingling of fates and bloodlines and a confusing interchange of common names. The first recorded non-Latin name for dianthus was the French, *gelofre*, which was Anglicized into gillyflower. No one seems to be in agreement as to the parentage of sweet Johns or the lineage of sweet swivelsfields. Carnations are often called pinks and vice versa.

I owe everything I know about dianthus to Rand B. Lee of Sante Fe, New Mexico, president of the American Dianthus Society and editor of *The Gilliflower Times*. He has devoted his life to dianthus, researching that genus and spreading the good word in all matters gilliflower-related. From Rand, I learned that the clove carnation symbolized gentleness in days when flowers were permeated with symbolism. I discovered that, in France, *D. caryophyllus* infused an aromatic liqueur swigged to cure the plague, that some tenants paid rent to Oliver Cromwell in roses and gillyflowers, and at one time inhabitants of the town of Ham in Surrey were levied a tax of three clove gillyflowers.... Obviously, dianthus have always been flowers of worth.

No longer known in the wild and difficult to find in commerce, the true single-flowered *D. caryophyllus* has spawned a tribe of progeny. Some say it was introduced from the Pyrenees and others claim it was native to southern Europe, but modern carnations are only hardy to Zone 8 much less hardy than this useful (Zone 3) parent, no longer to be found in the wild. The transformation of *D. caryophyllus* from wildling to highly cultivated "florist's flower" was accomplished early in the game. By the early 1700s, single, semi-double and double carnations were already common, while the color range included crimson, blush, purple, red, scarlet, white, and tawny petalled flowers. At that early date, there existed striped, stippled, spotted and veined carnations. In fact, even before Parkinson published his herbal in 1629, all those hybrids were herded into classes including Bizarre, Flake, Flame and Picotee Carnations with rules about how each should look. For example, the Flames bore red flowers striped with black, Bizarres were double and striped or variegated by four distinct colors. Few of those striking dianthus still exist.

Carnations have been so heavily bred that they retain only a vestige of their former perfume. Perpetual blossoms have long been considered crucial (in the greenhouse or window during the winter), with hardiness a less important factor. Vita Sackville-West proclaimed the 'Chabaud' strain (hardy to Zone 7), introduced by a French firm in 1870 and still available, superior above all other annual carnations. This race is still available in colors ranging from salmon ('Aurore'), through cherry ('Carmen') to 'Chabaud Yellow'. An improvement was the 1926 'Enfant de Nice' with double, clove-scented blooms on stiff stems, and this name has since been adopted by many highly fragrant double flowers that bloom the first year from seed. A more recent innovation, the 'Grenadin' strain with 2" wide, fringed flowers is recommended for its fragrance and hardy to Zone 6; 'King of the Blacks' is the most commonly sold member of this group.

D. plumarius, the grass pink or clove pink is much hardier (to Zone 3) than its finicky relative was, the pink that proved a mainstay of the cottage garden. The feathered foliage gives the species name of *plumarius*. It also sprouts in tufts, like grass, which earned it the common name of grass pink. Other common names allude to the fragrance which remains its signature. Gerard's twelve varieties of "wild gilloflowers" were all single-flowered and intensely aromatic. In fact, all pinks were single until the 1700s. The oldest known hybrid is the highly scented 'Sops-in-Wine', possibly used in brewing and introduced into England in the early 1300s.

At about the same time that carnations were developing, pinks were also witnessing flower-altering transformations. In the 1500s, the "starre pink" arose, described as a frilly, single-petalled plant with a darker pink eye and an overpowering scent, probably with *Dianthus plumarius* as one of its parents. In the early 17th century, the "starres" spawned several hybrids that could compete favorably with the upscale carnations. However, some names – such as 'Ragamuffin' – belied their status.

Although few of the truly ancient dianthus still remain, some 16th century hybrids have recently been rediscovered including several of the Painted Lady types including 'Nonsuch', 'Queen of Sheba' and 'Unique'. Among the most popular 19th century heirlooms is 'Mrs. Sinkins', with large, double, cabbage-rose type flowers and a mighty perfume. It was named for the wife of the Master of the Slough Workhouse by the same florist who introduced 'Cox's Orange Pippin' apple.

All pinks prefer full sun and a neutral to alkaline soil. For best results, try adding organic fertilizer and crushed rock phosphate when planting. Good drainage is crucial, and pinks will thrive in rock gardens; a raised bed is also helpful. Dianthus don't like

soil on their foliage; a bark mulch will prevent problems but don't mulch with compost, hay or grass clippings. Propagation is easy as pinks send out tufted side shoots that can be pinned to the ground (try using a U-shaped hairpin) and, if pinned to loose, friable soil, the offshoot will quickly send down roots. *D. caryophyllus* is also easily grown from seed, although most older hybrids will not come true from seed and must be reproduced vegetatively.

Fortunately, the blue-green leaved stems are easy to root. And carnations are easy to cultivate, given full sun, cool temperatures, well drained soil and regular feeding. They tolerate drought but are prone to red spider mites.

D. barbatus, Sweet William, is a biennial from the Pyrenees. The first written British reference notes Henry VIII's order of Sweet William roots to plant at his newly acquired castle at Hampton Court. The name possibly honors William the Conqueror or perhaps commemorates William of Aquitaine. Single sweet Williams could be found in most cottage gardens from early days, as well as some double varieties such as the double scarlet 'King Willie' of 1634. All sweet Williams were once much more scented than the varieties commonly available today.

Sweet Williams are biennials, but easily seed themselves in. They thrive in full sun and enjoy a soil rich in lime, enduring an occasional drought but blossoming over a longer period of time when watered regularly. Sweet Williams combine well with white blossoms, especially baby's breath and alyssum.

Dicentra spectabilis

FUMARIACEAE

bleeding heart, ladies' lockets

Not an ancient heirloom by any means, the bleeding heart didn't appear in cottage gardens until after 1850, but it immediately became such a firm fixture that it now seems to be part of the scenery. And who could blame 19th century gardeners for giving it space? The foliage is lacy and handsome and the

flowers are plentiful and whimsical. Dangling from a long, lily-of-the-valley-like stem, it's no stretch of the imagination to derive the bleeding heart image from the pink-petalled flowers broken asunder by an inner median white petal. Native to Siberia (where it was reputedly first unsuccessfully collected in 1816) and

Japan, *Dicentra spectabilis* was only introduced into Europe as recently as 1846 by Robert Fortune who found it cultivated in a Chinese garden. Needless to say, given its native region, the bleeding heart proved incredibly hardy.

The bleeding heart quickly made the jump to America, and was mentioned in Joseph Breck's 1866 *New Book of Flowers* (later referenced as *Dielytra* in Peter Henderson's 1881 volume, *Henderson's Handbook of Plants*). *The British Illustrated Dictionary of Gardening*, edited by George Nicholson in 1887, mentions a white form still prominent today.

Bleeding hearts are incredibly easy to grow and come up year after year despite abuse and neglect, making them as popular in the cemetery as the cottage garden. They prefer shaded conditions and a fertile, very friable, woodland-like soil. Propagate them by division in early spring (bleeding hearts are among the first plants to appear in that season), making sure that each division has sufficient roots to thrive apart from its parent plant. When content, bleeding hearts can grow up to 3 feet tall, with a similar girth.

Dictamnus

RUTACEAE

gas plant, burning bush, false dittany, fraxinella

You might accuse cottage gardeners of adopting *Dictamnus albus* (formerly known as *D. fraxinella*, alluding to the leaves of the ash tree which the leaves resemble) for the sole purpose of performing the burning bush trick, but in fact, that gimmick is a fairly recently discovered phenomenon. It is native to Southwest Europe, South and Central Asia to China and Korea and common in cottage gardens from the late 16th century onward.

Dictamnus is quite a handsome plant, with segmented pale green leaves topped to a height of 3 feet by spires of open-faced, azalea-like blossoms each bearing long stamens. Early gardeners valued it for the pyramid of showy white to purple blossoms that crown the plant, and for the aroma of lemon peel that the plant emits, mellowing to balsam when bruised and strongest around the flower spike. When some practical excuse had to be invented for retaining a flower in the cottage garden, dictamnus was recommended for nervous complaints and fevers. Later, the distilled water was popular as a cosmetic.

When Linnaeus's daughter set dictamnus afire in the mid 18th century, presumably by accident while wandering around the garden one evening by candlelight, a flurry of similar experiments followed, all of them unsuccessful, until a British scientist, Dr. Hahn, managed in 1857 to repeat the phenomenon on a sultry night, kindling the flowers without injuring them. He noticed that the peduncles and pedicels of the flower spike are covered with glands secreting ether and those glands don't mature until the flowers have faded. He noted that it all happened rapidly, like lightning, and the plant parts were too green to ignite.

Dictamnus is difficult to divide, so propagate it by sowing seeds as soon as they are ripe. Plants often take three years to flower but once established the plants tolerate drought, sun or partial shade. Although it grows in any conditions it is happiest in a heavy, rich soil. Four colors of dictamnus were available in the 17th century; at present, in addition to the natural diversity, there is 'Purpureus' with purple flowers, 'Ruber' with rose-colored flowers and 'Albiflorus' with white blooms veined in yellow.

Digitalis

SCROPHULARIACEAE

*foxglove, witches' fingers, fairy's gloves,
dead men's bells, fairy thimbles,
virgin's glove, bloody fingers*

Despite the fact that they are poisonous, despite the problem that they blossom only briefly and tend to die out if not replenished every few years, foxgloves have remained a crucial garden plant over the centuries. *Digitalis purpurea*, the common foxglove, is one of Britain's best known native plants, and different species of digitalis are found throughout Europe, North Africa and even Central Asia.

A handsome biennial, foxgloves display spires of tubular blossoms which could be conceived as resembling a cluster of gloves standing tall above a rosette of mullein-like deeply textured leaves. They were originally called folksgloves, an allusion to the fairies that shared the forest thickets that foxgloves frequent. Digitalis delights bees (which appreciate both the convenient landing platform and the prominent throat-markings) as well as people who love to weave folktales. The markings on the flower throats were said to be the traces of elf handling, or a warning sign that they are poisonous – a feature that gained Digitalis the common name of dead man's thimbles in Ireland. They have always been as common in the cottage garden as on the great estates.

Digitalis was traditionally widely used in country medicine, but not originally for heart-related ailments. Instead, it was recommended for healing "those who have fallen from high places" by Gerard and for sores and ulcers by Parkinson. The story goes that a witch (probably a local folk healer) passed the secret of digitalis to the doctor William Withering in the 18th century, and his experiments led to the discovery of its use as a heart stimulant, for which some species of digitalis are still commercially cultivated today.

Since foxgloves have an affinity for shade as well as fertile soil, they prospered more freely in the open gardens of Britain than in sunnier North American gardens. Traditional cottage gardeners valued and selected for the white varieties of foxglove such as *D. purpurea* 'Alba', and those sporting noticeable throat markings. Nowadays, the trend is toward stockier plants that bloom the first year, such as 'Foxy', as well as strains with blossoms surrounding the stem rather than being one-sided.

Early horticultural writers suggested that foxgloves were bound to appear wherever soil was freshly overturned and plants grown from seed do seem to thrive better than transplants. In fact, although foxgloves always seem to flourish unaided in other people's gardens, despite the fact they self-seed profusely, they are not always easy to establish in a garden and it can take many years to get a colony growing happily. Try fertilizing the plants heavily or feeding them with manure or comfrey tea to stimulate growth. This treatment also encourages the growth of very tall and majestic flower spikes.

Seed can lay dormant for years so the most reliable way of ensuring success is to collect some seed as soon as the capsule splits in late summer and sow it immediately in pots, overwintering in a cold frame for planting out in early spring. Seed requires light to germinate, so simply press it into moist soil. All species of foxglove will come true when sown in isolation, but some *D. purpurea* 'Alba' forms may include a percentage of reversions to the dominant purple color; those spires can be removed as soon as they begin to color.

Dipsacus

DIPSACEAE

teasel, card thistle, Venus' basin, barber's brush, brushes and combs, church broom

The name *dipsacus* is from the Greek "to thirst", applied because several teasels hold water in the dip that forms at the node where the leaves join the stem, but that wasn't the main feature of the plant. Native to much of Europe and later naturalized in North America to become a weed in the northeastern United States and Ohio Valley, teasel is an architecturally handsome plant with tiers of broad, opposite leaves joined by a web around the stem. Rising to heights of 6 feet and more, and bearing incredibly sharp prongs along the leaf undersides and stems, teasel is striking even before it comes into bloom. Bees enjoy working the flowers and it has some benefit as a honey plant, but teasels have historically been valued for their prickly, comb-like flowerheads that can be harvested after the lilac flowers fade and used to tease or raise the nap of woolen cloth. Three teasel heads figure on the coat of arms of the Clothworkers' Company: the plant proved so efficient for that purpose that its employment continued long into the machine age. It proved better qualified for its chosen task – early machines tended to tear cloth while doing the same job.

Originally grown by early settlers to North America, by the latter 19th century according to Henderson's *Handbook of Plants*, commercial teasel production in the United States was confined to the farm town of Skaneateles, New York, where conditions were particularly favorable. Although the seed is by no means common, teasel is available from the Seed Savers Exchange.

However, despite their attractive stature and history, think for a while before you invite teasel into your garden. They can be incredibly invasive, sending seedlings everywhere and these little plants are not easy to uproot as they establish long and strong dandelion like roots very quickly. Once established, it's difficult to dissuade teasles from growing even under the worst conditions, although they like sun best. They tolerate poor soil and happily reach 6 feet or more. Leaving the flowerheads intact after they've blossomed looks impressive, but will lead to an onslaught of seedlings that continue to germinate late into the following year requiring painful weeding – even the seedlings have spines.

Echinops

COMPOSITAE

globe thistle

Native to southern Europe and introduced into Britain in 1570, the name says it all – *echinops* is Greek for "like a hedgehog", and that designation fairly well sums up this thistle-like plant crowned by white or blue spiny globes. The echinops most commonly cited is *E. ritro*, standing 4 feet tall with felted, holly-shaped leaves topped by blue-tinted orbs of

blooms. By the 19th century, it was upstaged by *E. ruthenicus* from Russia, originally thought to be a form of *E. ritro*, with downier leaves and larger, deeper blue flowerheads.

Not wildly popular prior to the 19th century, globe thistle was a common Victorian estate plant. Peter Henderson dissuaded folks with "moderate-sized" gardens from attempting the plant, as "they are too rank growing and coarse to be useful," according to his *Handbook of Plants*, 1881. Certainly, like most thistles, globe thistle is not the sort of plant you want to site in close proximity to where children play or pets may roam.

Echinops can be propagated from divisions or seeds and grows in both full sun or partial shade, but the plant looks most handsome when given bright light. It tolerates most soils and is often suggested for naturalizing in wild gardens, although echinops don't increase with great speed. *Echinops ritro* makes a good companion for Lady's mantle *Alchemilla mollis,* and can also be dried and used in decorations year round.

Erysimum

CRUCIFERAE

wallflower, wall gilliflower

Erysimum cheiri (formerly *Cheiranthus cheiri*), the wallflower, is a southern European native, known to have grown in ancient times throughout all Mediterranean lands. Some cultivars are not entirely hardy in the British and northern United States climates and need to be treated as biennials. Their name is believed to derive from the Greek *cheir,* meaning hand, alluding to the bouquet of wallflowers that was traditionally carried by young women and girls at many ancient ceremonies.

We've come to associate wallflowers with unattractive debutantes who frequent the sidelines because they never get asked to dance, but the common name probably came from the fact that wallflowers were only introduced to Britain in the late 1500s at about the same time as the stone used to build Norman castles, abbeys and their surrounding fortress walls. Wallflowers have always been willing colonizers, thriving, as their name describes, in old walls and on stony ground. As with all gillyflowers, the early varieties were famed for their wonderful aromatic scent, a special treat in early spring, as wallflowers will bloom from the cold days at the end of winter until the heat of summer. Some of the older varieties will bloom from late fall right through a mild winter. Wallflowers were often employed as a filler in nosegays because of their intensely sweet perfume. Beyond pleasures of the nostrils, the flowers were used to cure ulcers, cankers, tumors and gout as well as apoplexy and palsy, depending upon which herbalist you read.

It's true, wallflowers aren't the most exciting of plants. The foliage is long, slender and lackluster, the growth habit is branching (with the help of some pinching) and 1–1½ feet in height. The earliest wallflowers all bore single yellowish orange flowers, rather similar to their humbler wild mustard relatives, but with a sweet and powerful fragrance, and they soon became so common that they could be encountered in any old rubble heap. However, double varieties have been cherished in cottage gardens since the 16th century and figured in the original order of seeds sent by Robert Hill of London to John Winthrop, the first governor of Massachusetts. By the 19th century – the heyday of the wallflower – cottage gardens boasted cultivars in shades of red-brown, yellow, crimson, orange, and cream. Named varieties were selected early in the game, and although they could only be propagated by cuttings, some have managed to endure through the generations. 'Bloody Warrior' (possibly also known as 'Blood Red'), a deep red double believed to stem from the 1600s, is still in cultivation. More common, 'Harpur Crewe', a chance seedling discovered by the Reverend Harpur-Crewe of Hertfordshire in the late 19th century, is brilliant yellow and intensely fragrant. However, for generations most wallflowers were dingy yellows verging on brown, which may account for the association with homely young ladies.

For their vigorous bloom and compact habit, wallflowers were common features in Victorian bedding schemes. The association with that type of gardening was probably their undoing. Gertrude Jekyll tarnished their image by accusing wallflowers of being rather too tender for her sensibilities. They smacked of bedding plants – and were frequently employed for that purpose. They probably also fell out of favor because more and more varieties were produced in astonishing colors and forms, but quite lacking the scent which was once the prime reason for growing these early spring bloomers.

They thrive in poor well-drained soil in full sun, and are perfectly happy on old paths and ruined walls once established. However, they are best in cooler gardens as they rapidly go to seed in hot weather, although they dislike harsh winters. Sow seed in a cold frame in spring and transplant to flowering positions in autumn. They will not thrive in heavy or waterlogged soils and plants should be trimmed lightly after flowering so they don't get too leggy.

Geranium

GERANIACEAE

*cranesbill, meadow cranesbill,
loving Andrews*

The name, *geranium* (not to be confused with the non-hardy pelargoniums listed in the Annuals section), stems from the Greek word for crane, referring to the seed pods that elongate into something that resembles a bird's bill. Although members of this large family vary greatly in their size and growth habit, most have broad, deeply cut leaves initiating from a central rhizome bristling with abundant coin-sized flowers in varying shades from white through pink and purple. There are eleven species of geraniums growing wild in Britain, and many of these were adopted early into cottage gardens. Gerard mentioned three prominent British natives, *Geranium pratense* (meadow cranesbill), *G. phaeum* (black widow or mourning widow) and *G. sanguineum* (bloody cranesbill). He also wrote of an early import, *G. tuberosum*, a Mediterranean native with violet flowers. The local hero among Gerard's list of geraniums was certainly *G. pratense*, the meadow cranesbill, also known as the crowfoot cranesbill or loving Andrews. Although used for making blue dyes in Iceland, the meadow cranesbill seems to lack the broad spectrum of medicinal applications that most early plants amassed. Parkinson listed *G. pratense* as a wound herb, applied to clot blood. Gerard and Parkinson grew both the white (now 'Albiflorum') and the striped version with violet streaks and spots ('Striatum'), but they weren't familiar with the double meadow cranesbill varieties that later ruled the day. Foreign species also entered the scene and took their place in the garden. In fact, the family reached such mammoth proportions that Robert Sweet devoted ten years (1820-1830) to chronicling its members in a several volume monograph, *Geraniaceae*, describing and picturing 500 geraniums (including pelargoniums as well), a work that was published at the crescendo of the family's fame. William Robinson (1838-1935), the feisty Irish-born garden writer and advocate of naturalist gardens, further fanned the fires of affection for geraniums when he recommended them in his plantings. In America, the native *G. robertianum,* or herb Robert, has always been prevalent in woodlands. It was joined by *G. pratense*, which arrived in America early and naturalized rapidly.

Geraniums enjoy diverse conditions. Although some can tolerate shade, most prefer full sun and tend to be very hardy. They grow lavishly, sometimes too lavishly. A stern cutting back after blooming will keep the plant from becoming too ragged while also stimulating a second flush of bloom on varieties that don't blossom throughout the summer. Propagation is by division or cuttings.

Hemerocallis

LILIACEAE

daylily, asphodel lily, lemon lily

Nowadays, there are daylilies galore. But the proliferation of daylily hybrids is actually a 20th century phenomenon, begun at the turn of the century by the British George Yeld and mushrooming in the 1940s. The ancients knew only a limited color spectrum. They were familiar with the rust-colored *Hemerocallis fulva*, whose origin is uncertain, but probably hailed from China and Japan where the flowers were harvested for culinary purposes especially added to meat dishes, soups and served with noodles. Another ancient day lily is the intensely fragrant yellow lemon lily, *H. lilio-asphodelus* (formerly *H. flava*), grown in ancient Egypt and Rome, mentioned by Dioscorides as a medicinal herb in the 1st century. Arriving in Britain in the 1570s with the immigration of French Huguenots, both hemerocallis were grown extensively in gardens. The fact that daylilies made themselves quite at home, were fruitful and multiplied was fine - the foliage was used for fodder, recommended to increase milk production in cows. Double hemerocallis appeared in Britain as early as 1576, common in China long before that date.

Hemerocallis were appreciated in Britain, but they truly found a happy home in North America. By 1695, they were omnipresent, adopted by every wave of immigrants that arrived, common in every ethnic garden. And that might explain why hemerocallis, especially *H. fulva*, is now naturalized. It has reached weed status, lining the streets and bedding bankings with orange blossoms that tend to clash with other flowers.

The introduction of *H. aurantiaca* from China in 1890 changed the tide of hemerocallis and launched them into superstardom. *H. aurantiaca* displays a tinge of red and, although it's self-sterile, it successfully expanded the color spectrum for day lilies, rendering them the darlings of every gardener who craves big midsummer blossoms with very little effort. Meanwhile, the blue daylilies that 19th century gardeners once glorified in were later reclassified as funkias, which then became hostas. Blue remains an elusive shade for hemerocallis.

Known for their robust nature, daylilies are often called carefree. Given sun and moderate water, they thrive and multiply extensively, crowding out weeds. They increase by sending up pups with frequency, and division is the most common way to propagate the plants. They also set seed with little provocation, which has led to the onslaught of daylilies currently available. One of the delights of daylilies is that the flowers are edible, and even tasty.

Hesperis matronalis

CRUCIFERAE

sweet rocket, dame's rocket,
rogue's gilliflower, queen's gilliflower,
damask violet, dame's violet

This southern European native arrived in Britain very early on to grow wild in marshy fields, from which point it was brought into the garden in the 14th century to become a popular cottage garden plant.

Hesperis means evening in Greek, referring to its wonderful evening scent, and although its existence in early utilitarian gardens was justified by herbalists' use of sweet rocket to sweat out a fever, it has always chiefly been grown as an attractive and fragrant addition to any border, with simple flowers in white or very pale pink. According to Gerard, a double white variety (later known as 'Alba Plena') was quite newly available in 1597, thanks to "the industrie of some of our Florists", but remained rare until the middle half of the 17th century.

The British were fond of the double version, but their affection was nothing compared to that of the French. In fact, it was such a favorite of Marie Antoinette's that she was comforted by nosegays of sweet rocket, pinks and tuberose in prison during the French Revolution, a courtesy for which the concierge was also briefly incarcerated.

By the late 1600s, there were double white, double purple and double striped versions, and they were well on their way to upstaging the singles in the garden. In 1725, the double white was reputedly brought to America. By the 1820s, striped sweet rockets were rare. The double white form under the cultivar name of 'Flore pleno' or 'Alba plena' can still be found in some specialist nurseries or at plant sales in Britain, but it is sadly no longer available in the United States.

Although sweet rocket is sometimes dismissed as a weed, *Henderson's Handbook of Plants* (1881) explains that, with a little tender loving care, the plant can reach splendid proportions. "They are all perennials," Peter Henderson advises, "and as soon as they have done flowering they should be taken up and transplanted into fresh and very rich soil, which must be of light and friable nature. Thus treated, the double white and double purple varieties of *Hesperis matronalis* will attain extraordinary size and will flower splendidly." Sure enough, the 3-4 foot wayside plant with phlox-like flower umbels can gracefully fill the lull between spring and summer, thriving best on fertile soil and in partial shade.

Although doubles are rare, they can be propagated by cuttings or root division. The species is easily grown from seed and generally self-sows, covering moderately fertile fields with abundant spring blossoms. It is among the easiest heirlooms to entertain, happy in sun or light shade.

Iris

IRIDACEAE

fleur-de-lis, sweet flag

Aptly named for the Greek goddess of the rainbow, iris was an early introduction. Although *fleur-de-lis* translates as "flower of the lily", many flowers were called "lilies" in the past. It was probably *Iris pseudacorus* that was adopted as the emblem of the French from the 6th century. A story relates that Clovis I, King of the Franks, found the flower growing in a bend of the Rhine and therefore realized that the water was sufficiently shallow to cross, delivering him safely from the army of the Goths. The name Fleur-de-lis came from Louis VII of France who carried the emblem during the Crusades. It has been a symbol of valor and chivalry ever since, and a royal emblem.

The moisture-loving yellow flag, *I. pseudacorus*, lined the waterways of Britain since earliest times, serving many functions for innovative peasants. Ink was made from the root, a beverage was brewed of the roots, while the long, sword-shaped leaves were used for caning chairs and thatching roofs. Similarly, thirteen other iris species had already been introduced and were common by the time Gerard wrote his herbal in 1597, including *I. biflora*, the parent of later remontant strains. Since iris bloom only briefly, extending the performance has been a goal throughout modern history, collectors are particularly keen on rediscovering varieties that blossom again in autumn.

Although the reddish remontant 'Autumn Sunset' was only registered in 1939, it is already among the missing. 'Morning Splendor', an American bred dark purple remontant introduced in 1923 appears to be in the same boat. Among the early remontants still in cultivation are 'Jean Siret', 'Lieutenant de Chavagnac', 'Autumn Queen', 'Ultra', 'September

Morn' and 'Sangreal', all hybridized in the 1920s and 1930s.

The oldest cultivated European iris was *I. germanica*, the bearded iris already well known in the 9th century when Walafrid Strabo reported from his monastery garden. It has survived from the 9th century until the present by sheer perseverance – although the plant is a sterile clone and cannot bear seeds, the rhizomes persist despite the worst conditions. Its sword-like leaves topped by plump blue, violet or purple flowers accented by a yellow fringe, or beard, have lingered in gardens throughout the ages. A white, more diminutive form of *I. germanica*, 'Florentina' (introduced into gardens by 1596), was the plant which supplied orris root, a common ingredient in perfume preparations. This iris had a multitude of other uses. It was employed to cure blemishes as well as to scent linen, make rosary beads and sweeten the breath. It also has cathartic and emetic properties which have been employed throughout history.

Although *I. germanica* has a lengthy history, it did not father the leagues of tall bearded iris which now frequent our gardens. They were a rather recent phenomenon, the progeny of *I. pallida* and *I. variegata*. Work began on tall beardeds in about 1800 when the German E. von Berg, and the Frenchman de Bure, began hybridizing. The first evidence of their efforts, *I.* 'Buriensis', was distributed in 1822. It's amazing how hybridizing escalated from that point. By 1840,

there were 100 tall bearded iris hybrids in cultivation. By the end of the century, Middle Eastern strains had been harnessed, further expanding the repertoire of tall beardeds in the garden. And in 1945, American breeders also pioneered a dwarf strain of beardeds by harnessing *I. pumila*, a 4-5 inch tall native of Europe and Asia Minor with bright lilac-purple blossoms introduced by 1596. At present, there is such a glut of cultivars great and small that you can easily choose any color of the rainbow. Fortunately, the signature bubble-gum fragrance is still a strong factor. Iris come and go, but some of the older tall bearded varieties still in cultivation include 'Aurea' (1830), 'Fairy' (1906), 'Caprice'(1904), 'Quaker Lady' (1909) and 'Monsignor' (1907), but there are many more early 20th century bearded iris afoot and efforts are being made to keep them in cultivation.

There are few plants easier to grow than bearded iris. They endure all sorts of neglect including prolonged drought and lean soil (although they appreciate being mulched in extremely hot climates). They thrive best if the rhizomes are barely buried and are given good drainage, especially during the winter when excess moisture can cause rot. Iris are best divided in early spring when they first break soil, or in summer after blooming. Iris blooms are fleeting; a flower lingers only 3-6 days before fading, and the display is also short-lived. If you have a certain combination in mind, make certain that your chosen flowering times will synchronize.

Lupinus
LEGUMINOSAE
Lupine

❸-❻ annuals in hotter regions

Native to the southern Balkans and the Aegean, the annual, 4 foot tall, white flowered *Lupinus albus* (alias white lupine or wolf bane), has been grown since ancient Egyptian times primarily as fodder, a purpose for which it's still planted in Italy and Sicily. John Parkinson suggests a more creative employment – the seeds can be burned to repel gnats. Half the height, *L. luteus* was also grown, valued for its intensely fragrant yellow blossoms as well as the leaves, often

described as resembling "expanded fingers." So lupines were in evidence in early gardens. Not only were they popular in Europe, but early American seedsmen listed, in addition to the white *L. albus*, *L. pilosus* (the rose lupine), *L. hirsutus* (the small blue lupine), and *L. varius* (the large blue lupine), none of which are still in cultivation.

Modern-day lupines stem from the introduction in 1826 of *L. polyphyllus*, native to the northwestern

United States. Most often, *L. polyphyllus* has spires of blue-purple blossoms, with infrequent white, pale pink and even bicolored forms popping up. The first step in the flower's improvement came when it was bred with the tree lupine *L. arboreus* which yielded a yellow strain and led to a vivid crimson version in 1912. But really, lupines were nowhere before George Russell, inspired by a display of lupines at the coronation of George V, began 25 years' of work on the plant, encouraging cross-pollination and selecting his favorites. In 1937, his strain was first put on public display to great acclaim. It included red, deep pink, orange and yellow monochromatic flowers as well as several dramatic bicolors (consider, for example, how people must have reacted when they first caught sight of a purple and gold flowered lupine) – completely overshadowing the species formerly grown. Of complex parentage, Russell lupines can only be propagated vegetatively, and yet they remain popular today.

There is something provincial about a stand of Russell lupines with tall 1½–2 foot spires plump with pea-like blossoms, and that's undoubtedly why they've taken cottage gardens by storm. We continue to patronize lupines despite the fact that they blossom for only a fleeting few weeks in most seasons. Late spring blooming plants, they tend to flag and fall victim to aphids with summer heat, but they usually rally the following season. However, lupines aren't long-lived plants, an individual rarely survives longer than half a dozen years but will often reflower in a single season if the blossom head is removed before the tip flowers open.

Russell lupines are propagated by division, but lupine species should be multiplied from seed which should be nicked and soaked for best germination. Species cross-pollinate easily, so you may wish to isolate strains to avoid eventually ending up with a bed full of predominantly blueish purple blossoms. They thrive in well-drained (but not parched), slightly acidic soil and partial shade. Early cultivated lupine species were edible, but *L. polyphyllus* and its progeny are poisonous.

Lychnis coronaria   ❸-❾

CARYOPHYLLACEAE

rose campion, gardener's delight,
bloody William, mullein pink

The rose campion is the flagship of the lychnis family, and believed to be the plant that inspired Theophrastus to affix the Greek name stemming from *lychnos*, or lamp - which some authors feel alludes to the vivid magenta blooms and others suspect is connected with the downy leaves, once used in making candle-wicks. Although the date of its introduction has been lost, this Southern European native has grown in gardens since the 1300s. Jovial and willing, gardeners welcomed this biennial with a rosette of felted lamb's ear-like leaves in the first year and a long display of striking magenta flowers on 2 foot stalks in its second season. The white form was also a common garden plant in Gerard's time, and still exists, under the name of 'Alba'. By 1614 there was a double magenta and by 1665 a double white form was available. In fact, early purists complained that the single rose campion was no longer to be found. Propagatable only by division, by 1835, the doubles were already reported as rare, according to the *Horticultural Register* of Boston. Now they are reputedly lost.

Native to Europe and Russia, *Lychnis chalcedonica* gained its common name of Maltese or Jerusalem cross due to the legend that the plant was brought to France by Louis IX from the Holy Land. Native to Russia, one wonders how it floated to that part of the world so early. The beauty of the flower lies in its form – it resembles a cluster of scarlet Maltese crosses – and its striking appearance allowed it early entry into gardens despite the fact that it was given few medicinal applications. A double scarlet variety was introduced by 1629 and was also prevalent, although it could only be propagated by division or stem cuttings and had a tendency to revert to the single state. It was already rare in 1835 and is now difficult to find. By 1710, there were white and flesh-colored forms. A double white appeared sometime thereafter and was "still more rare than the double scarlet" and needful of protection from full sun "to insure vigorous bloom" according to the 1835 *Horticultural Register* of Boston. It has now vanished.

A sun-worshipper, rose campion monopolizes little space, tolerates drought (better than heavy drenching) and yet lends a spark of color. Even gardeners who avoid strident shades can permit the tiny spot of magenta that a single 1 inch wide lychnis flower provides. For those who cannot even tolerate a small touch of magenta, a white version with a pronounced pink eye is available and comes true to seed.

While campions flourish in well-drained but fairly poor soil, seeding themselves shamelessly, Maltese cross prefers a richer loamy soil and should be propagated by dividing the roots in spring every second year. The color can be a tad uncompromising for modern tastes. You might opt for 'Rosea', with rose colored blossoms instead. Propagation is by division, however, even the early gardeners warned against acquiring plants that had spent too long in a container as they suffer if not planted early in the spring.

Monarda

LABIATAE

Bee balm, bergamot, Oswego tea

A native North American prairie flower, this species is named after the Spanish botanist Nicolas Monardes who, in 1571, wrote of the virtues of American medicinal plants. While the common name of bee balm refers to the plant's attraction for the pollinators often found frequenting the nectar-filled flowers, 'bergamot' is bestowed because the aroma of the leaves resembles the citrus scent of bergamot oranges. Although bee balm is reputed for its hardiness, when John Tradescant the younger brought the lavender-flowered, rose-scented *Monarda fistulosa* back to Britain from his voyage to Virginia in 1637, that initial introduction perished soon afterward. *Monarda didyma* was more successful; in 1744, John Bartram collected the scarlet-flowering version in Oswego on Lake Ontario and sent it to his British correspondent, Peter Collinson. This flower was traditionally made into a tea by the Oswego Indians, and this use earned it a place in history. Oswego tea was drunk by American patriots during their struggles with the British over import duties on Chinese teas.

Bee balm is the only North American source of the essential oil thymol, and monardas attract hummingbirds and butterflies as well as bees. The unadulterated scarlet whorls of the species *Monarda didyma* were handsome before breeders began to expand the color range. But the repertoire has been drastically increased to include a salmony red ('Adam'), pink ('Marshall's Delight'), purple ('Prairie Night'), violet ('Violet Queen') and white ('Snow White').

One beauty of bee balms is that, like other mints, they can grow and bloom in partial shade. In fact, they sometimes flag in noonday sun and their blooming period is expanded when they aren't stressed by beating sun. But, in that position, they often are blighted by mildew, which looks pitiful but doesn't effect their lifespan. *Monardas* are so hardy that they are rarely killed by winter cold and can become invasive, wandering by underground rhizomes and sending up 3-4 foot tall branches. If you want to encourage their ramblings, a moist, light soil makes them very happy. They are propagated easily by division or by rooting stem cuttings.

Myosotis

BORAGINACEAE

forget-me-not, scorpion grass

Although we associate the drifts of forget-me-nots with the romance of cottage gardens, its sentimental common name is of fairly recent vintage. It wasn't until the early 1800s that *Myosotis sylvatica* earned the nickname of forget-me-not. Based on a German legend, the oft-repeated story tells of a knight collecting the blossoms for his sweetheart along the banks of a river, only to fall in, yelling, "forget me not" as he was swept away by the current. Gerard knew it under its more ancient nickname, scorpion grass, which was bestowed due to the plant's curled flower stalks, reminiscent of a scorpion's tail. And just because the flower stalks happened to end with a curl, the plant was suggested as a cure for scorpion stings, but such associations between leaf or flower shape and medicinal application (laid out in the Doctrine of Signatures) ruled the day before mankind adapted more scientific means of healing.

The shape of the flower stems is not the main feature that sticks in our minds when we think of forget-me-nots. Instead, we usually associate the plant with its little periwinkle blue, yellow-eyed blossoms that appear in spring. Standing about ankle high, those flowers tend to carpet the garden – especially since the plant seeds itself in so rampantly. Once you've introduced the plant, you'll be weeding it out forevermore unless you cut it back before seed is produced. When the flowers begin to fade and you can

get a good look at the foliage, the reason for the Latin name *myosotis* becomes readily apparent, the leaves are shaped like a mouse's ear, which is what myosotis means in Greek. *Sylvatica* refers to the woods, the forget-me-nots' chosen haunt, as well as streamsides and riverbanks. However, in Britain, the plant has always been rare in the wild, which might explain why Gerard paid it scant notice. Henry IV, however, was totally besotted with forget-me-nots, embracing the flower as his emblem, stitching its likeness into the garments of his entire court.

Cottage gardeners used the plant, but the tradition of growing forget-me-nots in spring gardens is a relatively new tradition in Britain, beginning toward the latter part of the 19th century. Meanwhile, in Paris, forget-me-nots were sold as tokens of affection and in Germany they were planted in graveyards. Almost as popular at the moment is the white forget-me-not, known in one area of northern England as think-me-on. A pink variety is also gaining momentum with gardeners.

Forget-me-nots like a warm, shady situation to blossom best, and are usually grown from seed scattered where they are likely to thrive. As the story suggests, the roots prefer moisture. Myosotis can be propagated by seed, division or cuttings, although the plants usually die back after blooming.

Nepeta

3-9

LABIATAE

catmint, catnip

Although it is native to Europe and found in waste-lands and hedgerows, *Nepeta cataria* has been grown in British gardens since 1265, partly for the benefit of cats. With deeply textured silverish leaves and insignificant white flowers, catnip isn't really much to look at. But cats adore the plant, they roll in it, embrace it, eat it and generally destroy it. However, if you wish to dissuade this destruction, the ancient wisdom is to plant seeds rather than transplanting cuttings. The saying goes, "If you set it, the cats will get it; If you sow it, the cats won't know it."

Although cats have enjoyed the spoils, a more practical employment for catnip is for tea. Before tea was imported from China, a popular stimulant among the peasantry was catnip tea. Furthermore, rats are reputed to despise catnip, and so it's occasionally grown as a companion plant to vegetable crops such as squash and melons that rodents nibble. By the time John Josselyn wrote *New England's Rarities Discovered* in 1672, *N. cataria* had already escaped from European settlers and was reported in "the wilderness" of North America.

The catmint that parented the nepetas we now grow as ornamentals is of fairly recent vintage. *N. mussinii* arrived in Britain from the Caucasus in 1804 or so, and soon crossed with the less hardy *N. nepetella* (from North Africa) to give us a series of hybrids known as *Nepeta* x *faasenii*. They range from mauve to pale purple, their superabundant flowers nearly hiding leaves that vary from blue-grey to green and they are impressively hardy.

Unlike other members of the mint family, catnip and catmints don't require moisture or prefer shade. In fact, they bask in sunny spots despite poor, lean soil. They are among the easiest plants to grow and make wonderful borders, especially combined with the chartreuse blossoms of Lady's mantle. Because catmints are not fertile, they don't seed themselves in, moreover they don't usually run like other mints. However, most catmints become sizeable plants and require quite a bit of elbow room. Give them 3-4 feet between bedfellows. Catnip seed is known to be viable for at least 5 years.

Oenanthera

ONAGRACEAE

evening primrose, sundrops, suncups

Parkinson described *Oenanthera biennis* as the "tree primrose of Virginia" when recommending it to cottage gardeners in 1629. It was a new introduction at the time, arriving in Padua from North America in 1619 and thence to Britain two years later. Often grown as a biennial but occasionally blooming in its first year, oenanthera begins its career as a rosette. But the main attraction occurs when the 3-4 foot tall flowering wands appear, topped by 3 inch wide canary yellow flowers. The flowers are tightly shut

during the day, but expand dramatically in late afternoon, spewing forth their heady perfume. Each blossom is ephemeral, but replaced with further blooms throughout several months time. It was a thrilling experience for early gardeners, but there was also a practical excuse for cultivating evening primrose. In France, its tender roots were eaten while in their first year, like salsify. By the 19th century many gardeners had come to see it simply as a weed, if an attractive one, but we are now more familiar with the plant for its medicinal qualities: evening primrose has earned acclaim in the treatment of PMS, breast and menopausal problems, hyperactivity in children, eczema, acne, asthma, migraine, metabolic disorders, arthritis and allergies.

Evening primroses are a positive floral addition to any cottage-style planting, their rather untidy flowers complementing many other old-fashioned flowers. They are long rooted plants and will grow in sun in any except wet soil as long as it is reasonably deep. They are quite happy in drought and selfseed readily. Easily propagated by seed sown in autumn, some may flower in the first year but most will simply form rosettes that summer, to bloom the following year.

Paeonia

PAEONIACEAE

peony

Native to Greece and southern Europe the first peony to be grown in Britain was not *Paeonia lactiflora*, the parent of the common herbaceous garden peonies, but instead *P. mascula*, "the male peionie". It arrived so early that it was thought to be native, but probably came to Britain during the 6th century or so. The plant was immediately put to good, practical use, and can still be found on the site of ancient monasteries where it was grown to cure men of epilepsy. *P. mascula* had impressive large flowers around 5 inches across, available in pink, red or white. Also a European native, *P. officinalis*, "the female peionie" was its crimson counterpart, with blossoms of about the same size but of more compact stature (the plants are 2 feet tall as opposed to *P. mascula*'s 3 foot height). It came into cultivation before 1548 but after the "male" version. The reason for the split in gender has been lost to history. Gerard reported a double white variety in 1597, but it didn't appear in Britain until after his herbal was completed. *P. officinalis* 'Alba Plena', a double white form, is still in cultivation. By 1665, a carnation flowered version was reported, which may coincide with the double crimson 'Rubra Plena' still grown. At the same time, a red streaked with white *P. officinalis* was also cited, but we seem to have no current counterpart. *P. officinalis* was the first peony to arrive on North American shores.

Meanwhile, in China, *P. lactiflora*, native to Siberia, Mongolia and northern China, had been cultivated at least since the 10th century; the Mongolians were in the habit of adding the roots to their soups and grinding the seeds for tea. By the 12th century, the plant was sufficiently popular to warrant a monograph mentioning the 39 variations (both single and double) that had already been wrought. So *P. lactiflora* was quite well developed long before it reached British shores in 1784 when the first Chinese peony, a single white, arrived from Siberia. Other colors followed, but it wasn't until the 1820s that peony breeding began in earnest in the West. However, even the anemone-flowered types, which were touted as a modern breakthrough, are suspected of having their origins in 10th century China.

Peonies are now available with single, double, semi-double and pompom-shaped flowers in all shades from white to crimson with flecks, spots and picotee edges. Not much has been lost in this genus and the scent (sometimes likened to water lilies) remains an important feature.

Some of the oldest varieties still in cultivation include the tall and early blooming double pink 'Edulis Superba' (1824), the white with crimson flecked 'Festiva Maxima' (1851) and the pure white 'Duchesse de Nemours' (1856). The large, late, tissue pink 'Sarah Bernhardt', still readily available, was created in 1906. Even more intensely fragrant and bearing a huge blossoms, the tree peony, *P. suffruticosa*, (formerly known as *P. moutan*) was also cultivated in China since antiquity, but didn't arrive in Britain until 1787. Due to their high price, they were still rare in cultivation in the 1830s.

Herbaceous (or Chinese) peonies are long-lived plants; you are apt to find them lingering around old farm foundations decades after the house disappeared. They're tolerant of poor soil and partial shade, but prefer rich underfootings and ample moisture.

Drought can take its toll on a peony, although the plant usually returns, somewhat diminished, the next season. A clay subsoil with a light topsoil is reputed to be ideal. Peonies have been divided and shared for centuries among gardeners. If you need to transplant them do this in late fall, provide a generous hole and bury the eyes 2 inches below the surface.

Penstemon

SCROPHULARIACEAE

bead tongue

mostly ❸ and ❹

Penstemon hirsutus (the pale blue chelone) was introduced from North America in 1758 and *Penstemon laevigatus* (the penstemon chelone) was introduced (also from North America) in 1776. But penstemons didn't really raise eyebrows until the 19th century when *P. hartwegii* entered from Mexico in 1825. Hardy only to Zone 9, that plant was accommodated in greenhouses upon its introduction into Britain and didn't infiltrate the garden. Further hardier species came later with the introduction of 15 penstemons by David Douglas between 1827 and 1834. However, it wasn't until the herbaceous border gained a following that penstemons truly stepped into the limelight. The original colors were dull by modern standards, but nonetheless, the plants had merit. Penstemons grow like lobelias with similar long, shiny leaves, and the plants are crowned by long, tubular flowers in dense spires. Shortly after Douglas's introduction, fueled by those new species, penstemons were hybridized, their color range was increased, and named cultivars

entered the market. Nowadays there's scarcely a color that isn't represented from cherry reds through midnight blues with bicolored petals also part of the theatrics. And yet, they were neglected at home.

Formerly more popular in Britain than in North America, that situation promises to change. American gardeners are taking notice of penstemons with the introduction of *P. digitalis* 'Husker Red', developed at the University of Nebraska with deep maroon foliage topped by white blossoms. Not only will more new varieties undoubtedly follow, but heirloom types will undoubtedly become globally available.

Penstemons require a sunny location to thrive, on this point they are not negotiable. They will also survive where it is dry, but prefer even moisture (too much water is also a killer) and deep soil. Pinching early in the game will increase their flower stalks. Unfortunately, penstemons are particularly prone to thrips which cause unsightly damage. Penstemons can be propagated by seed and division.

Phlox ❹

POLEMONIACEAE

*perennial phlox, summer phlox,
autumn phlox, fall phlox*

Native to the United States from New York to Georgia and Illinois through Arkansas, the original rather drab mauve *Phlox paniculata* was first recorded in Britain in 1732. A pure white variety wasn't grown until 1812. It was the Europeans rather than the Americans who saw the beauty in the plant but even so, it wasn't until 1839 that the French began hybridizing. British breeders didn't start playing with phlox until the first decade of the 20th century. Not only was the color range expanded to include the pinks and periwinkle shades, but the density of the flower heads has also been improved. The syrupy sweet evening fragrance remains unaltered.

Phlox are farmyard rather than estate plants in North America, so collectors of heirloom types are often baffled by lack of documentation and many heirloom types are now known only by the location where they were found, such as 'Old Cellarhole'. One of the oldest varieties still in cultivation is 'Rijnstroom' introduced in 1910 and boasting salmon-pink flowers straddling 3 foot tall stems. Also available are 'Leo P. Schlageter' (1934), an early bloomer with brilliant carmine pink flowers on 3 foot stems and 'Widar' (also 1934) with 50" stems topped by reddish-purple blossoms enhanced by a white eye. 'Bright Eyes' was an early introduction in cultivation by 1934, but it was described as bright red in old catalogs. The plant we now grow as 'Bright Eyes' has white flowers with a pink eye, a heady fragrance and good mildew resistance. It is probably actually 'Daily Sketch', a daughter of the true 'Bright Eyes'.

Phlox are a good value for far northern gardens where they survive season after season without complaint. They're often subjected to poor soil, and they tend to be dwarfer when malnourished. When they are given a rich, limey soil, full sun, good air circulation, regular watering and occasional division, they are happier, healthier plants. In particular, they don't fall victim to mildew as prevalently when properly grown. Mildew doesn't harm the plants over the long run, but it certainly mars their appearance. Propagate by division in spring or fall.

Polemonium ❷

POLEMONIACEAE

*Jacob's ladder, Greek valerian, charity,
blue-jacket, poverty, ladder-to-heaven*

Native from Alaska to Europe and northern Asia, *Polemonium caeruleum* has a sufficiently broad range to make it a favorite wildflower over a vast range although it is now very rare in the wild in Britain. By Elizabethan times, Jacob's ladder was firmly adopted into gardens under the name Greek valerian, due to the shape of the pointed leaves that run up the stem in ladder-like fashion. Culpeper assigned all sorts of medicinal uses to the plant including a cure for distempers, headaches, tremblings, palpitations of the heart and nervous complaints as well as epilepsy, providing a good excuse to invite it into the cottage garden, where it was common. The medicinal uses were quickly forgotten so that Jacob's ladder was primarily valued for its purplish blue blossoms and their scent (which has been likened to grape soda by modern gardeners). The blossoms are transient, appearing early in spring and then shatter with warm weather, leaving foliage that is quite handsome. By the 18th century, a version with striped flowers was reported, but seems to have vanished. A white form was also available in the 18th century and remains in the trade under the name *P. caeruleum* 'Album', sometimes found as *P. alba*. A variegated Jacob's ladder was once popular, which could be propagated only by division and was already scarce by 1887. However, a variegated Jacob's ladder with cream along the margins of each leaflet has been newly introduced under the name 'Brise d'Anjou'.

A low-growing plant remaining under 18 inches in height, Jacob's ladder spends spring adorned with pale blue, bell-shaped blossoms. It prefers partial shade and thrives in a deep, rich, loamy soil similar to the sort of bedding you'd find in a woodland. The white form is a little taller than the blue, and blooms later. Jacob's ladder can either be propagated by seeds sown in the fall or by divisions made in early spring. However, when transplanting Jacob's ladder, keep the foliage free of soil – for some reason polemoniums dislike dirt on their leaves.

Polygonatum

LILIACEAE

Solomon's seal, David's harp,
ladder to heaven

Dioscorides, a Greek naturalist (and possibly a physician) who lived in the 1st century and wrote *De Materia Medica*, was the first to affix the Solomon's seal's name, *polygonatum*, meaning many knee joints, referring to the strangely bent rhizomes from which the plant's stems shoot up. The underground segments are unique, but the above-ground portion of the plant is much more rivetting from a gardener's perspective. The alternating deep green leaves fan out like wings and climb up the stem 2 feet to an arching tip. Handsome enough with no further gimmicks, Solomon's seal also adds white blossoms that dangle all along the stem. Although its difficult to discern Solomon's seal *Polygonatum multiflorum* from its counterpart, false Solomon's seal *Smilacina* before blossoms appear, when the flowers come out, the difference is marked – false Solomon's seal has blossoms only at the tip of the stem.

Solomon's seal was a woodland plant, not truly a garden flower until woodland gardens came into vogue relatively recently, although it was mentioned in late 18th century nursery catalogs. Even before that time, it was used extensively for medicinal purposes. Most prominently, Solomon's seal was mentioned by Gerard to knit broken bones – he suggested the results of its application were nothing short of miraculous. Gerard also recommended the roots for bruises, especially those gotten by wives "in stumbling upon their hastie husband's fists". The roots are edible, and the Turks reputedly dined often on those swollen tubers. Purple stemmed and double flowering types were available as early as the 18th century.

Although Solomon's seal is a woodland plant which increases by creeping runners (frequently a formula for disaster when plants are close bedfellows), it never really becomes invasive even in a tightly packed garden. There's plenty of space between stems, so Solomon's seal is a perfect companion to intersperse with other woodland plants. It likes a loamy, leafy underfooting and sprouts late in the spring. At that time of year, the plant is usually propagated. Look for Solomon's seal late in nurseries, although faultlessly hardy it's not usually on the market with the earliest perennials.

Primula

PRIMULACEAE

primrose, cowslip,
Jack-in-the-green, oxlip

Primula means first, and the plant is one of the first to flower, heralding the spring. Primroses and cowslips are native to much of Europe and particularly widespread through Britain, especially on limestone soil. There are over 400 species of primula, and so many have slipped from woodland thicket to become mainstays of the cottage garden that it's difficult to untwine their histories. They've also interbred, to further confuse chroniclers.

Primroses and cowslips were involved in many legends about fairies and elves, and praised in poetry and song. They were considered important healing flowers, used for everything from aching joints to paralysis as well as making useful cosmetics for refreshing or lightening the skin. Their medical uses date back to at least the ancient Greeks. One myth tells us that Paralisos, the son of Priapus (the garden god) and Flora, died of grief due to the loss of his sweetheart, and his body was transformed by his parents into a primrose.

Native to western and southern Europe, *Primula vulgaris* (syn. *P. acaulis*) is the common pale yellow primrose with lightly fragrant flowers, each held singly on a short stem. Mentioned by Jon the Gardener in 1440, the primrose was considered a woodland plant, and not sufficiently showy to be invited into gardens where space was at a premium. That changed by 1638 when the reddish-purple *P. vulgaris sibthorpii* had entered from the East Balkan peninsula, beginning the primrose's foray into the broader color spectrum. Before long, most colors of the rainbow were represented. By 1648, there was a double white version growing at the Oxford Botanic Garden, but it wasn't until the 18th century that double red primroses were common. Interestingly, British gardeners suspected that doubling was caused by frequent transplanting, and so they moved their primroses as often as possible. The doubles held great fascination. But it wasn't until the late 19th century that double primroses were sufficiently stable to garner specific cultivar names. Double primroses are now easily procured at garden centers.

The little cowslip, *P. veris*, is native to British meadows, holding its blossoms in a candelabra-like bunch on a stem above the rosette of leaves. They withstand more sun than primroses, making them easier to place in the garden. However cowslips seemed too wild to invite into captivity until the Elizabethans found aberrations that struck their fancy and seemed worthy of cultivation. There were hose-in-hose forms with a trumpet-like flower set within another trumpet-like flower, Jack-in-the-green versions with single flowers surrounded by a ruff of diminutive green leaves, and Jackanapes-on-horseback with a combination of leaves and petals in place of the flowers. However, it was the natural hybrids between primroses and the British native cowslip that really made an impact in the garden from the end of the 17th century on. Polyanthus primroses, as they were called, featured tall candelabra stems brandishing many open-faced flowers at the tip; the first is believed to have been red. By the beginning of the 18th century, polyanthus were common and came in many colors. A century later, they were bred to bear larger flowers and more in a panicle. Meanwhile, double polyanthus had appeared, known as pug-in-a-pinners. The high point in the polyanthus' career occurred when the golden-eyed, dark burgundy banded, and gold- and silver-laced polyanthus appeared on the scene in the 1750s, possibly a result of a natural cross between *P. veris* and *P. pubescens*. Like auriculas (*see below*), these were plants of the working class, largely cultivated in pots to permit easy transport to exhibitions. Gold- and silver-laced polyanthus can still be found through specialist nurseries.

In its native mountainous Switzerland *P. auricula* was apparently once distilled as a remedy to cure vertigo. Compared to the wild woodland primroses, auriculas have a more cultivated look with pale green leaves and rounded flowers about an inch in diameter dusted with what looks like confectioner's sugar. The flowers come in an incredibly broad spectrum of colors including green, mauve, yellow, burgundy, purple, baby blue and navy, often with bands of different shades (such as grey and black outlines) and all have an alluring aroma. Twenty or more kinds were available by 1629. To pigeon hole the many varieties, by 1665, auriculas had been divided into groups including border types and show varieties, bearing delightful names such as 'Mistris Buggs her fine purple' and 'The Virgin's Milk'. The most popular sorts, such as 'Rule Arbiter' were accented by a parrot green rim. Although 'Rule Arbiter' no longer exists, green edged auriculas are still to be found. From 1659 onward, auriculas with slashes of color were available, although they seem to have disappeared. Doubles were also grown and remain in the trade, although they are not common.

Auriculas truly hit the limelight early in the 19th century when members of florists' societies (*see page 73*), particularly silk weavers, invited the plants onto their windowsills to brighten their gloomy abodes. They cultivated the plants, competed in shows and vied for the most impressive hybrids. Auriculas still catch the excitement of the crowds at the Chelsea Flower Show, exhibited much as they were years ago

in handthrown clay pots set up on stages, or tiers of tables. The show auriculas are not as hardy as the tougher garden auriculas, and all detest hot summers with parching sun, which might explain why they never really caught on in North America with the same fervor they attracted in Britain. Auriculas thrive in a rock garden with a gentle eastern exposure or shade from noonday sun; they should be divided in spring when they first emerge and benefit from occasional division. The caveat is that they interbreed easily so seed is rarely true to form.

Cowslips and their hybrids will cope in sun as long as they have shade at some point in the day, but other primulas prefer woodland and its dappled shade, with damp, rich, leafy loam and most wilt rapidly in full sun. Ample moisture can substitute for shade, keeping primroses blooming over several weeks in spring and encouraging a second blossoming. Polyanthus can endure bitter winters, but they dislike dry summers. All garden primulas like to have their diet well-supplemented with rotted manure.

Primulas are easily propagated by division and seed. Plants should be divided in early spring and watered generously while they're being re-established. Try not to splash water on the leaves or the foliage may scorch. Seed should not be buried and prefers a moist seed bed to germinate.

Pulmonaria

BORAGINACEAE

lungwort, Joseph and Mary, soldiers and sailors, beggar's basket, Lady's milk sile, Jerusalem sage, Jerusalem cowslip

Native throughout Europe and indigenous to Britain, the string of common names that *Pulmonaria officinalis* has collected gives us some indication of how long the plant has been in cultivation. Interestingly, the one that has survived into the present, lungwort, is one of pulmonaria's earliest nicknames, dating to the 15th century. Both that nickname and the Latin name

refer to the belief that pulmonaria could cure lung problems because its leaves are naturally spotted and are shaped like a stylized lung. Those long, pointed, felted leaves are edible and form a broad rosette enhanced by clusters of flowers in the spring. And the flowers are not without intrigue, they open pinkish-red and fade to blue as they mature, which was the inspiration for the soldiers and sailors epithet. Not only was the blue species welcomed into gardens early in the game, but the white flowering version was being sold in catalogs by the late 18th century. The plant was also dispersed broadly. By the early part of the 18th century, pulmonaria was being sent to collectors in America.

Much later came *P. saccharata,* native to Europe and introduced into Britain by 1863. Although it looks quite similar to *P. officinalis,* the later introduction's claim to celebrity was the quirk that its leaves are nearly totally snow white, the flowers varying from white to violet. It has spawned many variations with more or less silver in the foliage, the most popular being 'Mrs. Moon' with a galaxy of silver spots.

It can endure almost any garden soil (although a fluffy, humusy bed is best), but pulmonaria prefers shade. Nearly pure white varieties will scorch and blotch in a flash in brilliant light and they also tend to deteriorate with the heat of midsummer. Just cut them back to the ground encouraging another flush of fresh growth. Although pulmonaria is sometimes lost in the wave of more colorful flowers during the spring rush when it blooms, I've brought the plant indoors in autumn, kept it going quite happily inside through the winter, and enjoyed very early spring blossoms just when forced bulbs are performing. Suddenly a plant that too often becomes a spaceholder in the garden is elevated to superstardom when sitting by my elbow.

Rosa ❹

ROSACEAE

rose

Roses have existed since antiquity, praised by each civilisation in turn. It was the Greek poet Sappho who first designated the rose as the Queen of Flowers. They were grown extensively by the ancient Romans – Virgil describes a farmer who received some criticism for converting a corn field to roses. They also began their romantic association with the Romans, woven into garlands to crown brides and bridegrooms, as well as crowning the likenesses of Cupid, Venus and Bacchus. The Romans dedicated the rose to Venus, the goddess of love, and to Bacchus the god of wine; no banquet was complete without rose petals strewn over couches, tables and floors; they floated on the surface of wine; garlands of roses decorated halls and were worn around necks and on heads. Beyond all its sensual delights, when a garland of roses was hung in a dining hall or around a person's neck it had the added meaning that any word uttered was 'sub rosa' - under the rose - and should therefore not be repeated outside the hall or out of the present company. One extraordinary report stated that Nero spent 4 million sesterces for

roses at a single banquet (a sesterce was a brass coin that was apparently equal in value to four donkeys). During the days of Roman decadence the demand for roses was so great that Roman colonies, including Egypt, grew roses in large numbers for export to Rome. On a more applied level, Pliny the Younger proposed an infusion of rose water, rose vinegar and honey for sore throats, ulcerated gums, headaches, earaches, piles, nausea, stomach-ache, toothache, diarrhea, hemorrhaging, eye trouble, mange and hypochondria.

The first garden roses were the Gallicas, *Rosa* x *alba,* damask roses, musk roses and *R. centifolia* – the cabbage rose. Those roses (along with lilies) played a leading role in monastery gardens. Roses were always popular with monarchs and rulers. King Childebert of France planted a rose garden in AD550 and later, in 1275, King Edward I put in a massive planting of red and white roses at the Tower of London. Rose fashions come and go. Most historians figure the cut-off date for modern roses as being 1867 when 'La France' was created, the first of the big flowering types.

Modern tidy roses bear little resemblance to the early types which boasted vigorous habits and were much more rambunctious than the staid bushes that followed. Their primary victory was repeat-blooming compared to the fleeting flowering of their predecessors. The remontant (repeat flowering) China roses caused such a flurry of excitement, they rapidly superceded the one-shot blooming antique types. In America the early Bourbons, Albas, Noisettes and Portlands went by the wayside to such a degree that heirloom rosarians were sending out distress calls by the 1880s. In the 1980s, a group of preservationists who called themselves 'Rose Rustlers' took to the small towns around Texas and other regions formerly rife with old roses, knocking on doors of farmhouses and begging cuttings of the old roses they found growing around homesteads. Thus many old roses have been restored.

It is often surmised that the prototypical red rose of the Greeks was *Rosa gallica* of a rich, velvety crimson color and reputed to have sprung from the blood of Adonis. Native to south and central Europe and naturalized throughout eastern North America, *R. gallica* adorned the shields of Persian warriors in 1000BC. The semi-double red flowering *R. gallica* 'Officinalis' was adopted as the symbol of the House of Lancaster in the Wars of the Roses, taken by Edmund (the first Earl of Lancaster) as his emblem in 1277. Meanwhile, *R. alba* was adopted by the opposition as the white rose of York. *R. gallica* is also called the apothecary's rose. In fact, the *British Pharmacopeia* stipulates that *R. gallica* must be the sole source of petals for apothecary purposes. Roses for apothecary use are harvested in bud during dry weather. Due to its strong scent, *Rosa gallica* is a primary ingredient in potpourri. A popular heirloom is 'Rosa Mundi', *R. gallica* 'Versicolor' named for Henry II's mistress, Rosamond Clifford. 'Rosa Mundi' has white semi-double blooms striped in pink and red. Reputed to flower more freely than any other striped rose, unfortunately 'Rosa Mundi' frequently reverts.

Rosa gallica was one of the original parents of *R.* x *damascena*, a hybrid so ancient that it was already portrayed on the walls of the Palace of Knossos in Crete built in 2000BC. Damasks are famed as the most fragrant of all roses.

R. rubiginosa, the sweet briar or eglantine rose formerly known as *R. eglanteria* is native to the British Isles and Europe and naturalized in North America, the single blush pink white-centered flowers are attractive although it was the apple-like scent released from glands on the undersides of the leaves that once caused it to be so popular with poets as well as gardeners. When the flowers have faded and the foliage has dropped, scarlet rose hips endure throughout the winter, giving the hedge perennial color. Gerard suggested the fruit as a substitute for red currant jelly in tarts. It was often grown in hedges or over arbours in cottage gardens. A double sweet briar was mentioned by John Worlidge in his 1677 *Systema Horticulturae*. The double pale pink sweet briar, 'Manning's Blush', dating back before 1797 is still available. The introductory date of another double still in cultivation, 'La Belle Distinguée', otherwise known as 'Double Scarlet Sweetbriar' is obscure. In the 1890s, Lord Penzance – an ardent proponent of rose preservation – performed breeding with the sweet briar, introducing most notably 'Lord Penzance' (a maize-colored hybrid from 'Harrison's Yellow') in 1894, 'Lady Penzance' (a yellow-centered pink from *R. foetida* 'Bicolor) in 1894 and 'Greenmantle', a large-flowering pink in 1895. All these hybrids are still available.

In general, roses like to be situated where they receive a minimum of 6 hours of sun daily, anchored in fertile, slightly acidic, well-drained soil with compost underfoot. Heirloom roses prefer organic fertilizers which should be applied at least 2-3 times a season, beginning in early spring when new growth begins, with a final feeding in August. Good air circulation is vital; roses are visited by fewer problems when situated at the crest of a hill as opposed to the foot of a valley. Mulching will help roses survive the winter and keep the roots moist and cool in summer.

Saponaria

CARYOPHYLLACEAE

soapwort, bouncing Bet, latherwort,
fuller's herb, bruisewort, crow soap,
sweet Betty, wild sweet William

Widespread in Europe, *Saponaria officinalis* was probably invited into gardens for purely practical purposes – its foliage was employed as a soap due to its lathering and scouring properties. For that purpose it was used to cleanse cloth before it was stamped with dye, leading to its appearance around old mills where it can still occasionally be found. Fragile tapestries are still sometimes washed with saponaria to ensure that the fibers will be treated as they were for centuries. Beyond its cleansing functions, saponaria was employed in venereal complaints or, as Johnson (1654) put it, "against that filthy disease, French poxes". If chewed, the leaves have an acrid taste and leave a numbing sensation in the mouth.

Certainly, the pea-green leaves of these 1–2 foot tall plants were useful, but the phlox-like flowers ranging in color from pink, red or white were handsome as well. And when the double variety, with its blowsy little tuft of pink and white petals, arrived in the 1600s, it completely upstaged the single version for garden purposes. Known as bouncing Bet in America, *S. officinalis* found another use in New England, where it was employed to cure poison ivy. It can be found spreading rampantly, surrounding old homesteads.

In fact, bouncing Bet spreads so bullishly that many gardeners warn against its inclusion in the garden. Tolerant of very poor soils and drought, it prefers a richer diet and predictable moisture, but even gourmet conditions fail to green up the leaves which are often mottled with bands of pallor. When not in blossom, soapwort is not a particularly showy plant, but flowers appear through late summer when the garden needs an infusion of color.

Tanacetum parthenium

COMPOSITAE

feverfew, featherfew, pyrethrum,
featherfoil, flirtwort, bachelor's buttons

Although this hedgerow herb was primarily valued for its fever-dispelling attributes, the lacy (although bitter-scented) leaves and handsome umbels of little daisy blossoms rendered it a favorite for cottage gardens. Native to southeastern Europe and formerly classified as chrysanthemum and matricaria, it has been growing in Britain since Roman times and might be native. The original species has flowers almost identical to chamomile. However, a double variety was common in Britain by the beginning of the 17th century and quickly displaced the single variety in gardens, eventually spreading into other lands. In addition to its fever-curing properties, Parkinson suggested the herb as a remedy "to helpe those that have taken Opium too liberally" while Gerard suggested it for vertigo and depression.

Currently, feverfew is frequently ingested to prevent migraines. However, the capsule form seems to work best – chewing the acrid foliage has been known to cause sores in the mouth. A tincture of the leaves is said to relieve pain and swelling from insect bites.

Feverfew is one of the many herbs to straddle the fence between practical and ornamental usage. Not only was the double variety adopted into gardens, but the single-flowered, golden-leaved version, *Chrysanthemum parthenium* 'Aureum', was popular in Victorian bedding schemes. It is still on the market as 'Midas Touch'.

Feverfew tends to seed liberally when introduced into a garden, and seed is a favorite method of propagation, along with division and cuttings. It transplants easily when dug and moved. However, it's wise to allow seedlings to germinate, individual plants are not particularly long-lived. Best planted in spring, feverfew prefers a sunny location and well-drained, fertile soil. Although feverfew is easily grown, it is prone to attacks from slugs and snails.

Valeriana officinalis ❹

VALERIANACEAE

valerian, garden heliotrope, all-heal,
amantilla, setwall, setewale, capon's tail

Native to Western Asia and Europe, valerian is common in marshy wasteground in Britain. Due to its lacy-flowerhead composed of many tiny white blushing to pink blossoms clustered in a Queen Anne's lace-like bunch, valerian has often been likened to centranthus and heliotrope. However, valerian flowers have a signature pungence, warranting the common name of "phu", a word that Dioscorides used for plants of offensive odor. First found mentioned in the 9th and 10th centuries for its medicinal virtues, valerian was so often employed for epilepsy and other ills that it earned the name "all-heal" in Medieval times. Its roots are said to send cats into a state of euphoria and the roots are also used to cure toothaches in human patients.

Equally content in sun or shade, valerian can most often be found growing in moist areas by streams or marshes. Not only are the flowers handsome (and some people find their pungent scent delightful), but the deeply segmented leaves are also an ornamental feature, making valerian a welcome addition to the cottage garden. Spreading rampantly, valerian can be propagated by pieces of root. The plants prefer a fertile soil and ample moisture, especially when transplanting. Valerian can also be propagated by seed. However, for medicinal purposes, transplanted roots tend to contain the strongest alkaloids. *Valeriana officinalis* remains readily available at most garden centers. Not quite so common is *V. phu* with white flowers and undivided lower leaves. Rarer still, but a nice slant on the common theme, *V. phu* 'Aurea' has golden leaves in the spring which fade gradually by midsummer.

Viola

VIOLACEAE

violets

With 500 known species in the viola family, native throughout the globe, violets entered cultivation early in the game. They were among the first flowers grown commercially, sold in the Athens markets in 400BC. Mentioned by Homer and Virgil, violets were used by the ancient Greeks to induce sleep and "comfort and strengthen the heart". Pliny suggests a liniment of violet root and vinegar for gout and disorders of the spleen; the Romans made a wine from the flowers of *Viola odorata*. Much later, in Britain, violet blossoms were used as a cosmetic to enhance female beauty. Violets were commonly grown in monastery gardens and in the cottage gardens of country folks. They have always been popular in cooking, especially in France where they are the main ingredient in a syrup. In the late 18th century, syrup production for the chemical industry was the goal of the first large commercial violet fields in Britain.

Violets are popular in confectionery, but the blossoms are also employed as a coloring agent and a perfume, although the essential oil could not be extracted from violet flowers until the 19th century. Before that date, the roots of *Iris germanica* 'Florentina' provided the constituents of violet perfume. Certainly their scent is headturning, the term shrinking violet refers to the fact that the flowers of many species nod. One theory is that the blossoms form a canopy to protect the developing seed from rain until ripe, at which point the flowers turn upward. Violets are primarily at home in woodland and prefer a rich, loamy, friable soil similar to the floor of a forest. They prefer even moisture and dislike dryness underfoot, which might explain why their major flush of bloom synchronizes with spring showers.

Native through much of Europe, *V. odorata* or sweet violet is the violet of commerce, valued since antiquity for its culinary and medicinal uses, grown in cottage gardens since their birth. It was *V. odorata* that Napoleon chose as the emblem of the House of Bonaparte, and it was also a favorite flower of the Empress Josephine. Upon his banishment to Elba,

Napoleon pledged to return to France when the violets blossomed again. When Josephine died, sweet violets were planted on her grave. Napoleon plucked some flowers from that grave, tucked them into a locket and wore it into exile on St. Helena. His former officers stubbornly wore violet blossoms in their buttonholes to show support, inspiring the monarchy to ban the wearing of that blossom. Napoleon's nephew, Louis, reinstated the violet, the favorite flower of his bride, the Empress Eugenie.

In America, violets were incredibly popular at the end of the 19th century, with huge violet farms supplying flowers to all the major cities. The most famous violet fields were in San Francisco, with glassed counterparts along the Hudson River. Bundled in bunches of 50 or 100 and surrounded by a ruff of heart-shaped violet leaves, those nosegays were worn to the opera, affixed at the waist when corsets were in vogue. Later, when fashions went waistless, the corsage emigrated to the shoulder. *V. odorata* is a handsome little creeper with heart-shaped leaves and small blue, lavender or white flowers, but it is the violet's perfume that truly earned its reputation. The fragrance is so sweet, in fact, that a person's scent receptors can shut down and refuse to recognise the smell if it is sampled too often, a trait that only wallflowers share. Unfortunately, in the rush to breed violets with larger blossoms, longer stems, better keeping quality and disease resistance, hybridizers completely forgot the scent and over years the scent of sweet violets shrank into oblivion; many newer varieties, such as *V. odorata* 'Freckles', have little scent. For a time in the 1940s to 1970s, fragrant violets were nearly impossible to find. However, the deep blue *V. odorata* and its pink counterpart, *V. odorata* 'Rosea' can again be found from specialty nurseries. And some of the older, intensely fragrant hybrids such as the blue-violet blooming 'Baronne Alice de Rothschild' (1894), deep purple 'Czar' (1865), rose red 'Madame Armandine Pages' (1900) and the classic lavender blue 'Princess of Wales'

(1899) have been ferreted out and are again available.

The double flowering parma violets are not quite as handsome as the adorable single violet. However, the parma's perfume is superb. Stemming from *V. odorata pallida plena*, also known as the Neopolitan violet, and probably originating in Asia Minor or the Levant, doubles were cultivated by the Empress Josephine at Malmaison. By 1816, they were being grown in Britain. Cultivation in pots has always been the standard method of accommodating parma violets. The flowers – which are a nest of many stubby petals in varying shades of blue, purple, lavender and white — are most easily seen when allowed to cascade over the rim of a container, and their long stems make them useful for cut flowers, ideal for bunching. Once the darlings of the floral industry for corsage purposes, parma violets disappeared from the scene for several decades following World War II. At present, it is possible to find 'Marie Louise' (1865), 'Duchesse de Parme' (1870), 'Lady Hume Campbell' (1875) and 'Swanley White' (alias 'Comte Brazza', 1880). This handful of hybrids are all that remain of nearly the 50 varieties once popular.

The bedding pansy *V.* x *wittrockiana* is a fairly recent phenomenon, the result of crosses between *V. tricolor* and *V. lutea* (the mountain pansy native to western and central Europe) with several other species playing minor roles. Modern garden pansies were widely developed during the 1820s and 1830s; by 1835 over 400 named varieties of garden pansy existed in England alone! The Hammersmith Heart's-ease Society held its first show in 1841, exhibiting plants subscribing to specific rules: to be suitable for competition, pansies were expected to have a perfectly round flower with a yellow or white background. There were equally strict regulations as to acceptable petal color combinations. It was a British phenomenon, and as soon as French and Belgian breeders began working with pansies, the color repertoire increased and the central blotch expanded to cover nearly the entire petal. These 'Fancy' pansies came back to Britain in 1848 but weren't accepted onto the show tables until 1871. Among the heirloom varieties of pansy still available are 'Bullion', a 19th century variety with golden yellow blossoms and 'Jackanapes' with crimson upper petals contrasted by yellow lower petals.

Like other violets, pansies fail to flower during the heat of midsummer, but are valued primarily for their spring performance, whch can be prolonged by cutting plants back severely, keeping the soil moist and growing them in partial shade. A similar display occurs in fall if the plant has been pruned back. Pansies are also suitable in cool rooms indoors, blossoming simultaneously with forced bulbs. They make splendid companion plants for daffodils, Jacob's ladder, pulmonaria and other spring attractions and are often exhibited in seasonal windowboxes. Plants should be propagated by division or cuttings in spring. Seed will not be true to form.

Pansy development was followed by work on hybridizing violas from *V. cornuta*, the pale blue flowered horned violet, which was introduced into Britain from the Pyrenees in 1776. Beginning in 1860, violas became the subject of improvement, culminating in the work of Dr Charles Stuart in 1872, striving to produce a "tufted viola" with no streaks (or whiskers) in the face. His new creation was perennial and handsome but had smaller blossoms than the pansies of the past. *V. cornuta* and its cultivars grow to form large carpets of colour, very effective as underplanting in a border and more tolerant of hot and dry conditions than most violets which prefer semi-shade and moisture-retentive soil. In most regions they bloom in spring and autumn; cut them back when they become straggly to encourage new growth. The only reliable way to propagate most named violas is by layering young shoots in spring or dividing plants in autumn. However a few do come true from seed. And non-named strains are available by seed.

Although most violets will survive the sun they tend to prefer cool evening temperatures and cease flowering when temperatures consistently rise above 50 degrees F. at night. Parma violets are much more tender than other violets, not reliably hardy north of Zone 7. Most violets can be propagated by divisions, preferably in spring. Seed rarely comes true to type although there are some exceptions, such as the popular small-flowered pansy *V.* 'Bowles Black', a cultivar of *V. tricolor*. Grown by the horticulturalist E. A. Bowles in his famous 19th century English garden, this plant forms generous dark mats of tiny flowers, ideal for underplanting or the front of a border.

Annuals

Amaranthus

AMARANTHACEAE

love-lies-bleeding, velvet flower,
tassel flower, amaranth

Native to Peru, Africa and India, *Amaranthus caudatus* was called the "great purple flower-gentle" by Gerard and Parkinson. But by 1665 it was established as love-lies-bleeding, well describing this 3 foot tall annual tipped by slender, chenille-like plumes. The plumes are deep magenta and cover the tip, dangling in one long dramatic streamer. The name *amaranthus* means "never waxing old", referring to the plant's everlasting qualities. Gerard mentioned that love-lies-bleeding was a popular dried flower, so commonly preserved for that purpose that it came to symbolize immortality. It was popular in cottage gardens from its introduction but reached the peak of its popularity in Victorian gardens, when the chartreuse tassled 'Viridis', or 'Green Thumb' was popular.

A. hypochondriacus is native to the southern United States, Mexico, India and China. The prince's feather (as it was quickly nicknamed) boasts tall, upright, crimson plumes, valued for nutritious seed as well as being an extremely ornamental plant. It was among the plants taken to Europe by John Tradescant from Virginia in 1684.

Amaranths love sunny weather but wilt easily when conditions are dry. Tall plants by nature, the Victorians were fond of encouraging them with generous doses of manure, with the end result of stems that stretched so tall that their tassels towered over anyone walking through the garden. For best effect, several amaranths should be clustered together; they make wonderful companions for *Centaurea*, *Nicotiana* or amongst sunflowers.

Antirrhinum

SCROPHULARIACEAE

snapdragon

The original purple-flowering *Antirrhinum majus*, native to southwestern Europe and the Mediterranean, was probably brought to Britain with the Romans. In 1564, Thomas Hyll mentioned that snapdragons (named and nicknamed for the long jaw-like blossoms) were perfectly capable of reseeding themselves with little assistance from the gardener. Elizabethans were fond of snapdragons which were then available in five colors: purple, white, pink, red with yellow throat or red with yellow veins. These early snapdragons stood 3 feet or taller, and were scentless. Most heirlooms lost rather than gained

scent, but snapdragons are an exception, the first scented versions only being produced in 1963.

In the early 19th century the color range increased; a yellow and an orange form were the first to be selected but by the 1850s the first striped snapdragon appeared, debuting as *A. hendersonii*, although it wasn't, in fact, a separate species. Double snapdragons were also on the market in the 19th century, each with its own cultivar name. Those double hybrids were sterile and had to be propagated by cuttings, which isn't always an easy feat with annuals that blossom on a terminal spike, so they soon disappeared from the scene. In the 1880s the dwarf 'Tom Thumb' series became very popular bedding plants.

Modern innovations include multi-colored series of snapdragons (such as 'Madam Butterfly') with open-faced flowers that render the snout imagery irrelevant and cheat children of the pleasure of making snapdragon jaws "talk". Monticello sells an heirloom snapdragon, but contrary to the original species description, its flowers are burgundy.

The seed of snapdragons should be started early (February is not too soon) to see blossoms by midsummer. The plants prefer full sun and well drained soil. For best performance deadhead the plants as soon as the seedbuttons begin to form, although seed savers must of course let the spire develop into seed, which shortens the floral performance but preserves the strain.

Calendula

COMPOSITAE

ruddes, pot marigold, common marigold, Scotch marigold, Mary Gowles

Although ancient identification is notoriously nebulous, the "gold flower" of ancient Greece is often considered to be calendula. If this is the case, calendula would be the flower that Theophrastus, in the third century BC, mentioned for a variety of ailments of the head. Named for the *calends*, the first day of the month in the Roman calendar, *Calendula officinalis* has earned a reputation for blooming constantly throughout the year. The first record of calendula's garden cultivation is from 5th century France.

Native throughout Southern Europe, marigolds were widely grown in British gardens by the 15th century, and probably centuries before, as a staple ingredient of every cottage and kitchen garden. The single flowered types were traditionally used as kitchen and medicinal herbs, and the doubles, known since at least the 16th century, were grown in flower beds. The flowers were suggested (by Stevens in *Maison Rustique, or the Countrie Farme*, 1699) for headache, jaundice, red eyes and toothache. But they were most commonly prescribed for complaints of the heart, especially palpitations. A modern usage is to rub the flower (or salve made of calendula) on a wasp or bee sting to alleviate the pain. Pot marigold was a common flavouring, a "sweet herb" used for centuries in puddings, pottages and possets (a popular Tudor milk and herb based drink to which beer or ale was added).

Gerard described large double marigolds "like pure gold". In addition hen-and-chicken forms, now known as 'Prolifera', where miniature flowers appear around the central blossom, were apparently common in the 16th and 17th centuries. If you grow pot marigolds in quantity, such sports sometimes still occur. The blossom heads of calendula (like most of the daisy family) face the sun, and Charles I of England wrote before his execution, "The marigold observes the sun, More than my subjects me have done."

Pot marigolds grow to 2 feet in the wild in Southern Europe, with pale yellow to dark orange blooms up to 4 inches across, many with darker centres. Many late 19th and early 20th century cultivars have been bred to boast very dark centres. Sow pot marigolds in autumn or spring in any reasonable soil, in sun, covering seeds with a layer of soil as they need dark to germinate. Make a second sowing in early summer for late blooming marigolds furnishing attractive bright autumn color. Spacing should be generous so the plant has room to expand; pinching will encourage side branching. With a little care, calendulas can blossom from June until hard frosts. Although grown as an annual, calendula can survive winter in regions warmer than Zone 6. Seeds ripen by late summer and are easy to collect, often seeding themselves in.

Celosia
AMARANTHACEAE
cockscomb

Celosia argentea var. *cristata*, the cockscomb, was formerly classified as an amaranth, and is generally mentioned in the same breath. When the break was made, the name *celosia* was selected from the Greek *kelos* meaning "burned", referring to the color of the prototypical flower. Native throughout the tropics, it was the dark red-colored *C. cristata* that was first introduced into Europe in 1570. This had a colorful crest straddling a little mound of deeply textured foliage: the plumed and feathered types came later. Although all these different guises are currently lumped together as variations on *C. argentea*, they were once divided into separate species.

In 18th century Britain, these plants were segregated as potted plants, but at the same time they were eagerly embraced into colonial gardens in America. Always interested in unique plants, Thomas Jefferson included celosia (probably the crested one) at his Monticello garden in 1767. Later, due to their color-ful plumes and compact stature, they were important components in Victorian bedding schemes. Although Nicholson mentions only the dark red *C. cristata* in Britain in 1887, by 1928, L. H. Bailey stated "There are 8 or 9 well-marked colors in either tall or dwarf forms, the chief colors being red, purple, violet, crimson, amaranth, and yellow. The forms with variegated leaves often have less dense crests." Cockscombs became popular exhibits at small fairs, the object seeming to be to produce the greatest crest on the smallest plant; one report of 1928 recalled an award-winning specimen bearing a whopping 21 inch crest.

Like most amaranths, cockscomb is a sun worshipper. It prefers warmth, it likes generous root room and it's always hungry. The roots must be kept moist at all times – if they dry out, even once, the flowers drop. They are easy to propagate from seed, and growing them in pots guarantees better results than using them for bedding in open ground.

Centaurea
COMPOSITAE
cornflower, blue-bottle, bachelor's buttons,
hurtsickle, ragged sailor

The Egyptian boy king Tutankhamen was buried *c.*1340BC with a funeral wreath around his head made of cornflowers, olive leaves and waterlily petals. We know that beautiful deep blue cornflowers have grown for many centuries, throughout Europe and into Asia.

Their Latin name *Centaurea cyanus* comes from the mythical centaur who reputedly healed himself with cornflowers after he was wounded by an arrow poisoned with the blood of Hydra. In later centuries the Doctrine of Signatures suggested that they be used to ease eye complaints – comparing the blue of the flowers with the blue of people's eyes. The practice of using cornflowers as an eye salve persisted for many centuries.

Cornflowers have wiry silver leaved stems growing up to 3 feet tall with many fringed deep blue brush-like flowers. They were once so common in cornfields that the farmers called them "hurtsickles" as their stems could (apparently) blunt a sickle. They were also called bluebottles because of their resemblance to little blue pouches of ink, and people used to make a blue ink from the petals. By 1629, Parkinson recorded several colors which he wasn't particularly keen on, judging from his description, "wholly blew, or white, or blush, or of a sad or light purple, or of a light or dead red, or of an overworne purple color." Philip Miller (1692–1771) wrote that when the bright pink version became available, it totally upstaged the blue in the garden. Call them faded if you will, but all these colors are still available. By the early 20th century, interest in cornflowers had increased to the extent that several named varieties were on the market including dark blue 'Emperor William', 'Flore Pleno' with the outer disc flowers converted to ray flowers, 'Nana Compacta' which was dwarf, 'Pure White', and 'Victoria', a dwarf for pots and edging. These separate varieties might correlate with some of the cornflowers in modern mixes, but they no longer available by name.

Cornflowers were once very common in Northern European arable fields, appearing in nearly every rural garden. But they are one of the casualties of 20th century farming methods and are now a very rare sight in the wild. They remain a popular garden annual, particularly with children, as they are easy and rewarding to grow. In America, they frequent prairies, which are also endangered ecosystems.

The cornflower's other common name of bachelor's buttons may come from their popularity as buttonhole flowers in Victorian times, as their stems are very resilient and the blooms keep fresh even when cut, but it is more likely to refer to their shaggy headed habit resembling the traditional buttons worn by

bachelors – small pieces of cloth stitched on top of one another.

The sweet sultan *Amberboa moschata* was *Centaurea moschata* until recently, and considered a close relation of the cornflower. Native to southwestern Asia, but introduced by 1629 from Persia, sweet sultans were reputedly popularized by the Sultan of Constantinople who wore them in his buttonhole (or equivalent). Looking similar to cornflowers in blossom but with a more paintbrush-thick cushion of petals, the flowers are handsome, coming in lilac, carmine, white and purple on dusty miller-like foliage. But it was the musky-thick scent, strongest when the sun isn't in full glory, that won sweet sultans a strong following. Of that fragrance, John Parkinson remarked, "it surpasseth the finest civet there is." 'Imperialis' is the most readily available strain, standing 2–4 feet tall. 'The Bride' is pure white and shorter in stature.

Cornflowers are easily grown. They prefer sun and like to associate with other plants of sturdier stem, making them perfect for a meadow or prairie. Cornflowers are made for drought and dislike abundant moisture. They tolerate poor soil but prefer the relative fertility of the cultivated field. They make handsome companions for yellow flowering plants such as lady's mantle, or mix nicely amongst poppies to tone down their bright colors.

Cleome
CAPPARIDACEAE
spider flower, spider plant, cleome

By no means an ancient cottage plant, cleome was introduced from the West Indies in 1817. Although a latecomer, it immediately attracted notice because of the broad topknots of spider-like blossoms with pistils and stamens protruding similar to honeysuckle blooms, crowning tall stems of palmate foliage. The original cleome was misidentified as *Cleome pungens* or *C. spinosa*, a plant that has only 1 inch wide, dingy white blossoms. That original entry was probably *C. hassleriana*, with 2 inch wide flowers and a color range

that includes white, pink and purple on 4-5 foot tall plants with slightly prickly stems. Usually cultivated under glass in Victorian times and exhibited in pots, cleomes were later adapted into the neo-cottage style garden, more so in America and continental Europe where summers are hot. An 'Alba' form was available in the 19th century, which was probably identical to the flower marketed as 'Helen Campbell'. The darker shades have been selected out as 'Violet Queen'. All make excellent cut flowers.

Cleomes prefer full sun and light, rich soil. They tolerate drought bravely, and seem to prefer dry, warm conditions. Most importantly, they want plenty of room to spread without competing with bedfellows but they look best displayed *en masse* rather than sprinkled lightly here and there. Cleomes tend to get naked ankles, which can be remedied by a skirt of shorter plants in the foreground, such as geraniums or *Centaurea montana*. Cleomes are propagated by seed which should be started early.

Coleus

LABIATAE

flame nettle, painted nettle, coleus

In 1879 Joseph Breck pointed out in his *New Book of Flowers* (1879), "the beauty of the plant consists entirely in the leaf; the flowers are of no consequence." Although it is the colorful leaves that create the show rather than its pale blue blossoms, coleus are still generally classified alongside flowers – the raucous foliage serves the same function.

The nomenclature of coleus is fraught with confusion. The brashly colored and many branched member of the Labiatae arrived in Britain from Java in 1825 as *Coleus blumei* var. *Verschaffeltii*, but botanists later found that the supposed species had intermingled and hybridized frivolously before reaching cultivation. So all the many festively-colored progeny of unknown parentage were then lumped together into *Coleus* x *hybridus*. Not content with that slight rearrangement, the colorful-leaved coleus have been reassigned to *Solenostemon*, but will still undoubtedly remain coleus for common reference.

Coleus arrived in Britain just in time to take their place in the gaudy carpet beds and ribbon borders popular in the 19th century landscape. Ideally-suited for the job, they are easy to grow and tolerant of the shade that often happens when you tuck many plants cheek-to-jowl. They hybridized and set seed with such abandon that all sorts of color combinations – both subdued and otherwise – were soon widespread. Many went unnamed, but old-fashioned named cultivars included 'Pillar of Gold' with divided yellow leaves tinted rose, 'Sunbeam', green veined with yellow, 'Kentish Fire' with divided purplish-crimson leaves, and 'Renown' with light green reticulated leaves irregularly mottled in maroon. They were incredibly simple to propagate, rooting rapidly in a glass of water. However, the old-fashioned varieties could tolerate neither the slightest frost nor bright sunshine, and those two traits were their undoing.

Vern Ogren, the coleus expert from Color Farm in Florida, claims that the only Victorian cultivar to survive to the present day is 'Pineapple Queen', a maroon and yellow hybrid. However, other equally eye-riveting types have taken their place. The names have changed, but there are at least 400 named varieties currently in cultivation, displaying all the characteristics that the Victorians adored.

Coleus prefer partial shade and tend to wilt easily if not given sufficient water. Although they might tolerate poor soil, they would prefer a rich, friable underfooting and, most importantly, plenty of room to spread their branching stems. Plant them no closer than $2\frac{1}{2}$ feet apart and inflict an initial pinching when you plant them out. Continue pinching to encourage branching, and nip off the blossoms when the spires begin. 'Pineapple Queen' is particularly sensitive to sun.

Consolida

RANUNCULACEAE

*Larkspur, rocket larkspur, lark's heel,
lark's toe, lark's claw, knight's spur*

Formerly known as *Delphinium ajacus* and currently classified as *Consolida ambigua*, larkspur was introduced to Britain from its native Mediterranean area sometime before the mid-16th century and was soon naturalized, growing as a weed in cornfields. Larkspurs are often mentioned in the same breath as delphiniums which have similar characteristics but are perennial and biennial while larkspur perishes promptly after blooming. The common name refers to the spur behind each flower that makes single blossoms look like shooting stars. Parkinson and Gerard were both familiar with double larkspurs, with stems surrounded by little many-petaled mops.

At one time larkspur was probably applied as a wound herb because the name *consolida* reputedly stems from consolidating wounds. Tournefort (1656-1708) mentioned that the juice of the distilled flower strengthened the sight. The seed was also used as an insecticide, especially to rid the scalp of lice.

Larkspurs were common in gardens throughout the 17th and 18th centuries, with a peak in fame in the middle of the 19th century when American gardeners embraced the romantic cottage style. There are numerous larkspur strains on the market, the taller hybrids, reaching 20 inches or more, most closely resemble the older types. The originals were probably non-branching, resembling today's Giant Double Hyacinth hybrids.

Larkspur likes sandy or chalky but fertile soil. They prefer full sun and should be clustered together to make a worthwhile show – seen alone the plants seem spindly, especially when they shoot up into blossom. Larkspur goes to seed easily which tends to self-sow but rarely becomes a nuisance. All parts of larkspur are poisonous, the seeds being the most dangerous, causing vomiting if consumed.

Cosmos

COMPOSITAE

cosmos, Mexican aster

Cosmos were only introduced to Britain from their native Mexico in 1799. The feathery foliage of *Cosmos bipinnatus* complements its large daisy flowers held on tall stems and traditionally pale pink, lightly fragrant after dark. They make attractive plants for the back of the border, blooming at the end of summer into autumn. By 19th century standards, the daisy-like flowers of cosmos must have appeared splendid, even though they were only an inch in diameter compared to our current 3–4 inch extravaganzas.

In 1838 the entrepreneurial New York garden sundries and seed supplier Grant Thorburn was offer-

ing his customers six-foot tall "late Cosmos", and there was little development of the species through the 19th century, but the disadvantage of traditional varieties of cosmos is their late blooming – the original cosmos didn't blossom until late summer, just in time to be smitten by hard frost. So in the early 20th century new earlier flowering strains of cosmos were developed, and the blossom size was increased a bit.

Before that crucial improvement, the color spectrum had been increased to include brighter shades by 1895. The 'Sensation' strain, coming in a full complement of colors including white, pink and deep rose and still readily on the market, dates back to 1930. White forms also date to approximately 1895. At present, 'Sonata' is available in a full color collection as well as simply pure white and it's a primary player in moon gardens. Semi-double cosmos were a 20th century phenomenon.

Cosmos are easy to grow; benign neglect is the key. Seed should be sown in fairly light warm soil, and barely covered. The flowers self seed profusely, but they almost always revert to the most vigorous pale pink form so save seeds from preferred cultivars to keep the colors true. The white forms are least vigorous, so it is particularly important to save seed from them.

Fuchsia

ONAGRACEAE

ladies' eardrops, fuchsia

Native throughout Central and South America and named for Leonard Fuchs, a 16th century German botanist, the first fuchsia was introduced in 1788. *Fuchsia coccinea* came from Mexico via a sailor and, set in the windowsill of a London cottage, caught the eye of James Lee, the wily nurseryman of Hammersmith. Promising the sailor's wife that he'd replace the shared plant before her husband returned from his next ocean voyage, he took his booty home and propagated it. By 1793, he was selling *F. coccinea* for the equivalent of $50–$100, the sailor's wife having received only a pittance for her treasure.

Between the 1820s and 1840s, a flurry of species arrived in Britain from South America and breeding of these valuable plants began, with a special interest in elongating the oboe-shaped blossoms that dangle like earrings (thus the common name of ladies' eardrops) from the tips of broad, oval leaves. Leaning most heavily on *F. megellanica* from Chile and *F. fulgens* from Mexico, the color range increased. However, only flowers with a red or pink tube and sepals contrasted by a blue or purple corolla were available prior to the 1850s. In the middle of the 19th century, a variety with a white corolla appeared, and that innovation was followed rapidly by double flowers. At the height of the fuchsia's popularity in the latter part of the 19th century, there were 1,500 varieties available.

At present, double-flowering fuchsias have all but overshadowed their single counterparts. Older miniatures such as 'Tom Thumb', 'Display' and 'Liebriez' are nearly impossible to find. Of the single-flowering fuchsias available in the 1880s, we still have the rosy-carmine 'Earl of Beaconsfield' (now sold as 'Laing's Hybrid', after the original breeder), 'Beauty of Swanley' (pink and white), 'Charming' (red) and 'Sunray' (with ornamental crimson and bronze leaves accenting the scarlet flower), among others.

The first fuchsias were hothouse or windowsill plants thriving in filtered light. But the hardier (to Zone 6) *F. megellanica* (often listed in 19th century references as *F. macrostema*) was introduced in 1823 and it became a resident of the shady flower border outdoors. British gardeners grew fond of fuchsias in their gardens, but Americans never caught on – fuchsias can't survive northern winters and they dislike the humidity in the South. Popping the little flowers as they swell is a lasting summer childhood memory for many British children!

Fuchsias require a light, friable soil and prefer slightly moist underfootings as they wilt easily. Most importantly, shade is essential, as they detest noonday sun. Most varieties blossom heavily (to the tune of several hundred flowers simultaneously) in spring and early summer. To reach ample proportions, they must be given lots of elbow room. Fuchsias are propagated by cuttings.

Helianthus

COMPOSITAE

sunflower

Native to the southern states of Northern America, sunflowers must have traveled into South America in very early days as sunflowers were a staple Inca crop, grown for the oil and the seeds. Native Americans used seeds of the wild plants to make meal cakes as a source of protein. The Spanish took sunflowers back to Spain in the 16th century, and they were first mentioned in English in 1577 in *Joyfull News out of the Newfounde Worlde*, a translation of an earlier work by the Spanish botanist Monardes. Gerard was growing sunflowers in his garden at Holborn in 1596. He said that he ate the flowerbuds like globe artichokes "surpassing the Artichoke far in procuring bodily lust."

Helianthus annuus had already evolved into a variety of shapes and sizes in the wild long before Europeans collected their first sunflowers. All had large, prominently colored inner disks with seed packed in a spiraling formation, invariably surrounded by a ring of yellow or orange petals. But the growth habits were vastly different. The western types branched frequently, while the eastern versions had larger flowerheads. The single-stemmed feature that we've come to associate with the mammoth sunflowers so popular today was probably a mutation, encouraged by Native Americans for the largest seedheads. Depending upon the region, types were bred with different soil preferences, maturity dates and germination needs (arid region tribes developed sunflowers that could be sown deep). By the time Europeans happened upon the scene in the 16th century, *H. annuus* was a highly variable plant.

Both Gerard and Parkinson were impressed by sunflowers. Perhaps to dissuade predators in a land of sparse vegetation, the leaves have a strange signature scent, likened to turpentine by both herbalists. Sunflowers were welcomed as a curiosity rather than a food plant when they first entered Europe.

Meanwhile, in North America, sunflowers had many uses – the Hopi Indians bred a purple seeded variety to be used for dyes, other tribes used the petals to make a yellow dye, and they were also grown for fiber, but the most inventive use came from the Mormons. Setting out from Missouri to find a place where they would be free from religious persecution, they scattered sunflower seeds on their way to Utah so that later excursions need only follow the sunflower trail.

The flamboyant Oscar Wilde began a cut flower sunflower fad in 19th century Britain. Meanwhile, in Russia, the sunflower was embraced with a fervor unparalleled in the rest of Europe, and grown commercially as a major oil crop. The red-flowered hybrids so popular as ornamentals nowadays are of fairly recent vintage stemming from a single flower discovered by a Briton named Mr. Cockerell vacationing in Colorado. He dug the sunflower, brought it home and began breeding it in 1910, selling the results to a seed company. The double sunflowers that are currently the rage, touted as the latest novelty, with a mass of quill-like disk flowers and no evidence of ray petals remaining, were known to Gerard and Parkinson.

Many named varieties of heirloom sunflowers are available including the classic 'Mammoth Russian', 'Rostov' (also a Russian version with 12 inch flowerheads), 'Taiyo' (with chocolate center) and 'Romanian' (a giant flowering type with petals facing initially inward, giving a cup-like effect).

Given as much sun as possible, sunflowers forgive poor soil and lack of rain. Needless to say, ample space between plants is advisable. Sometimes used as a screen to hide compost heaps and outbuildings, sunflowers are best grouped together, providing mutual bracing against high winds. Sunflowers freely cross-pollinate, so segregation is vital for seed saving, or else plant different sunflowers in succession to stagger blooming times. The heads may need support and protection from birds when the seeds form. At all stages of growth they are beloved by deer.

Heliotropium
BORAGINACEAE
heliotrope, cherry pie, turnsole

Not an ancient plant, but nonetheless legendary from the moment gardeners first inhaled its vanilla-perfumed scent, heliotrope is now classified as *Heliotropium arborescens* but was originally known as *H. peruviana*, honoring its place of origin. Introduced by Joseph de Jussieu into France's Jardin du Roi in Paris, it flowered in Europe for the first time in 1740. From there heliotrope traveled to Britain in 1757 where the headily fragrant flower became an instant favorite. The name indicates the flower's affinity for facing the sun; in Greek *helios* means sun and *trope* means to turn. And that growth habit was also reflected in another common name, turnsole, now rarely used.

Heliotrope has long, slender, velvety, deeply veined leaves carrying dense clusters of many lilac-colored, verbena-like flowers, and a wonderful fragrance that ensures its continued popularity. The scent varies according to cultivar, but it encompasses baby powder, vanilla and baked apple or cherry cobbler. For the best scent, propagate through cuttings as seedlings can be disappointing.

Heliotrope made an immediate impact on the garden, primarily grown as a bedding plant, sheltered in glasshouses as soon as the first chill threatened. In the 19th century specific winter-flowering varieties, such as the snowy-hued 'White Lady', were developed for the conservatory and heliotropes were traditionally trained into standard (or tree) form. 'White Lady' is probably the white flowering hybrid still in cultivation as *H. arborescens* 'Alba'. Toward the middle of the 19th century, there were at least ten cultivars of heliotrope grown, ranging from 'Miss Nightingale', a dwarf variety hybridized for bedding, to 'Bouquet Perfumé', a towering hybrid. Books described heliotropes with golden variegated leaves as well as double flowers. All shades from lilac to deep purple were represented, occasionally with dark foliage enhancing the trusses. By contrast, few catalogues now offer anything other than *H. arborescens*. Cultivars still popular until the middle of the 20th century most probably disappeared with the Second World War when many plants that had to be propagated vegetatively and overwintered in heated structures were lost.

Heliotrope is very tender and should be the last plant put out in spring and the first to be taken in at the end of summer. Heliotropes have to be grown from cuttings and overwintered in a frost-free place as plants grown from seed have diminished fragrance. Heliotrope tends to attract white fly, red spider mite and aphids. Of the named varieties currently on the market, 'Iowa' displays the richest fragrance of baby powder, vanilla and mulled cider. The dark-leaved 'Dwarf Marine' is barely scented.

Iberis
CRUCIFERAE
candytuft, candie mustard, Spanish tufts,
Sciatic cress, Billy come home soon

Native to Southern Europe and first grown by Gerard in 1596, *Iberis umbellata* earned its common name from its tufted habit and its place of origin – Candia, otherwise known as Crete. In 1629 Parkinson called the plant "Spanish tufts" receiving his plants from Spain, or Iberia, explaining the botanical name .

Initially, candytufts were used as a substitute for mustard (hence one name, candie mustard), the flowers also being used to counteract poisons. Although candytuft is not mentioned in early herbals, it appears to have been commonly known as sciatica weed in the 18th century, and since its introduction it has been a universal cottage garden plant, although never fashionable in sophisticated gardens. Low-growing plants with many branches of small, dark green leaves tipped by clusters of flat-topped flowers similar to verbena, candytufts rarely exceed 18 inches in height. In the 18th century, versions with lilac, purple and rose blossoms were also cultivated.

Although the hardier (to Zone 4) *I. sempervirens*

was growing in Britain by 1679, it wasn't as popular as its annual counterpart. Another European native candytuft, *I. amara*, became a favorite of florists in the 17th century due to its sweet scent when an elongated version (often listed as *I. coronaria*), the Giant Hyacinth-flowered candytuft, was bred for bunching purposes in nosegays.

The problem with candytufts is that they slip out of flower quickly, especially in hot weather. They enjoy rich soil, and liquid manure in particular. In North America it has long been the custom to sow candytuft seed during the first two weeks of May.

Impatiens
BALSAMINACEAE
balsam, sultana, lady's slipper

An Asian native, *Impatiens balsamina* had arrived in Britain by 1596 but was recorded earlier in Germany where Fuchs' *Herbal* of 1542 referred to it as a "recent introduction planted already in many gardens." The flowers are white, cream, pink, lilac, red, and crimson with a columbine-like spur behind. By 1706, there were two-tone balsams with flowers that bloomed scarlet and white as well as purple and white. Apparently these colors were most apt to occur if you selected seedlings with spotted stems.

In the 17th and 18th centuries it was the custom to sow seeds of this and other heat-loving introductions on "hot beds", piles of fresh manure covered by a layer of soil to keep the heat rising. The earliest plants grown in Britain were single with purplish-pink flowers but a white flowered form was recorded growing as early as 1620, and Philip Miller was growing red, white and striped singles and doubles at the

Chelsea Physic garden in 1768. These double balsams were very popular in the 18th century, called camellia balsams because the blossoms resembled camellias. Unfortunately, they were a thorn in the side of many gardeners as the seed was often unreliable.

It takes patience to grow balsams from seed. Those started indoors in March will not blossom until the end of July, and they must be kept well watered and shaded. Although the camellia flowered types are still available, as well as 'Double Strawberry Ice' and 'Double Blackberry Ice', balsams aren't as popular as they used to be.

I. walleriana, the busy Lizzie, came from Zanzibar in 1896 and was little grown until the 1950s. It was still a rare plant in 1930 but 20 years later it had quite stolen balsams' thunder. *I. noli-tangere*, the touch-me-not, has been a rampant weed in Britain for centuries.

Lobularia

CRUCIFERAE

sweet alyssum, sweet alison

Confusion abounds with sweet alyssum. Firmly classified as *Lobularia maritima* at present, it has gone through several name changes previous to this point, including *Alyssum maritima* and *Koeniga maritima*. The alyssum part of the name coincides with the Greek word for "abating rage", but several plants seem to have shared the name, so no one is certain whether the sweet alyssum that we grow is the same plant that was once used for curing the bite of a mad dog! However, it is fairly certain that *Lobularia maritima*, the sweet alyssum that we know today, is native to Southern Europe and was included in gardens dating back to the 16th century.

By 1900, sweet alyssum was one of the most popular flowers invited annually into gardens: the plants naturally form neat little mounds, covered throughout the summer with tufts of honey-scented blossoms, much visited by bees. Advertised as a bee plant, the original sweet alyssum grew slightly taller (averaging 9 inches) than the compact version now common. The smaller type was sold as 'Benthamii' or 'Compacta' in the 1900s, as opposed to 'Giganteum', described as robust and broad-leaved.

Sweet alyssum is delightfully easy to grow. Useful as edging, it is perhaps most useful of all in window-boxes where it tolerates drought, beating sun and requires neither pruning nor deadheading. It likes friable, moderately fertile soil and full sun, but will give as good a show as possible, virtually regardless of conditions, as long as it isn't waterlogged. Propagate by seed, which germinates easily.

Matthiola

CRUCIFERAE

stocks, ten week stocks, stock gilliflowers, night violets

Stocks were probably brought from southern Europe into England by the Normans, and both perennial and annual stocks were certainly well established by the 16th century. They were once divided into two species, *Matthiola incana*, the day-scented stock and *M. annua*, the fast-growing ten week stock. Now the ten week stock is recognized as a variety ('Annua') of *M. incana*. Both versions were in cultivation by 1597, with single and double forms of each readily available at that early date. Standing 1–2 feet tall with soft, hoary gray leaves crowned by many spires of blossoms (if the plant is pinched in its youth), stocks come in gentle shades like chartreuse and peach (one catalog describes them as reminiscent of old chintz), as well as lilac, purple, faded blue and pink.

William Turner grew a purple and single white form in 1548 and by 1597 Gerard had added pink and striped forms, singles and doubles. In the 17th century they were sold by color with names affixed to each, the most colorful being the yellow sort that Parkinson referred to as 'The Melancholick Gentleman'. At the time, stock blossoms were accented by spots and lines, a trait which seems to have disappeared. All stocks have a wonderful scent which does not seem to have diminished through time. Even single stocks are worth growing with their broccoli-like heads in a broad spectrum of shades, but the open-faced, $1/2$ inch wide singles pale beside the doubles, with their wands of closely stacked buttons of rosebud-like blooms.

An unbranched biennial strain was developed at the end of the 17th century by the nurserymen

London and Wise, and it came to be called Brompton Stock after their nursery. Brompton stocks are very worthwhile fragrant bedding plants, standing 1–2 feet tall with soft, hoary gray leaves crowned by 8–10 inch spires of dense fragrant blossoms in shades of pinks and blues, as singles and doubles. Seeds sown in summer may flower the following spring, and sowings throughout the year give a display from spring through to late summer. Double forms are sterile but plants raised from garden-sown seed produce a high proportion of doubles.

Stocks thrive in deep, moderately rich soil and don't like to dry out. Although they don't wilt without great provocation, they swoon in a drought, which will shorten their lifespan considerably; hot weather also ends the blooming cycle. *Matthiola incana* 'Annua', ten week stocks, blossom quickly, but will also fade rapidly. It helps to pinch out the center stalk and deadhead as soon as a flowerhead opens halfway – the harvested spire will keep quite a while in a vase. Stocks are open-pollinated and set seed readily, so selection and segregation are essential if you plan to save seed of a specific color. Propagation is by seed.

Mirabilis

NYCTAGINACEAE

marvel of Peru, four o'clock, umbrellawort, false jalap, belle de nuit

Some very worthy plants slip out of fashion for no apparent reason, and Marvel of Peru is a good example. Native to Peru, *Mirabilis jalapa* was introduced into Britain by the end of the 16th century, via Spain. Linnaeus classified it as *jalapa* because he mistakenly thought it was the source of the drug jalap. Its floral antics won the plant its nickname marvel of Peru, a title already in place when Gerard wrote his herbal.

Quickly reaching 3 feet in diameter, the plant is covered with umbels of oboe-shaped blossoms, each fluting to an inch wide skirt at the mouth and producing an evening scent touched with citrus. The drama begins at 4:00 p.m. promptly, and it continues until the next morning, making the flower ideal for gardeners who work elsewhere during the day. Not only is the perfume a delight for anyone who happens by, but it's particularly enticing to hawk moths who pollinate the plant. Furthermore, the flowers come in several strident shades including white, rose, magenta, butter yellow, and bicolors, a range that was also available in 1659. However, the fascinating feature of the plant is that the colors can vary on a single plant, resulting in a Jacob's coat effect, these color variations seem greatest when the plant grows in cooler areas, such as in Northern Europe or the northern United States.

All things considered, four o'clocks are the perfect flower for a child's garden, and cottagers found it equally appealing. Thomas Jefferson received seeds from the Jardin des Plantes in Paris, and wrote that he found the floral timepiece "very clever." It wasn't until the mid-20th century that it slipped out of favor, for no apparent reason. Perhaps the clownish blossoms were a little too outlandish for the conservative taste of the times. *Mirabilis jalapa* is a garden escape in North America and can be found frequenting old foundations. Fortunately, none of the once-popular varieties have slipped away, and selections have been made of the yellow version 'Lutea' and red 'Rubra'. A Spanish heirloom called 'Don Pedros' with a large proportion of striped and spotted flowers has become commercially available.

Although it can be grown as a tender perennial in some parts of the world, in northern areas mirabilis has to be treated as an annual. It makes tubers which can be dug after the first frost and stored during the winter but seeds germinate rapidly and plants reach impressive proportions and bloom freely in one growing season, so seed is the most common method of propagation. Four o'clocks tolerate poor soil, but prefer friable loam. Similarly, a sunny location is ideal, but partial shade will be tolerated.

Nicotiana
SOLANACEAE
flowering tobacco

Nicotiana was named for Jean Nicot (1530–1600), the consul from the King of France to Portugal who first obtained tobacco from a Belgian merchant in 1560 and presented it, first to the court of Portugal and then, back in France, to Queen Catherine de Medici. The tobacco he brought back was *Nicotiana tabacum*, native to northeast Argentina and Bolivia, and the source of smoking tobacco, grown by Native Americans for that purpose long before Europeans arrived on the continent. It was introduced into Britain by Sir Walter Raleigh in 1586, prohibited by several kings and wasn't widely grown in gardens, despite the handsome broad, felted leaves topped by tubular blossoms. *N. tabacum* has been used for many purposes, good and evil, over the centuries, but it is not our garden flowering tobacco.

Ornamental flowering tobacco has a different origin. *N. alata*, native to northeast Argentina and Southern Brazil, wasn't much grown in gardens until the end of the 19th century, although it was undoubtedly discovered earlier. The cream-colored blossoms crown stems whch typically vary from 3–6 feet tall, releasing a strong perfume in the evenings. Victorian gardeners particularly welcomed nicotiana as it perfectly fitted into their night-scented gardens, popular so fair-skinned ladies could walk into the gar-

den in the evening when all danger of being burned by the sun was long past. The flowers not only release a wonderful scent, they also seem to glow at dusk, attracting their pollinators. Like *N. tabacum*, their leaves can be made into an infusion to deter aphids, as they have insecticidal properties.

Seed savers have introduced a strain of *N. alata* from Russia with purple, white, salmon, fuchsia, pink and rust colored blossoms, increasing the color range drastically while preserving the perfume. Unfortunately the most common flowering tobacco plants at local garden centers are the new Nikki hybrids which have larger flowers but little or no scent. *N. sylvestris*, with plump umbels of long pure white, tubular blossoms, is also of recent vintage, arriving in cultivation from Argentina in 1899.

Flowering tobacco is easy to grow on any well-drained soil. Seed generally self-sows in loose, fertile soil (it is reputedly fond of potassium), but it tolerates poor conditions as well. The plant thrives in full sun and wilts in a lengthy drought, but also dislikes over-watering. Seed left on the stalk to ripen will attract finches, the remainder self-sows for the following season. Flowering tobacco looks best *en masse*, but also compliments baby's breath and *Centaurea*.

Nigella
RANUNCULACEAE
love-in-a-mist, devil-in-a-bush, nigella,
jack-in-the-green, lady-in-the-bower

Although it isn't among the prima donnas of the cottage garden, *Nigella damascena* is a nice addition and a good weaver amongst more brazen blossoms. Native to Southern Europe and Northern Africa and grown in gardens before 1548, the botanical name refers to the black seed pods. They found multiple uses

throughout history, in the 16th century they were apparently crushed to make one of many cures to banish freckles.

The blossoms of love-in-a-mist resemble open-faced, sparkling-petaled, pale blue stars surrounded by a collar of lacy bracts. The original *N. damascena* stood about 2 feet tall with a delightful mist of frilly leaves that matched the floral bracts, but dwarf versions have followed consolidating the show into 8 inches or less. The seed pods look like little blowfish, and they last indefinitely in dried arrangements.

The end of the 16th century brought double forms and whites, and although these apparently disappeared for a while, both double blue and double white are again available under the names 'Cambridge Blue', 'Miss Jekyll', and 'Miss Jekyll Misty White'. There's also a pink version that goes under the names 'Persian Red' and 'Mulberry Rose'.

Nigellas hardly need to be encouraged, they just seem to sow themselves and grow happily if left undisturbed, particularly in poor soil, although they will spread into virtually any area of the garden. They can easily be uprooted if they end up somewhere you don't want them. Sow the seed in fall just below the soil surface, where it survives the worst winters. They tolerate drought as well as heavy rain. They will branch more freely if deadheaded regularly, just leaving the last seedpods to form at the end of the season. They make excellent cut flowers as well as dried.

Papaver

PAPAVERACEAE

poppy, opium poppy, lettuce poppy

Native throughout Europe and Asia, poppies figure strongly in mythology. Even Pliny knew the dangers of overdosing on poppies, warning that over-indulgence could bring death. Gerard warned, "It mitigateth all kindes of paines, but it leaveth behinde it oftentimes a mischiefe worse than the disease."

At least 50 species of annual and perennial poppies are native to Europe, another 100 growing throughout the northern hemisphere and in California. *Papaver somnifera*, the opium poppy or lettuce poppy was probably introduced into Britain from southern Europe by the Romans. Poppies have often been seen as symbols of fertility because of their large seedpods. A single plump pod can hold as many as 32,000 seeds – Linnaeus is alleged to have counted them! Gerard mentioned red, white, purple, purple streaked and scarlet flowers.

Poppies are linked with fecundity, but interestingly, poppies also signify death and have been used as a token of remembrance. American legend has it that the first poppy reputedly sprang up in the West on the battleground where Custer was slain. In Western United States, poppies were called Custer's heart. Poppies were being grown in European cottage gardens for the beauty of their blossoms long before 1794 when they were first grown commercially in Britain for the opium. Notorious for its sleep-inducing qualities, and infamous for its narcotic properties, the latex was extracted by making incisions in the seedpod. The original *P. somnifera* probably came in pale lilac with a purple spot at the base of each petal. However, there were white, rose, violet and striped types early in the game, all boasting the telltale blackened spot at the center. Dutch painters adored opium poppies, gardeners invited them onto their property, and governments throughout the ages have had mixed emotions about them. At present, it is legal to sell opium poppy seeds in the United States, but not to grow them, although this has not been enforced. And it should be mentioned that, although drugs from poppies have wreaked all kinds of havoc, they were also responsible for morphine and codeine. Their cultivation for that purpose was attempted commercially in Britain, France and Germany, but was abandoned due to the expense of labor.

P. rhoeas, the corn poppy, is another ancient species that grows wild throughout Europe as well as Africa and Asia. In ancient mythology, Somnus, God of Slumber, created poppies to force Ceres, in charge of the corn crop, to slip into sleep when she had grown too filled with worries to rest. She woke up refreshed and the crop revived, which explained why her crown for evermore was interwoven with corn and poppies. These foot tall plants with their ephemeral red blossoms and grayish, tooth-edged leaves were once a common sight on arable land and also long cultivated in gardens. Modern strains of *P. rhoeas* date back to 1880, when the Reverend William Wilks, Vicar of Shirley, noticed a scarlet poppy with white edges on its petals growing in a cornfield next to his churchyard. He selected seed from this poppy and over a number of years managed to stabilize a reliably white-edged strain of poppies, as well as lilac, mauve and white forms, all of which became known as Shirley poppies. They are just as popular now as then, and there are singles as well as doubles with the characteristic pale hem.

Poppy seed can be stored or left buried for many years, and will germinate when soil is turned and the seed is exposed to light. This is why they become nuisance factors in cornfields where the ground is regularly turned. No one can forget images of the battlefields of Northern France where red corn poppies sprung up all over the ground disturbed by trenches and mass graves as the scars of the First World War began to settle. All annual *Papaver* species like sun, while perennial species such as the Oriental poppy *P. orientalis* – which came to Britain from Armenia in 1714 by way of France – are content in dappled shade.

Pelargonium
GERANIACEAE
geranium, bedding geranium, zonal geranium

Pelargoniums are often still referred to as geraniums although they were separated from that genus in the last century. One telling difference would be that pelargoniums are tender and geraniums are the hardy garden crane's bills. Native to the Cape of Good Hope, the first pelargonium arrived in Britain in 1632 and was probably one of the scented-leaved varieties, but the first pelargoniums were probably grown in France by nurseryman Rene Morin in Paris in 1621. However, the major influx of pelargoniums didn't occur until the Dutch fetched several species in 1690. By 1710, Britain had introduced several species, mostly scented-leaved types as the scented foliage was originally the primary attraction for pelargoniums. These vary in appearance from 18 inch plants (in the case of apple-scented *P. fragrans*) to 3–4 foot tall plants (in the case of peppermint-scented *P. tomentosum*) with leaves that are sometimes smooth, sometimes heavily felted and which give off a strong scent if they are even slightly bruised.

Attention moved away from the foliage toward the blooms in 1710 when *P. zonale* was introduced to Britain with its thick truss of bright scarlet blossoms.

P. zonale effectively changed the way gardeners looked at pelargoniums, but that species was probably not one of the parents to father what became known as the zonal geraniums, although later references usually credited it with parentage. Experts now believe that *P. frutetorum* played a more important role. This species has a black horseshoe marking on notched, rounded leaves which have a strange musky odor; its distinguishing characteristic was the bounty of large dark salmon flower trusses held proudly above the leaves. By modern standards, it was a straggly plant with 4–6 naked inches between leaf petioles, and yet it obviously had potential. In 1714, another important player arrived; *P. inquinans*, the scarlet geranium, also came from the Cape of Good Hope. The rush began to breed a more comely strain.

By the time the first pelargoniums arrived in America in 1760, they were already much improved. And by the beginning of the 1800s, zonal geraniums were no longer straggly, and their petals were larger. The color range had increased to include rose, scarlet, magenta, and salmon although white wasn't added until some time around 1850. The first double flowering hybrids came in 1864 and were available in salmon only, with a white double version following close on its heels.

Not content merely to improve the flowers, the foliage was also subject to changes. In the mid-1850s, fancy-leaved, or tricolor geraniums (as they were called) began appearing. It all began with 'Attraction', a silver-variegated pelargonium, no longer available. Then a gold-margined plant appeared on the scene, beginning a group of plants with several colors intermingled on the leaves. Hundreds of fancy-leaved types were developed at first, but only a few survive,

including 'Mrs. Pollock' (one of the oldest), 'Miss Burdett Coutts', 'Happy Thought' and 'Mrs. Cox'.

Pelargoniums should be grown in moderately fertile soil in full sun. Water them when they're dry but don't overwater (it's best to err on the side of drought rather than drowning, although drought will lead to yellowing leaves). Too much root room might discourage flowers and heavy fertilizer has the same effect. Frequent pinching is essential. Propagate the hybrids by leaf cuttings and scented-leaved species by seed or leaf cuttings.

Petunia

SOLANACEAE

balcony petunia, climbing petunia

Petunias haven't been with us very long. In 1823, *Petunia axillaris*, the white petunia, arrived from its native South America, picked up by an explorer at the mouth of the Rio de la Plata. And as *Vick's Flower and Vegetable Garden* stated in 1880, "For seven years the florists were delighted with this poor, white flower." Gardeners were contented until the deep magenta *P. integrifolia* (formerly *P. violacea*) arrived from Brazil. Without any improvement, *P. integrifolia* is a lovely plant, branching with only a little encouragement, sprawling densely over the side of pots, producing prolific blossoms with a delicious scent, especially after dark. The trumpet-shaped flowers are not much larger than an inch, but they're plentiful. Fifteen years after the initial introduction, a semi-double white was introduced. Although it pales in comparison to modern doubles, it was very popular in the mid 1800s.

By 1880, there were doubles (although they had fewer petals than our pompom extravaganzas) and grandifloras, with flowers 4–5 inches in diameter. Fragrance was still an important factor until 1931

when the first truly double petunia was produced. From that point on, petunia hybridizing went frenetic. The color range was increased so that every shade of the rainbow was represented. The flowers were immense, smothering the foliage and featuring wavy, frilly petals. But they lacked the wonderful scent that was once the petunia's main attribute. Fortunately, the fragrant *P. integrifolia* is coming back into fashion and can be found at specialty nurseries. Mailorder seed specialists are also offering early hybrids, called balcony, climbing or pendula petunias, selected for the whites and purples that emit the best fragrance.

Most petunias can be self-pollinated and seed tends to pop up when the ground is tilled in gardens that have been neglected for many decades. The older varieties are just as easy to grow as their modern counterparts. Moderately fertile soil should be offered – very rich soil will inhibit flowering. Water petunias when the soil is dry (they wilt easily) and pinch the stems to encourage branching. Deadheading is crucial for the older types. Just like their modern cousins, heirloom petunias are wonderful for windowboxes.

Reseda

RESEDACEAE

mignonette, sweet reseda, bastard rocket

It is strange that mignonette seems to have fallen completely out of fashion in gardens and is now rarely seen, despite its powerful scent and ease of cultivation. The Romans reputedly brought it into northern Europe from the southern Meditteranean before the 1st century and used the little herb as a sedative, dubbing it *resedare*, meaning "to calm". However, it wasn't a popular garden plant until the early years of the 18th century when it was adopted by the French who called the plant mignonette meaning 'little darling'. But mignonette reached the crescendo of its popularity in France after Napoleon conquered Egypt and sent seed back to Josephine so she could raise plants in her garden at Malmaison. It became widely grown in southern France and its flowers were used for making perfume.

Despite its rather dull pale flowers and sprawling habit mignonette became equally popular in England in the second half of the 18th century, and the strong fragrance rose from town windowboxes everywhere, particularly in London where it seemed to thrive despite pollution. In fact, in 1829, one resident complained that London had become "oppressive with the odor." True, their perfume might be strong, but it's pleasant; the aroma of mignonette has been likened to honeyed raspberries.

In the 1860s, with 'Machet Giant', the length of the flower spike was increased with reddish or purple highlights added. But the innovations weakened the scent and modern versions are often criticized as lacking the original aromatic wallop. Even so, mignonette is still extremely fragrant.

The only way to smell reseda in the garden is on all fours, so it is often grown in pots – Victorians often grew it into shrubby standard bushes in pots in cold conservatories and used it as a fragrant indoor decoration for parties. You can encourage the stems to become woody by pinching off sideshoots, producing a shrubby bush in three years.

R. odorata is a perennial plant in its warmer native countries where it can often be seen as a wild garden escape. In cooler areas it is best to sow the seed directly into a warm flower bed where they are to flower, although some people raise seedlings in a greenhouse for planting out in position. Seed sets rapidly in hot weather.

Tagetes

COMPOSITAE

marigold

Long after the African marigold *Tagetes erecta* and the French marigold *Tagetes patula* were identified as originating in Mexico, they still stubbornly clung to their deceptive common names. Both arrived in the late 16th century, and both were immediately adopted into gardens. The reason for retaining the erroneous names probably stems from the fact that *Calendula* was already firmly entrenched as marigold. Early gardeners wanted no confusion, especially as tagetes odoriferous leaves were said to be poisonous.

T. erecta, the African marigold, had naturalized along the North African coast before it came into Britain. The species varies in flower color from pale lemon to deep orange, standing 4–5 feet in height balancing 2–4 inch flowers on top. By the mid-18th century, double African marigolds existed, but they disappeared sometime afterward, being reintroduced as a 20th century novelty.

The French marigold, *T. patula*, was discovered toward the end of the 16th century in the wilds of

Mexico and Guatemala, and was quickly adopted into Europe. French marigolds are bushy annuals growing up to 18 inches tall with feathery scented leaves and showy daisy-like flowers. The earliest French marigolds were always pale yellow. Later, the range was increased to include orange and reddish brown blossoms, in single, double and quilled varieties.

The early French marigolds were rather small and failed to blossom well unless it was reliably hot and sunny. In 1929 the first sure-flowering French marigold, 'Harmony', was created, but it wasn't until the 1950s that popular modern dwarf French marigolds were created. Meanwhile, there was a major effort afoot to render the rank foliage (described by Lyte in 1578 as "of a naughtie strong and unpleasant savour") of marigolds scentless.

Curiously, many people once considered the leaves of marigolds to smell offensive, particularly florists using them widely for bouquets, and a scentless variety was reputedly first available in the mid-18th century to render the flower more pleasant for use in handheld bouquets. In 1937, David Burpee was proud to announce the first scentless marigold, 'Crown of Gold', and a race of non-scented hybrids

followed. Another family member, the edible flowered *Tagetes tenuifolia*, or Signet marigold, with its bright yellow single flowers and lacy foliage is a vast improvement, with lemon-scented leaves.

Many gardeners mourn the loss of the marigold's signature aroma. Marigolds are traditionally considered very useful companion plants, their roots produce an exudate that deters nematodes, especially in carrots. They also reputedly confuse rabbits from nibbling neighboring crops. However, modern scentless hybrids are of little use, as Diane Whealy of the Seed Savers Exchange points out, "The plants are now virtually useless for companion planting," they dissuade few of the predators they originally deterred. The original tall African marigolds seem to have the strongest effect, so look for older forms if you want to use marigolds among your vegetables.

Marigolds are easy to please. They can tolerate the worst soil, frequent drought as well as torrential rain. However, they prefer a sunny location. Deadheading will encourage branching. Marigolds are propagated by seed. In fact, many home gardeners throw caution to the wind and save their own marigold seed.

Tropaeolum

TROPAEOLACEAE

nasturtium, Indian cress, flame flower

Native to Colombia and Bolivia, the common nasturtium wasn't the first member of the family to come into cultivation. It was preceded by *Tropaeolum minus* (now almost impossible to find) with small yellow flowers accented by a purple blotch, brought to Europe from Peru in the 15th century. *T. majus*, its big brother, was introduced in the 1600s and immediately won favor as a camouflage for whatever needed a quick makeover in the cottage garden.

Dense with abundant, peltate leaves that creep or climb, depending upon the terrain, *T. majus* is bedecked with brightly colored, gaping, almost pansy-like blossoms in early summer with the performance continuing (if sufficient water is provided) until frost. Naturally occurring in shades of red,

orange, and yellow with a spur jutting from the rear of each blossom, nasturtiums must have provided a rare festive element in the early garden. More than just a pretty face, culinary applications were found for the plant as well — the seeds were used as a substitute for capers in pickles while the foliage was eaten in salads, giving the common name Indian cress. Furthermore, not to waste any part, the flowerbuds were also pickled.

Nasturtiums were most often grown by early gardeners for their climbing habit and ability to encase trellises and arbors. It wasn't until the late 19th century that dwarf, free-blooming types more appropriate as bedding plants were developed. By the end of the 19th century, varieties with spots, blotches, shading and bands of color were available and from the 1850s onward the Tom Thumb series became popular, a dwarf mixture (still available) resulting from crossing *T. majus* with *T. minus*. Another late 19th century novelty was 'Empress of India' with dark leaves and brilliant crimson flowers; it is still standard. Double nasturtiums were introduced from Italy in 1769.

Nasturtiums were latecomers to North America, introduced by Bernard McMahon in 1806. A few years later, Grant Thorburn, a seedsman in New York City, was offering a "variegated-leaved Queen of Tom Thumb Chameleon" which boasted not only marbled foliage, but also many flower colors on a single plant. In 1931 a semi-double nasturtium was found in a Mexican convent, fathering 'Golden Gleam' which sold for 5 cents a seed in the midst of the Depression; the Gleam hybrid mixture is still available.

Give nasturtiums poor soil otherwise they will produce masses of leaves and precious few flowers. They grow in both sun and partial shade, making them ideal for city windowboxes. However, an occasional heavy pruning is essential to prevent nasturtiums from becoming straggly, and nasturtiums should be deadheaded regularly. Easily propagated from seed, you can also reproduce nasturtiums by rooting cuttings in a glass of water.

Zinnia

COMPOSITAE

zinnia, youth and old age,
Brazilian marigold, medicine hat

Native to Mexico, the first zinnia to migrate into Britain was *Zinnia peruviana* (formerly *Z. pauciflora* or *Z. lutea*) which came from Paris in 1753. It's an untidy plant, branching loosely to 3 feet in height and topped by small, muddy yellow or burnished scarlet composite flowers, like little marigolds. Much more exciting was *Zinnia elegans* which arrived from South America in 1796 and was equally tall, but topped by slightly larger scarlet and crimson blossoms, each topped by a Mexican hat-like disk surrounded by a skirt of ray petals. It's *Zinnia elegans* that brings us the hybrids we know today.

Interest in zinnias really took off in Europe when the first doubles appeared in France in 1856; unfortunately it wasn't a stable strain, and considerable grumbling ensued when it arrived in America in 1861 and two-thirds of the seed turned out to be single. However, zinnias later came into their own in America, probably due to the sunny, warm climate. By 1864, there were purple, scarlet, orange, and salmon doubles. And by 1880, Vick's *Flower and Vegetable Garden* was boasting that 75% of their seed could be relied upon to be as double as dahlias.

Meanwhile, another introduction was stealing the stage. 1861 saw the arrival in cultivation of *Z. haageana* (formerly *Z. ghiesbrightii*, *Z. mexicana* and *Z. angustifolia*), a dwarfer species also from Mexico. In 1872 a double form appeared, and in 1876 *Z. haageana* was being crossed with *Z. elegans* to produce a thicker, broader, more branched zinnia.

Zinnias have gone up and down in stature. By 1886, a 40 inch strain was available under the impressive name of *Z. elegans robusta grandiflora plenissima*, called the Giant or Mammoth strain for short. On the other hand were the pompoms of Liliputians, which reached only 3–12 inches in height. The zenith of the dwarfs was the Tom Thumb type which was described as "the largest possible flower on the smallest possible plant." Both large and small zinnias continue to be prevalent. But the latest novelty in zinnias is 'Envy' with large, parrot green flowers.

Propagate zinnia from seed sown early under cover and transplanted before the ground warms – seedlings seem to thrive best if they experience a bit of spring cold and damp to toughen them. Plants flourish in any deep, good soil, whether loamy or sandy.

Vines

·····················

Clematis   ❹

RANUNCULACEAE

traveler's joy, old man's beard, virgin's bower, leather flower, vase vine, grandfather's whiskers

Native to Europe, Lebanon, the Caucasus, Northern Iran and Afghanistan, as well as the chalky southeastern regions of Britain, *Clematis vitalba* was the first clematis to come into cultivation. Originally suspected of being a grape and called Viticella-Woodebinde by the Anglo Saxons of the 11th century, it was also called traveler's joy, according to Gerard, because anyone on a long journey was grateful to rest in its shadow. Despite the fact that it was a rampant vine, *C. vitalba* was invited into cottage gardens but it is far too vigorous to allow into modern gardens unless you are fortunate to have a piece of woodland or large wild garden; its small white flowers are fragrant but not terribly exciting compared to other early clematis. The common name of old man's beard applies to the hairy seed that overtakes the vine after blossoms have faded. *C. vitalba* is still important as the primary rootstock for grafting less rampant species. A better old-fashioned garden species is *C. flammula*, also grown in the 16th century, a vigorous species not unlike a refined *C. vitalba* covered in tiny white sweetly scented flowers from August to October followed by silky seed heads.

The first import into Britain was *C. viticella*, a native of Southern Europe with nodding dusky-rose blossoms, arriving in cultivation sometime before 1659. Its common name, virgin's bower, was credited to the apothecary of Elizabeth I. It was first hybridized through its accidental crossing with *C. integrifolia*, a non-vining species, but large-flowered hybrids didn't appear until the 1850s, when several Chinese species arrived in Britain by way of Japan. *C. alpina* was an earlier introduction from southern Europe, arriving in 1792. It is ideal for small gardens,

blossoming in April and May with small nodding blue flowers with a white central tuft. Some years it can bloom again in midsummer.

The first work on hybridizing clematis was accomplished in 1855 by Isaac Anderson-Henry of Edinburgh. Using one of the newly introduced Oriental clematis, *C. lanuginosa* (an introduction made by Robert Fortune and blessed with the largest blossoms of any species), Anderson-Henry created the white flowered 'Henryi', still popular. In 1858 George Jackman, a nurseryman from Woking, enlisted *C. lanuginosa* to create *C. x jackmanii* in 1858, a novelty that caused an instant sensation in exhibition. Its abundant masses of 4-5 inch wide, star-shaped, purple blossoms remain popular, smothering the vine in spring and again in late summer. This introduction was the start of a storm of hybridizing, producing older cultivars that can compete favorably with all of today's novelties. Popular early hybrids include 'Mme Julia Correvon' (rosy-red), 'Elsa Späth' (purple) and 'Madame Grangé' (maroon).

Some gardeners find clematis difficult to grow, but if you follow a few basic principles you should have little trouble. Plant any clematis in a generous hole laced with well-rotted manure and bonemeal to encourage strong root growth. Plant them deep because clematis are subject to a fungus disease called clematis wilt which makes plants wilt from the top and die; the fungus doesn't affect anything below ground so deep-planted clematis have plenty of buds to regrow if the plant does succumb to disease and has to be cut back hard. Clematis require shaded roots but sunny stems, so it is a good idea to grow a low-growing plant at the foot of the clematis to act as an umbrella. You can place a stone at the base of the plant but this can impede water flow which can be a problem as clematis like to be well watered, especially the large-flowered hybrids. However, many of the *C. viticella* hybrids ('Madame Julia Correvon' being one) have proved drought-resistant.

Feed clematis every year with seaweed or an organic fertilizer. Pruning is often also a question: as a rule of thumb you can leave the early Montana types to fend for themselves, simply cutting back to shape when they become too vigorous. Large free-flowering clematis which flower early, before June, should be cut back immediately after flowering to within a couple of buds away from the main branches. Those that flower later in the year should be cut back hard to within 6 inches of the ground in February.

Cobaea

POLEMONIACEAE

cup and saucer vine, Mexican ivy, monastery bells

Native to Mexico, *Cobaea scandens* was discovered by the Spanish botanist Cavanilles in 1789 and named for Father Cobo, a 17th century naturalist and Jesuit monk. Even without flowers, the vine is a handsome sight with trumpet vine-like segmented leaves accented by bronze undersides climbing via abundant curly tendrils which arise curiously from the tips of the leaf segments. Added to the comely foliage are midsummer flowers which begin life as 4 inch long, gaping green trumpets and change gradually from lilac to dark purple. Rapid growing, this tender perennial quickly gained a place in the garden. By 1850, Andrew Jackson Downing was recommending it highly in *The Horticulturist*, urging gardeners to plant it as a camouflage plant, suggesting that it could be used to cover a "wall or trellis, 20 or 30 feet square, by November, growing and blooming till the black frosts overtake it." In addition to the standard violet, a white form, 'Alba', is also available.

This ambitious climber likes rich soil and a sunny location is also crucial; it can climb very fast with little support – any rough surface is sufficient for its tendrils to grasp and gain a leg-up. By midsummer, the vine should be sporting its trumpet-shaped flowers. Propagate by seed, which will only have a long enough season to ripen south of Zone 6. Plant the seed in moist earth, pointed edge downward.

Humulus

CANNABACEAE

common hop, European hop, bine

Humulus lupulus is native throughout northern temperate regions and was so valued that it was used by the peasants of Bohemia and Bavaria in the 9th century as legal tender to pay land debts. The vine was named for *hoppan*, the Anglo-Saxon word for climb, and some authorities suspect that hops were native to Britain while others suggest they arrived in 1525. Hops gain vigor with age and climb so strongly that they sometimes choke their hosts, but they are attractive plants – the hop vine has broad, glove-shaped, pale green leaves and cone-shaped female flowers which nod in long catkins of blossoms.

Young hop shoots have been considered a delicacy since Roman times but most people wait for the flowers which are used in brewing. This role led hops to be banned in England in 1528. That law was rescinded in 1603, but hop production wasn't widespread until the end of the 17th century.

In 1629, the Massachusetts Bay Company began hop production, followed by a similar enterprise in Virginia in 1648. In America, hops became a common fixture around the cabins of settlers, not only employed for brewery but also to leaven bread. Wherever the vine was planted, it tends to endure - one hundred year old hops vines are commonplace.

Hops are gently but reliably sedative, and an infusion of steeped hops is reputed to temporarily relieve pain and inflammation.

The name humulus gives some clue as to the vine's preferred soil conditions, referring to the moist humus that hops like underfoot. A sturdy trellis is essential. Hops can harbour various pests including Japanese beetles, aphids and weevils hiding in the flower catkins.

Hops can be too rampant for many gardens, but a slightly more compact golden form, known as 'Aureus', is now more popular than the old mainstay.

Ipomoea
CONVOLVULACEAE
morning glory

Morning glories are native to tropical America, arriving in Britain in 1621 when John Goodyer received seed from correspondents abroad. *Ipomoea purpurea* (originally *Convolvulus major*) came from Italy and *Ipomoea tricolor* (originally *Convolvulus tricolor*) arrived the same year from Spain. However, those original morning glories suffered from guilt by association: they were too similar to *C. arvensis*, the bindweed (or wild morning glory) that chokes food crops at a lightning pace, so they weren't whole-heartedly adopted into cottage gardens. Although *I. purpurea* and *I. tricolor* are actually far removed from (and will not cross-pollinate with) bindweed in the size of the flowers that smother their trailing stems and in their more neighborly manners, morning glories were largely neglected until the Victorian era. When moveable privies became commonplace in North America, annual vines including morning glories were enlisted as camouflage – their foliage grows rapidly to cover and smother although the original morning glories didn't usually flower until the tail end of the season.

Another reason for their late adoption was that the original morning glories were gorgeous only at dawn and closed shortly thereafter. As Vick's *Flower and Vegetable Garden* declared in 1880, "but a sight of a good 'patch' of these flowers in the 'dewy morn' is a feast for a whole day, and quite enough to tempt any lover of the beautiful to rise early to see and enjoy their glory."

Convolvulus major (later classified as *I. purpurea*, the common morning glory) was the variety that John Goodyer received by way of Italy in 1621. He described the blossoms as "redd darke crimson velvet", noting that the blooms tend to last only a day, folding toward evening. Native to Mexico, this vine has rounded leaves and prolific blossoms smaller than the more popular *Ipomoea tricolor*. This is the species responsible for 'Kniola's Purple Black', a nearly black flowering hybrid discovered on an abandoned farm in Indiana, as well as the famous 'Grandpa Ott's' morning glory. Not only is 'Grandpa Ott's' a handsome bloomer with a deep purple blossoms accented by a red star in the throat, but it was also responsible for the creation of the Seed Savers Exchange in Decorah, Iowa. Seed was originally brought over from Bavaria by Baptist John Ott who grew the vine religiously every summer. Following his death, his granddaughter, Diane Whealy, realized that the strain would be lost if she didn't continue to save the seed. That realization led to the birth of the Seed Savers Exchange in 1975, which branched into the Flower and Herb Exchange in 1990. Both exchanges are now very popular means of acquiring heirloom varieties.

Morning glories were ignored in many parts of the world, but in the 1830s they enjoyed some fame in Japan: using *I. nil*, hybridizers created a strain of scarcely twining, large-flowering, brightly colored blossoms, often with double flowers and bands of color. Called *Ipomoea* x *imperialis*, those morning glories were used to honor the emperor, sums comparable to $18.00 often being spent on a single seed. Although there wasn't much interest in the *Ipomoea* x *imperialis* strain elsewhere, *I. nil* was introduced into the United States in 1895. It is the parent of many red-flowering hybrids, most notably 'Scarlett O'Hara'.

The moonflower *I. alba* (formerly classified as *Calonyction*), has an enticing jasmine-like scent and white blossoms creased in cream that open at dusk. It was very popular during the Victorian era when white evening gardens were in vogue (so that fair-skinned ladies could walk among the blossoms without marring their delicate complexions by exposing them to diret sunlight). *I. alba* is best suited to warm climates, disliking cool evenings.

I. purpurea and *I. tricolor* were the two species that figured strongly in morning glory breeding, especially in America where morning glory-mania underwent a crescendo in the 1940s and 1950s. In 1963, it was discovered that chewing the seeds could cause hallucinations; the sales of morning glories dropped off drastically in the United States and their purchase was prohibited briefly in Britain. Because of that character blight, many varieties were lost to cultivation. At present, morning glories are enjoying a resurgence, and several seed savers are laboring to recover what was lost.

John Goodyer was the first to procure seeds of *Convolvulus tricolor* (later *I. tricolor*) in 1621, but his source also sent a packet to Parkinson who described the flowers as "most excellent fair skie-coloured blew." This morning glory (sometimes referred to as *I. rubro-caerulea*), has slender vining stems covered by pale green, heart-shaped leaves. Known as 'Heavenly Blue' from its onset, the species has sizable blossoms in rich deep blue. However, the original 'Heavenly blue' wasn't often grown due to its late season schedule until an amateur gardener by the name of Clarke discovered a mutation in Colorado and saved the seeds. Not only was 'Clarke's Early Heavenly Blue'

free-flowering and early blooming, it had larger blossoms than the species in an incredibly vivid sky blue. Clarke shared his seed with the Dutch wholesaler, Sluis & Groot, who grew fields full of that hybrid and made it available to retailers in 1931. It was an instant success. In fact, the improvement made the original morning glory so obsolete that Clarke's name was eventually dropped, although all 'Heavenly Blue' morning glories on the market today are actually Clarke's early strain. 'Blue Star', which is now scarce but still available, was offered by Denholm Seed of California in 1949. It is covered by 4 inch, icy blue blossoms marked by a sizable dark blue star in the center.

Efforts have been made by morning glory preservationists such as Thelma Crawford of Kansas and Adrian Kencik of New York *(see page 65)* to reintroduce lost tricolors. Their successes include 'Flying Saucers', a 1960, blue and white striped introduction by Darold Decker of California and 'Wedding Bells', a white centered rose lavender also introduced by Darold Decker in 1962. Their most recent victory was the discovery of a storehouse of seeds, locked in a closet for 37 years, from the defunct Mandeville Seeds. Due to the discovery of that treasure, 'Candy Pink' and 'Cornell' have been reclaimed. However, 'Summer Skies', 'Darling' and 'Tinker Bells' appear to be lost, despite the short hiatus since they were listed for sale.

In heirloom gardens, the cypress vine, *I. quamoclit* (formerly *Quamoclit pinnata*), was even more popular than the large flowering, large-leaved ipomoeas that are currently the rage. Introduced from tropical America in 1629, the cypress vine has long, oboe shaped, bright scarlet blossoms amid airy, ferny leaves and grows to a height of 6 feet (although the more optimistic catalogs bill it as a 25 foot climber). Gaining prominence during the Victorian era, it was described in catalogs as resembling a "constellation of stars" and was recommended for trellising over porches, patios and covering walls in conservatories. Unlike other ipomoeas, the blossoms remained open all day, blooming from early summer until frost. A white flowering version, available as recently as 1989, appears to have vanished.

Morning glories prefer a sunny location but their blossoms will remain open longer into the day if placed on the east rather than the south side of a building. Strong support is necessary as the weight of a fully grown morning glory can easily topple something too slight, especially in high winds. Seed forms readily, but different varieties will cross-pollinate so should not be grown together if you want to save

seed that grows true to form. Seed germinates rapidly; when sowing, nick the seed coats and soak them first. You can wait until May and sow seed direct into the ground or start seeds earlier indoors. In fact, there's little advantage in starting seeds early as they bloom late in the summer whatever your schedule.

Lablab

LEGUMINOSAEA

dolichos bean, hyacinth bean, bonavist, Indian bean, Egyptian bean

Formerly known as *Dolichos lablab*, now classified as *Lablab purpureus*, the hyacinth bean is native to tropical Africa but widely in cultivation throughout India, Southeast Asia, Egypt and the Sudan. Grown as an annual, it was introduced from India in 1794. Although Europeans and Americans valued its large, flat, brick-red seed pods simply for their beauty, the hyacinth bean is an important food crop in its native region, used like kidney beans. Not only are the bean pods handsome, but they are also preceded by purple blossoms against dark, deeply textured, segmented leaves.

Before the hyacinth bean began its tenure in latter day cottage gardens, where it neatly straddled the gap between food and flower, it began its career under

cultivation in the 19th century in the glasshouse. Later, it was grown in gardens. For example, Thomas Jefferson is believed to have grown hyacinth beans at Monticello. In Victorian times, the violet-colored variety was known as 'Darkness', and a white-flowering variety from Japan was known as 'Daylight'; this one is still available. However, a non-twining bush form with showy pink flowers that was quite widely grown at the beginning of the 20th century has since disappeared.

A vigorous vine, the hyacinth bean can climb to heights of 10 feet if given full sun. Don't give a hyacinth bean too much fertilizer and keep plants moist. Sow seed under cover and transplant seedlings as soon as the soil turns warm.

Jasminum

FAMILY: OLEACEAE

jasmine, jessamine

Native to Asia Minor, the Himalayas and China, *Jasminum officinale* was probably the first jasmine to arrive in Britain, coming into cultivation sometime before 1577. The flowers are single white stars about an inch in diameter on wispy stems scantily clothed with deep green segmented leaves. But the fragrance of the flowers is unparalleled.

By 1629, John Parkinson wrote that *J. officinale* could be encountered "ordinarily in our Gardens

throughout the whole Land." In Britain, it became as popular in cottage gardens as it was on estates. By 1809, Thomas Jefferson had succeeded in tracking down *J. officinale* to grow at Monticello. In addition to their scent, the flowers have been employed medicinally to cure coughs and hoarseness, boiled in a syrup and combined with honey. Jasmine is still used as an ingredient in most expensive perfumes; it has never been reproduced artificially.

J. sambac, the Arabian jasmine, has an entirely different, bush-like growth habit with round-petaled flowers which give off a delightful perfume at night. Although they are rarely used in the garden, these plants make excellent houseplants, blooming sweetly all the year round.

Jasmines prefer reasonably rich soil but are quite happy to grow in partial shade, and make very good companions for other climbers. They don't need much water but they can be rather shortlived and should be freshened with new stock every few years. It is essential to prune jasmine hard in autumn when it is not blossoming to maintain a good shape and a healthy plant. They are not reliably hardy and should be grown against a south or west wall in a sheltered situation, or under glass.

Lathyrus

LEGUMINOSEAE

sweet pea

Native to Italy, Crete and Sicily, *Lathyrus odoratus*, the sweet pea, was so potently fragrant that it caught the eye (and nose) of the Franciscan monk, Father Cupani. In 1696 he found the plant in Sicily, collected it and planted the seed in his monastery garden to better enjoy the handsome flower with deep blue lower petals (known as the "standard") and topped by purple upper petals (referred to as the "wings"). The flower of the tendril-climbing sweet pea is pretty, but the fragrance is extraordinary – resembling the mixed perfume of honey, propolis and wax that rushes from a freshly opened beehive. The whole package provoked the monk to send seed in 1699 to a horticultural friend in Britain, Dr. Robert Uvedale of Enfield. That same seed was made commercially available in 1724 and is again offered by specialist seedsmen under the name 'Cupani's Original', alias 'Matucana'.

The original sweet pea remained untouched but very popular for the next century. Then, in the early 19th century, the color range was increased until varieties were available in colors including pinks, blues, purples, white, and bicolored combinations of those shades. All of those original sweet peas were spicily fragrant. However, the look of sweet peas altered most dramatically in 1870 when Henry Eckford created the Grandiflora class with larger blossoms than the original sweet pea; and this innovation was followed by the Unwins, a group with slightly waved petals. However, the most momentous alteration came in 1900 when Silas Cole, the gardener at Althorp, the estate of the Earl and Countess Spencer, discovered 'Lady Spencer', a rose pink mutation of Henry Eckford's 'Prima Donna' sporting very large flowers with wavier edges on longer stems. This new development was more florist-worthy than the original sweet pea, to be sure, but the scent was forfeited.

The Spencers revolutionized sweet peas, rendering them the most popular annual flower by 1910. However, as the flowers were further developed, so most of the pre-Spencer sweet peas disappeared, overshadowed by the bigger, showier modern varieties.

It wasn't until 1986 that efforts were made to reclaim the original ultra-fragrant varieties. That's when Peter Grayson of Derbyshire put out the call for *Lathyrus* heirlooms, corresponding with growers throughout the world. Mr. Grayson managed to rescue 'Painted Lady' (1737), collected from an Australian family who kept it in cultivation over several generations, as well as over 50 heirloom sweet peas. His success stories include Henry Eckford's pink flowering, wavy-edged 'Prima Donna' (1896); white tinged pink 'Fairy Queen' (1873); deep mauve 'Captain of the Blues' (1891), and deep maroon 'Black Knight' (1898).

Given a chicken wire or twine trellis on which their 3-4 foot stems might lean and their tendrils grasp, sweet peas are easy to grow. Most importantly, they prefer cool temperatures and quickly slip out of bloom when the weather becomes warm in summer. So they are best sown indoors or as soon as the ground has thawed in spring. Sweet peas have shallow roots, but prefer a loose, friable soil. Shelter from the noonday sun and ample moisture will prolong their performance. Since they are self-fertile, sweet peas will not interbreed readily with their neighbors. However, like most legumes, sweet pea seeds begin to lose viability rapidly if not planted within a year of harvest.

Lonicera

CAPRIFOLIACEAE

honeysuckle, woodbine

Native to Europe, Asia minor, Caucasus and Western Asia, *Lonicera periclymenum* was a common fixture in cottage gardens from their inception, valued for the rich scent from the common honeysuckle's gaping yellow and white blossoms. Threading throughout the hedgerows and wrapping itself around any support within reach, honeysuckle is one of the rich components of summer. Sipping its sweet nectar, accomplished by pulling the sepal through the trumpet's tube, lingers in memory among the delights of childhood.

The family name, *Caprifoliaceae*, refers to the fact that honeysuckle vines have always been much appreciated by browsing goats. For human consumption, Dioscorides suggested honeysuckle for fatigue, shortness of breath and hiccups as well as diseases of the lungs and spleen. Honeysuckle has been used as a laxative and for respiratory ailments and asthma. Still a favorite plant in Britain, the wild honeysuckle has become a nuisance plant in America, strangling trees and covering ground invasively. Its planting is generally frowned upon.

Honeysuckle adapts well to any sort of growing environment, and can hardly be dissuaded. It grows happily in sun or shade, and is perhaps most at home when twined around an old apple tree, a porch or front wall, wafting its scent through bedroom windows. It tolerates drought as well as torrential rain. Its seeds are easily spread by birds – and therein lies the hitch.

Passiflora

PASSIFLORACEAE

Passion flower, maypop

Never has such a combination of religion, rapture and outrageous beauty been bound up in a single vine. Native to tropical America, many took for a hoax the sketches of passiflora an Augustine monk took back from the New World to Rome in the early 1600s. However, papal scholars immediately recognized the passion flower's symbolic potential and used the strangely configured flowers to help South American missionaries tell the Passion story to potential converts. According to their interpretation, the 10 petals and sepals represented the 10 apostles at the crucifixion of Jesus. The filaments were the crown of thorns or halo, the five anthers were the wounds and the three stigmas symbolized the nails. That prototypical passion flower was probably *Passiflora incarnata*, which was also the first passion flower to successfully arrive in Britain in 1629. Later dubbed the maypop, native as far north as Virginia and prone to a long dormancy period, *P. incarnata* didn't lend itself readily to cultivation. It was followed in 1690 by *P. caerulea* with fingered leaves and prolific 3-4 inch white flowers overlaid by a thick halo of blue filaments. This is the passion flower most commonly grown today, as popular now as it was in early cottage gardens, sufficiently energetic to reach blooming size quickly, and produce large numbers of attractive flowers, and it could be persuaded to bloom in winter under glass.

At the end of the 19th century passion flowers gained the attention of collectors and hybridizers. The best cultivar was the athletic, floriferous and fragrant hybrid *P. alato* x *caerulea* with large flowers of alternating white and pink petals. New species have recently been popularized, notably the red-flowering *P. vitifolia* and *P. coccinea,* as well as many new hybrids.

Passion flowers require light sunny warm sites, with plenty of room to send their energetic arms and legs roaming - several climb 9 feet or more in a single season. They like a rich soil and should be fed with organic fertilizer throughout the growing season to achieve the best blossoms. You can grow them in containers, but make sure the pot is large enough. Passion flowers have plentiful roots and can be difficult to untangle without a lot of damage if they must be transplanted.

Phaseolus

LEGUMINOSEAE

scarlet runner bean, Dutch case knife bean

Native to tropical America, the scarlet runner bean is a good example of the crossover between food and ornamental flowers typical of a cottage garden. If a perfectly delicious bean looked handsome as well, gardeners felt compelled to select it rather than a less visually exciting alternative. Found in South America in the 1600s and successfully introduced into Britain in the 1700s, *Phaseolus coccineus* was pleasing to both eye and palate. Although the foliage doesn't look markedly different from any other pole bean, the clusters of scarlet blossoms are headturning, especially against the chartreuse foliar background. Furthermore, the long, slender beans are of excellent eating

quality, either as snap beans (harvested when the pods are no longer than 4 inches for best flavor) or dried.

The scarlet runner bean is actually a tender perennial, but is most often treated as an annual. In addition to fertile, friable soil, good sun and water when dry, give scarlet runner beans a sturdy support for their 6 foot plus vines to climb. Scarlet runner beans attract both bees and hummingbirds and are likely to cross-pollinate with neighbors if they are not isolated, befuddling seed savers. 'Painted Lady', an heirloom variety from Britain with coral and white blossoms, is available from specialty nurseries.

Bulbs

Anemone   ❽

RANUNCULACEAE

windflower, garland anemone,
rose parsley

According to a Greek legend, Anemos, the wind, sent anemones to the ground as the earliest harbingers of his spring arrival. The Romans collected anemones to ward off fevers, while Gerard and Culpeper both suggested bathing in an infusion of the native European wood anemones or windflowers, *Anemone nemorosa*, for leprosy, as well as suggesting the plant for a number of other ailments. A keen observer of nature, Linnaeus noticed that the blooming of *A. nemorosa* always coincided with the return of the swallows to Sweden.

Tradition suggests that *A. coronaria* earned its name when the Greeks and Romans made garlands or coronets of the flowers. Possibly the 'lily of the field' of the New Testament, *A. coronaria* is native to Southern Europe and the Mediterranean. It gained further religious significance during the Crusades when the Bishop of Pisa suggested that ships returning from the Holy Land fill their holds with sacred soil on their return voyage resulting in the "miraculous" appearance of cherry red anemones wherever that soil was spread, prompting the church to suspect divine intervention. *A. coronaria* was widely distributed in monastery gardens because of its sacred connotations and by the 16th century a double form was often found. One of its common names, rose parsley, provides an apt description of the many-petalled, prominently-bossed blossoms that crown ferny, deep green foliage.

There were so many anemones growing in Britain by the 16th century that Gerard was sated, drawing the line by planting merely a dozen favorite sorts in his garden, turning away many others. The lines of species identification were blurry at the time, but by the end of the 17th century, there were no fewer than 300 varieties of anemones in cultivation. Much later, at the end of the 19th century, double anemones became known as the 'St. Brigid' group, in honor of an Irish columnist who wrote a celebrated garden column under the pen name of St. Brigid. Although few named varieties remain from the early St. Brigids, 'Mount Everest', a semi-double snow white with a red band, is similar to the original garland anemones.

Although *A. blanda* wasn't widely cultivated until the 20th century, it appears that Theophrastus was familiar with it more than two thousand years before. The Japanese anemone, *Anemone japonica* (now *A. hupehensis*), is a recent cottage garden plant, arriving in 1845 thanks to Robert Fortune. By the 1880s, pure white Japanese anemones were available, first called 'Alba', then 'Honorine Jobert' , still available under that name.

Anemones prefer a loose, alkaline, well-drained soil. The blossoms come quickly and also go rapidly, especially in hot, dry weather. Red spider mites and aphids are pressing problems for anemones, especially *A. coronaria*, which is not reliably hardy and is sometimes treated as a greenhouse forcing bulb. Besides that one caveat, anemones are among the easiest bulbs to grow and multiply rapidly. They make colorful and handsome companions for hyacinths. Propagate them by division.

Colchicum ❺

LILIACEAE

autumn crocus, meadow saffron,
naked boys, naked ladies,
naked nannies, upstart

The name Colchicum is derived from the plant's native Colchis, the ancient name for an area on the eastern side of the Black Sea. Colchicums extend from North Africa through Europe and Asia as far as the Himalayas. The leaves and corms of the plant contain a substance called colchicine which is poisonous to humans and animals; an ancient remedy was drinking cow's milk as an antidote to the poison, but this remedy failed to be effective when the poison had built up in the body, with lethal results. Nevertheless, colchicum was often prescribed for gout. More recently, its primary usage is in plant breeding - colchicum increases the chromosome count in plants, causing all sorts of aberrations in the progeny.

Colchicum autumnale is commonly known as autumn crocus or meadow saffron, known to Gerard. A more whimsical epithet is naked boys applied because their clusters of flowers emerge straight from the soil naked, without leaves, a striking sight in glowing shades of pinks, purples, and white. Leaves come after the flowers. The soft lilac pink *C. byzantium*, (*C. autumnale major*) praised by Clusius in 1601, is still a popular hybrid. Some colchicums flower in spring, these are largely tender species and are best grown in an alpine house or tunnel.

Colchicum can be planted in full sun but they also thrive on the edge of shrubberies or woodland. They appreciate light soil as long as it never dries out, preferring a slightly damp environment. Colchicum look best when grown in clumps of several plants clustered together. The flowers are close to the ground, but the foliage is rather rank and so the bulb is rarely placed at the front of the border, but is at its best scattered among autumn-blooming *Sedum*. Unfortunately, slugs love all parts of colchicum.

Crocus ❻

IRIDACEAE

crocus

The original crocus was the autumn-blooming saffron crocus, *Crocus sativus*, grown in Palestine during Solomon's time and used in commerce in ancient civilizations as well as modern. Saffron comes from the Arabic, *sahafarn*, which translates as "thread", referring to the stigmas that have proved so valuable economically. Probably brought to Britain by the Romans, and cultivated in that country by 1330, *C. sativus* was introduced into Essex as a commercial venture, the stigmas providing a yellow dye for fabrics and also used as a substitute for gold leaf in lettering. Saffron's use today is as a flavoring agent and to color food, but it is almost all imported from the Middle East and very expensive.

Less valuable for practical purposes is the popular spring flowering ornamental *C. vernus*, the spring crocus. Also an early introduction, *C. vernus* was introduced to Europe by Clusius at the end of the 16th century, and swiftly spread. *Crocus vernus* was among the tubers credited with founding Holland's bulb industry. By the 1600s, there were white, purple, and striped forms. *C. vernus* became such an integral part of the garden that the bulbs came to North America with the earliest settlers, following rapidly behind crop plants. And their dispersal in the New World was quick, spreading throughout Virginia, Maryland and New England colonies.

Other ornamental family members also came from the near East, especially the bright yellow *C. chrysanthus* which was much used as a parent of modern hybrids, expanding the color range of spring crocus. The species crocus which are popular in modern gardens were not commonly grown until the early 1900s. Although species crocus are now gaining

momentum, at the same time we're losing varieties from the past. The number of crocus cultivars, primarily *C. chrysanthus* hybrids, which have been lost is rivaled only by the number of Oriental poppies on Britain's Hardy Plant Society's Search List. Over 80 varieties of crocus are currently listed as lost.

Crocus prefer a light but fertile alkaline soil and perform most impressively when they are taken up and divided every third year. Unfortunately rodents love to eat them.

Cyclamen

PRIMULACEAE

Persian violet, alpine violet, sowbread

Native from southern Europe through Turkey, *Cyclamen hederifolium* (formerly *C. neopolitanum*) was given all sorts of inappropriate common names, the most colorful being sowbread, referring to the swine that once rooted up its tubers. And cyclamen tubers, sitting just below the soil's surface, must have been easy fodder for pigs. Those tubers reputedly taste repugnant, and some say that they can do foragers harm. But that little detail, apparently, did not dissuade the wild boars of Sicily. Of greater interest than the tubers, from a gardener's point of view, is the foliage – handsomely marked with wonderful patterns of silver and green on the top, blushing to red underneath. Even when the plant has finished blossoming, it's a handsome sight, especially when many tubers are clustered together in the dappled shade of a thin woodland. The rest of plant's common names allude to the flowers that appear on long stems in late summer when the tuber is still bereft of leaves. Although cyclamen are related to primroses, their nicknames reveal what they resemble more closely: violets, but with petals slung upward like shooting stars.

The Latin name, from the Greek *cyclos,* or circle, refers to the curlicues that develop while a seed capsule is ripening. Gerard grew *C. hederifolium* in 1597 (both pink and white flowering versions), as well as *C. coum.* But these were new introductions at the time because William Turner mentioned that they

hadn't arrived in Britain in 1551 (although he'd apparently caught wind of their existence) when he wrote his *New Herbal.* Another popularly grown hardy cyclamen, *C. purpurascens* (formerly *C. europaeum*), came into cultivation by 1605, followed by *C. repandum* in 1629. Both were once suspected of being native to Britain because they became so rapidly plentiful, but both were later deemed imports.

C. hederifolium was not lacking in medicinal applications. It was said to cure baldness, counteract poisoning and act as a love potion. Not only that, but it was rumored to be such a potent aid in childbirth that it could cause miscarriage if an expectant woman stepped over the bulbs.

The parent that fathered the cyclamens grown as houseplants was *C. persicum*, introduced from Cyprus and native to the Mediterranean. It arrived during the early 18th century and was prevalent by the 1840s. In 1870, a giant form appeared in both Britain and Germany, which led to the beefed up cyclamens sold for the winter holidays.

Cyclamens can be found growing seemingly unbidden throughout Britain, as well as in gardens, but they seem unable to survive the winter in North American gardens, except on the Pacific coast where conditions are never too hot or bitterly cold. Cyclamens prefer dappled shade, a cool environment and humusy soil. The same sort of conditions should be given to members of the family grown as houseplants, which might explain why they rarely live long in a toasty family room. When grown in pots, cyclamen like plentiful root room and prefer clay rather than plastic pots. Allowing them to slip into a wilt can be their undoing.

Dahlia
COMPOSITAE
dahlia

Travelers to Mexico in 1575 found the native dahlia growing in cultivation, already in double form. But the first plants weren't introduced into Europe until they reached Madrid in 1789. Then the Swedish botanist Dahl introduced the single red *Dahlia coccinea*, accompanied by the semi-double *D. pinnata*. They weren't originally introduced as ornamentals, but the botanists who brought them back hoped that the dahlia's edible tuber would become an important food crop, along the same lines as the potato. But there was general disinterest in the culinary possibilities of dahlias – apparently they tasted foul!

Dahlias have always been handsome plants. The thick, almost succulent stems are thickly covered with long, broad leaves, the flowers coming in shocking colors and looking like daisies. Even though the original single dahlia had only relatively slender ray petals, it obviously possessed potential.

By the beginning of the 19th century efforts were poured into expanding the flower size and broadening the ray petal's wingspan. By 1806, 55 single and semi-double cultivars were in flower at the Berlin Botanic Gardens and by 1808, the prototypical double pompom type appeared, the first of many innovations. The year 1809 brought the first single white; followed in 1814 by large-flowering doubles, a Belgian innovation. The same Belgian breeder who gave us the pompoms, Monsieur Donckelaar, introduced dwarf dahlias in 1838. By 1818, the color range had increased to include the full complement of rainbow shades now available. And public interest kept abreast. In 1841, one British dealer stocked over 1,200 varieties. At the turn of the century, 3,000 different dahlias were on the market. Meanwhile, in America, their crest of popularity came in 1840 and continued into the next century, if the pages devoted to that one plant in reference books of that period are any indication.

Dahlias fell out of favor for the first two decades of the 20th century, but by 1927, they were on the rebound, described as taking a leading position of all bulbs grown in America. Unfortunately, although thousands of dahlias (with wonderful names such as 'Acme of Perfection', 'Dauntless' and 'Prince of Liliputians') were available in the 19th century, all the older varieties disappeared in the interim. Scott Kunst of Old House Gardens (*see page 56*) has ferreted out the oldest dahlias and can find none prior to the 1920s. So far, the only survivors are 'Betty Anne' (1928) with dusty rose pompoms, 'Edith Muellar' (1933) a yellow accented by pink pompoms, 'Jersey Beauty' (1923) a pink formal, 'Mary Munns' (1928) with fuchsia-colored pompoms and 'Thomas Edison' (1929) a large royal purple. 'Bishop of Llandaff' (1927), with dark burgundy foliage accented by plentiful single, scarlet flowers, is readily available. Scott Kunst is hopeful that there may be 19th century dahlias preserved in private collections in Britain and Germany.

Plant dahlias at least 6 inches deep in the fertile, friable soil of the sunniest location you can muster. Many gardeners suggest removing all but one or two upshoots, which are then pinched to encourage branching. And the original dahlia growers were prone to disbud their plants, forcing the plant to pour its energies into only a few blossoms. Dahlia tubers should be left in the ground until the tops are touched by frost, at which time they should be dug and stored in a dry, cool place. Dahlias are propagated primarily by division of the tubers and cuttings, although they can be raised from seed.

Fritillaria

LILIACEAE

crown imperial, fritillary, Persian lily, tears of Mary

Native to Southern Turkey, it's little wonder that the crown imperial, *Fritillaria imperialis*, was greeted with enthusiasm when it first appeared in Vienna in 1576. Traveling from Vienna to Holland and then on to Britain, Gerard already had "great plenty" in 1597 and Parkinson was so taken with the plant in 1629 that he let it preface the rest of the entries in his herbal, explaining that it "deserveth the first place."

Crown imperials are majestic plants, holding their blossoms on tall, 3 foot spikes. The lower third of the stem is well-clothed with long, pointed, pale green leaves, but the drama is increased by a long, naked section crowned by a cluster of big, brightly colored tulip-shaped blossoms all nodding downward but accented by a topknot of leaves, similar to that of a pineapple. Droplets of nectar cling to the base of each petal, and in Persia a legend suggests that these are the tears of a queen who, accused of infidelity, was turned into a fritillary and weeps for her husband forevermore. Unlike tears, the droplet is supposedly sweet to the taste, like honey, much to the delight of early herbalists.

Early crown imperials were always orange and there is a legend that the crown imperial was originally white but failed to bow down during the Crucifixion, and so spent the rest of its days blushing and nodding in shame. Introduced in 1665, the bright yellow version, 'Lutea', was considered a great rarity in America in 1739, according to Scott Kunst the bulb historian at Old House Gardens (*see page 56*). 'Aurora', introduced in 1865, is an even brighter, raging orange than the species. Thomas Jefferson would not be deterred from having crown imperials at Monticello although he found them difficult to establish – he put in five orders before finally receiving three roots which evidently thrived so well in the garden that they could be distributed to other locations. He reputedly received a coveted silver striped type as well. Double versions were available by the mid-18th century.

Crown imperials have a commanding presence, often used as a focal point. L. H. Bailey suggested in 1900 that crown imperials should be afforded "deep planting, rich soil and much room," and he suggested digging a 12 foot trench filled with manure before setting in the bulb. However, all this labor is not essential as the bulbs will thrive in any reasonably rich soil in partial shade; they should be divided every three years to avoid overcrowding which can impair flowering. Although the bulbs are perfectly hardy and can reach the size of a child's head, late frost can critically damage the emerging flower spike in spring.

Galanthus

AMARYLLIDACEAE

snowdrop, Candlemas bell, Mary's tapers, February fair-maids

Currently in vogue with collectors, snowdrops weren't all the rage until recently. Some feel that *Galanthus nivalis* is native to Britain, others insist that it arrived from Italy in the 15th century. Whichever, it is an ancient plant and certainly widespread throughout Europe. The tiny, dangling bells, white with green markings, sprouting from a little tuft of deep green, grass-like leaves, are such welcome harbingers of spring, it's amazing that they didn't get more play in history. Theophrastus mentioned them in 320BC while St. Francis is said to have embraced snowdrops as an emblem of hope. Gerard suspected that they were a "bulbous violet" and so did Parkinson. Before Gerard happened upon the scene to coin his name, they were called Candlemas bells, because the flowers were used to decorate the altar of the Virgin Mary on that day, their white bells providing a symbol of purity. The perfectly appropriate common name of snowdrops wasn't recorded until 1633. And it's little wonder that it stuck. Few people know snowdrops by their Latin name, which isn't particularly image-provoking. Linnaeus dubbed them *galanthus,* translating as milk flowers.

The weather is generally too chilly and the ground too patchy with snow for sampling the fragrance of snowdrops outdoors in situ, which might explain why many early chroniclers failed to mention these spring bulbs. But Gerard and Clusius both note its scent, which is much more pronounced when you bring a bouquet of the tiny flowers indoors to enjoy.

At present, there are several variations on *G. nivalis* available to collectors, and collecting is rampant in

Britain. The names rival anything given to a rose. A double version is known as 'Lady Elphinstone', 'Magnet' is a larger flowering version and 'Poculiformis' is devoid of green markings. A less petite version, *G. plicatus,* accused of lacking delicacy in George Nicholson's 1887 *Dictionary of Gardening,* was mentioned by Parkinson in 1629 but disappeared afterward, requiring reintroduction in 1818.

Among the early versions of *G. plicatus* are 'Warham Variety', brought home from the Crimean War by a Captain Adlington in 1855. Thanks to the Captain, we now have the results of a marriage between *G. nivalis* and *G. plicatus,* especially 'Ophelia' and 'Jacquenetta' with double flowers and larger than the common snowdrop.

Galanthus are reputed to grow in absolutely any soil and location. But they don't particularly like to be moved around or divided. Unfortunately, snowdrops aren't easily forced and most historic books claim that it isn't possible. I've succeeded in a nearly freezing sunporch after pre-chilling the bulbs.

Gladiolus

IRIDACEAE

gladiolus, corn flag

Amazingly, the gladiolus was once considered a weed accused of invading cornfields when the farmers really just wanted to harvest a food crop. The name was derived from the shape of the leaves, the Latin *gladius* translates as "sword". Although there is one rare species, *G. illyricus,* native to Britain, gardeners were more intrigued with imports from the start. Gerard mentioned the red-flowering *G. communis* (still available) from Southern Spain, which thrived so well in its adopted home that it became an agricultural weed. In addition, Gerard was familiar with the purplish-magenta *G. italus* (formerly *G. segetum*) native to Southern Europe. As for medicinal applications, a poultice of the roots was apparently employed to draw out splinters. *G. communis* and its 'Albus' (white) form were the gladioli available in the trade by the late 18th century.

Other species entered at regular intervals – such as *G. imbricatus* which came from Southern Europe sometime before 1604 and *G. tristis* (a native of South Africa known as the marsh Afrikaner) with greenish-yellow, night fragrant flowers, which arrived in the 1700s. But the species gladioli didn't really shake up the botanical world. They are interesting and colorful, to be sure, but the blossoms are loosely held and patchily displayed on the stem compared to modern versions. It wasn't until hybridizers began to fiddle with the gladiolus that it began to flirt with fame. Of the early hybrids of gladioli, only the scarlet-flowering *G. x colvillei,* created in 1823, is still available in the United States, but is not listed as being sold in Britain. This was the first in a long string of hybrids. Much more important were the large flowering Gandavensis hybrids created in 1837 in Belgium, holding their blossoms snugly bunched on the stem and blooming primarily in shades of red and yellow, with occasional blotching on the petals. From that point, there was a fray of breeding toward a large-flowering gladiolus, with many species thrown into the gene pool and work being done in England, France, Germany and finally in America. The introduction of *G. dalenii* (formerly *G. primulinus*) from tropical Africa in 1904 expanded both the color range (allowing for more subtle shades) and giving rise to ruffled flowers.

Gladiolus were much more popular in the 19th century than they are at present. Once all the rage but mostly as a cut flower, they began to suffer from their heavy usage in funeral floral arrangements. Although the flowers appear in the same rainbow of colors that iris boast, although they have gorgeous spires of frilly-petalled blossoms, people tend to find the gladiolus depressing. This sad turn of events will probably change with the tides of fashion. In fact,

species gladioli from South Africa are gaining a following in North America. Grown indoors during the winter, they promise to rival forced bulbs for cold season entertainment. However, besides *G. x colvillei*, few older hybrids can be found. Scott Kunst, of Old House Gardens in Ann Arbor, Michigan (*see page 56*), has been searching for years, and cannot find gladiolus hybrids dating before 1930.

Actually, gladioli sprout from corms rather than bulbs and those corms are not perennial. Each year, the flowering corm shrivels but is supplanted by another viable corm formed above the spent tuber. These should be planted in full sun and well-drained soil plowed to at least 8 inches deep. The soil should be fertile. In fact, many vegetable farmers slip a few gladioli into their plantings to sell at roadside stands. The flower stalk's greatest foe is wind, which can wreak havoc and has led to the development of a dwarf strain.

Hyacinthus

LILIACEAE

hyacinth

Native to Turkey, Syria and Lebanon, *Hyacinthus orientalis* arrived in Europe in 1560. Prior to that, hyacinths were worn as headdresses by bridesmaids in Greek weddings and were mentioned in Homer's *Iliad*. Although the thick succulent leaves are comely and the plump flower spike densely packed with open-faced blossoms is handsome, it was the unique, intense fragrance (likened to the grape by Pliny) that really caught the imagination. Although the Elizabethans found the intense aroma rather melancholic, nevertheless double white, blue and pink varieties were available by 1613 and there were 2,000 hyacinths in cultivation by 1730.

The early doubles didn't pack the stem in a solid, seamless mass as they do today, furthermore each flower on the spike drooped downward. The development of the early hyacinths into our modern forms was the work of Dutch bulb merchants from the 18th century onward. During the 19th century increasing

numbers of hyacinths were produced for forcing indoors in hourglass-shaped vases of water. The bulb was balanced in the top cup, its roots barely touching the moisture below. Many strong colors became available then, such as 'Baron von Tuyll' described in a 1872 edition of *The Garden* as "dark porcelain blue", and 'La Citronière' described as "deep citron yellow". Few of the early forcing hyacinths are available now, although the colors included delicate azure blue ('Grand Lilas'), bright dark carmine red ('Robert Steiger') and lively violet ('Charles Dickens'). In fact, of the 84 hyacinths mentioned in an 1897 catalog, only two are still available - 'Marie' an indigo-purple single introduced in 1860 and 'King of the Blues', a deep purple single introduced in 1863. The Roman hyacinth, with nodding, fringed petaled bells, is no longer commercially available.

Besides the need to support the plump drumstick of blossoms, hyacinths are foolproof bulbs if given fertile soil, ample water and filtered sun.

The related English bluebell, *Hyacinthoides non-scripta*, with its smaller spires of packed blue bell shaped blossoms, is another heirloom flower that has been gracing patches of woodland and shady waste-

land in temperate climates for thousands of years. It makes an excellent companion for other members of the family. Supposedly, if you plant hyacinths near an ant's nest, the formic acid will turn all blue blossoms pink.

Lilium

LILIACEAE

lily

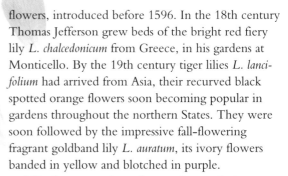

❻

The Madonna lily, *Lilium candidum* is thought to be one of the oldest plants in cultivation, appearing as a motif in the art of ancient civilizations, a symbol of purity, grown for its beautiful flowers and also for its edible bulbs. Apparently the Greeks and Romans made healing lotions from the underground parts, but the bulbs had to be dug according to a prescribed ritual which involved ceremoniously drawing a circle around the plant, then facing eastward to beg permission to remove the bulb.

L. candidum was the only lily known to European gardeners prior to the 16th century. The broad, unwaivering white trumpet of the Madonna lily produces a wonderfully rich perfume from its numerous 3-4 inch wide waxy white flowers. Known as "the fair white lily" it was brought to the Plymouth settlement of America in the 1630s although weather conditions in the northerly parts of the country were not conducive to either its survival over winter or blossoming in summer. It might have been grown for largely sentimental reasons, a nostalgia for the blossoms of the homeland, but was probably most used as a medicinal plant, providing the main ingredient for an ancient healing salve. In order to blossom, Madonna lilies require about three months of sunshine, so from the mid-19th century it was most often used as a forcing bulb. It was upstaged in the 1800s by *L. longiflorum*, the Easter lily from Asia, that truly caught the eye of economically savvy Americans, forced in pots for Memorial Day and Easter.

Some lilies, easier to cultivate than the fussy Madonna lily, became popular in North America early on, particularly martagon lilies or turk's cap lilies *L. martagon* with their numerous hanging pink-purple

flowers, introduced before 1596. In the 18th century Thomas Jefferson grew beds of the bright red fiery lily *L. chalcedonicum* from Greece, in his gardens at Monticello. By the 19th century tiger lilies *L. lancifolium* had arrived from Asia, their recurved black spotted orange flowers soon becoming popular in gardens throughout the northern States. They were soon followed by the impressive fall-flowering fragrant goldband lily *L. auratum*, its ivory flowers banded in yellow and blotched in purple.

Lilies have experienced waves in popularity - being wildly popular with the Elizabethans, falling from fame in the 18th century, rising again with the Victorians and reaching a crescendo with the Arts and Crafts movement at the end of the 19th century. A double form of the Madonna lily was grown in North America in the mid-17th century, and a purple striped form a century later. Although the double version was lost for a time, it seems to have resurfaced (although it is rare) under the variety name 'Plenum'. The regal lily *L. regale*, introduced from China by the great plant hunter E. H. Wilson, is an extravagant competitor to the Madonna lily, and is easier to grow. Regal lilies grow to six feet tall with stems packed with wonderfully fragrant flowers white on the inside and pinkish purple on the outside.

The most important thing to remember when cultivating lilies is that they must have good drainage in deep friable soil. If they sit in wet ground they will fail. They prefer dappled shade and need to be staked. As with other bulbs, when plants begin to go straggly and produce fewer blossoms, divide them. New divisions may not bloom for two or three seasons after transplanting.

Muscari

LILIACEAE

grape hyacinths, pearls of Spain

Originally known as *Hyacinthus botryoides* and later classified as *Muscari botryoides*, grape hyacinths were in cultivation by 1576, originally collected from Spain. The 5-6 inch tall, grape-like clusters are a piercing blue, yet the color didn't seem to draw any fans among the ancient herbalists. The white *M. botryoides* ('Album') was known to Parkinson, who called it affectionately "Pearls of Spain" and seemed to prefer it to the blue variety. And older gardens were rife with other species of muscari beyond the familiar grape hyacinth. Parkinson grew *M. comosum*, the tassel hyacinth, which was also a favorite of Thomas Jefferson's who naturalized it at Monticello. That species is still readily available as is *M. comosum* 'Plumosum', the feathered hyacinth, which Jefferson ordered under its former name of 'Monstrosum'. The little spikes of feathery purple flowers are delightful, but the bulb isn't quite as vigorous as the common grape hyacinth.

Grape hyacinths are very accommodating. They survive in almost any soil and naturalize happily in short grass, but do best where the soil is rich and the location sunny. They can be propagated by offsets or seeds, and it isn't necessary to divide clumps to keep the bulbs healthy.

Narcissus

4 however *Narcissus tazetta* is **8**

AMARYLLIDACEAE

daffodil, daffodowndilly, daffodily
Lent lily

Native to the Mediterranean as well as Southern Europe, Northern Africa, Western Asia, China and Japan, the first cultivated daffodils were probably *Narcissus tazetta*, known as the bunch-flowering narcissus or polyanthus narcissus. This yellow and orange multi-headed scented daffodil was grown by the ancient Greeks. Although it is not reliably hardy throughout northern Europe, it is widely naturalized wherever climate suits. The oldest form is 'Grand Soleil D'Or', which might well coincide with Parkinson's *Narcissus africanus aureus major,* the yellow daffodil of Africa. By the 1880s *N. tazetta* var *orientalis*, the Chinese sacred lily, or Lien Chu lily was very popular, billed by Victorian catalogs as producing no fewer than 97 flowers from a single bulb.

It is often assumed that the Latin name, narcissus, is connected with the youth who was so obsessed with his own physical beauty that he drowned while trying to embrace his image in a river, but Pliny insists that the name comes from *narkao*, to benumb, alluding to the bulb's narcotic qualities. Juice from the bulb, applied to an open wound, was said to cause instant numbness of the nervous system and paralysis of the heart. For those properties, it was viewed as a portent of death, often planted beside tombs, although the Arabs viewed the plants more optimistically, using the oil as an aphrodisiac and to cure baldness.

N. poeticus, the pheasant's eye narcissus, was mentioned by Theophrastus in 320BC. However, the actual *N. poeticus*, with its broad glistening white petals radiating around a small cup-like corona and producing a heavy perfume, seems to have vanished from the industry. Perhaps the loss was due to plant's reputation: according to 19th century writers, the scent of poeticus flowers in any quantity in a closed room was capable of causing headache and vomiting. What survives are the varieties *N. poeticus ssp.*

radiiflorus (dating from 1796) with its tiny red-tipped cup and windmill-like appearance and *N. poeticus var. recurvus* (from the early 1700s) with recurved petals. The most commonly sold *N. poeticus* hybrid, often billed as the 'Old Pheasant's Eye' is 'Actaea' which, according to Scott Kunst the bulb historian at Old House Gardens (*see page 56*), is of very recent vintage, dating only to 1927.

Daffodils were grown in European gardens for 300 years, doubles were popular in the 17th century and many of the older doubles such as 'Butter and Eggs' (1777) are still available. However, the daffodil's popularity peaked in the 19th century: the first hybrids were developed in the 1820s, commercially available from the 1860s. The famous bright yellow 'King Alfred' first appeared in 1899, but the 'King Alfred' currently sold is actually a beefed up version of the original. And recent years have brought many

improvements in daffodils. Early narcissus tended to have nodding heads, relatively small flowers and spindly flower stems compared to their modern counterparts. Between the years 1860 and 1900, one thousand new daffodils were introduced with a further 6,000 appearing by 1930. The year 1923 brought the first pink daffodil, 'Mrs. R. O. Backhouse', which could more accurately be described as apricot ("pale almost-pink" says Scott Kunst, "like a sunrise"). It remained the sole representative of that color for several decades.

Daffodils are ideal candidates for naturalizing, tolerating most soils and light conditions, from full sun to semi-shade. The only prerequisite is well-drained soil, which should ideally not be too light. Plant bulbs 4-6 inches deep in autumn, and divide after a few years when clumps begin to get established, as they always flower best if they aren't too crowded.

Polianthes

AGAVACEAE

tuberose

Although *Polianthes tuberosa*, the tuberose, was cultivated in pre-Columbian Mexico and is native to the Andes of South America, it is no longer found in the wild. The nickname refers to the tuberous root and the rose-like blossoms that appear in spires on tall wands that jut from the center of grass-like, pale green leaves.

Introduced into Europe by 1530 and growing in Williamsburg, Virginia by the 1730s, tuberoses were extremely popular garden plants until the latter 19th century. However, their flirt with fame was short-lived and toward the end of the 1800s, they were abandoned in North American gardens, due to their heavy perfume (accused of being too powerful) and funereal associations. The double version was discovered in 1870 by Peter Henderson, a New York nurs-

eryman and appeared as 'The Pearl' or 'Excelsior'. However, double versions were known to revert frequently back to the single. Peter Henderson also offered 'Albino', a single that he billed as having an odor "less powerful, and therefore more pleasant, than that of the ordinary tuberose." If you can find any old named varieties, try them, their lush vanilla-like scent would grace any garden.

Tuberoses grow best in conditions similar to potatoes, they dislike chilly soil and require a long growing season with warm evenings. They are traditionally grown in pots, the bulb buried an inch below the soil surface. Outdoors, plant the bulbs when the soil has warmed in June, and don't expect flowers before October, assuming frost hasn't intervened. Propagate by division.

Ranunculus ❾

RANUNCULACEAE

Asiatic ranunculus, Persian king cup

Although *Ranunculus asiaticus* was reputed to enter Europe from Turkey with Louis IX of France as a gift to his mother upon returning from the Crusades in the mid-13th century, the Middle Eastern native didn't reach the general public until the end of the 16th century. It came to Britain in 1596, and by 1629, Parkinson proudly boasted that he was growing 8 varieties. Even in the wild, *R. asiaticus* displayed plenty of diversity. From densely clad stems thick with celery-like leaves sprout plentiful poppy-like flowers. Although red is the standard shade, yellow, purple, pink and white *R. asiaticus* were also to be found growing wild in the plant's native habitat. Not only were there various color forms, but doubling also occurs unbidden in the wild and so double flowers were part of the initial influx. In the early 18th and 19th centuries, the ranunculus was further improved by hybridizers. In 1792, there were at least 800 named cultivars available.

By the early 19th century, hybrid ranunculus were divided into classes for exhibition purposes with colors that included coffee, red and yellow striped, mottled, olive, light purple and gray. They had flowers that were fully double, like a rosebud, and many were subtly shaded to a different hue at the tip of the petals. Furthermore, there was a form that was described as black, although it was probably the deep purple. Of those early colors, the olive, the grey and coffee colored versions have been lost. And for some reason, ranunculus fell from popularity in the mid-19th century. By the end of the century, there were complaints that only "a few dozen – or perhaps less than a score" remained in catalogs. At present, they are sold only as mixed colors.

The plant's name, *ranunculus* from *rana*, a frog, gives you some indication of the environment where the corms prefer to grow. Ranunculus wilt at the slightest provocation. Interestingly, the corms were traditionally planted in autumn in the 18th century but this shifted to late winter planting in the 19th century. Good soil, plenty of compost and excellent drainage are essential. But even when grown in the best of conditions, the foliage and buds are ravaged by aphids. In North America, they are usually treated as greenhouse plants.

Tulipa

LILIACEAE

tulip

The first cultivated tulip came from Turkey, but no one is quite certain from which species it sprang because tulips had long been cultivated in the area. In fact Babar, a conqueror of India, wrote in his journal of 1505 that he found 32 or 33 different tulips of many colors in the foot-hills near Kabul, some sweet scented like the rose. We do know that Ghiselin de Busbecq, ambassador from the Holy Roman Emperor to Suleiman the Magnificent, first encountered the bulbs in 1555 during a trip between Adrianople and Constantinople and shared them with Clusius. Apparently, those original bulbs were stolen, and tulip bulbs became incredibly sought after.

Tulips were cultivated in the Middle East in the 12th and 13th centuries, but the first Dutch plantation was not established until 1562. Meanwhile tulips had already reached a high degree of development in their native lands, with flamed and streaked types already available by the 16th century. In 1578, tulips arrived in Britain and by the time Gerard wrote in 1597, seven types were commonly available including a red, a yellow, and a streaked sort.

A virus spread by aphids caused the famous striped and streaked "Rembrandt" tulips so often depicted on the canvases of the Dutch masters, but it was only in 1928 that the reason for the mutations was discovered. The virus caused flames, slashes and featherings of various shades and in 1634 it fired the Dutch economic and horticultural trend known as Tulipomania. Gardeners and businessmen alike were fascinated by the exotic appearance of the radiantly colored tulips and fortunes were gained and lost over tulip speculation, with bulbs selling for magnificent sums to people who knew nothing about horticulture; tulips were briefly an important trading commodity. The virus generally weakened the Rembrandts and few tulips survive from that time. However, Hortus Bulborum, the Dutch national bulb museum, has recently made some excess bulbs available so that 'Lack Van Rijn', a red pointed-petaled tulip with white edging (c.1620) and 'Zomerschoon' with ivory petals flamed in red (also dating from 1620) are now available.

Trends in tulips changed with time. Parrot tulips, with their frilly edges, date back to the 1600s. Most cottage gardeners from the 17th century on also grew the short-stemmed 'Duc Van Thol' types, which slipped from fashion in the early 20th century and are rare at present. In the mid-19th century, rules governed "model tulips"; unlike the original pointed-edged tulips of the 17th century, these show tulips looked like a half-cup with an edge as smooth as possible. Darwin tulips, developed from antique Flemish varieties, were all the rage in the early 20th century; 'Clara Butt' (pink flowering, circa 1889) was the most popular and is still available. Of the parrot tulips, 'Fantasy' (pink, with apple-green markings, c. 1910) is the oldest still to be found.

Plant tulips in late fall, sinking the bulbs 4–6 inches into sandy soil enriched with loam and leaf mould. Tulips can tolerate most conditions, but they dislike soggy soil. Unfortunately, rodents seem to seek out tulips and many gardeners advise sprinkling ground oyster shells around the bulb for "bulb insurance". Propagate tulips by dividing the clumps of bulbs every three years once groups are established.

The Directory – Resources

While we have done our best to ensure this information is accurate and up-to-date at the time of publication, from time to time companies change, new individuals start trading and some others take a break. No list such as this can ever be complete, there are sure to be others out there providing a wonderful service in saving and supplying seeds as stewards of the future. We apologize for any omissions.

We have not included information relating to catalog prices, as these are also subject to change. Please, don't just expect something for nothing, but contact the nurseries or seedspeople first, and see how much you can contribute for a catalog.

ALASKA

Seeds of Alaska
PO Box 3127
Kenai, AK 99611-3127
Tel: 907/262-5267
Fax: 907/262-3755

Seeds and plants of species native to south central Alaska.

ARIZONA

Native Seeds/SEARCH
2509 N Campbell Ave, #325
526 N Fourth Ave/Retail outlet
Tucson, AZ 85719
Tel: 520/622-5561
Fax: 520/622-5591
email: jhosofaz@aol.com
web: http://desert.net/seeds/home.htm

Many varieties of heirloom seeds from traditional crops of the southwestern US and northern Mexico.

Southwestern Native Seeds
Box 50503
Tucson, AZ 85703

Over 400 species of almost exclusively wild-collected seeds of wildflowers, trees, shrubs, and succulents native to the southwest.

Wild Seed
PO Box 27751
Tempe, AZ 85285
Tel: 602/276-3536
Fax: 602/276-3524

Seed native to the southwestern US – especially the Sonoran Desert. Wildflowers, trees, shrubs and native grasses.

ARKANSAS

Holland Wildflower Farm
290 O'Neal Lane
PO Box 328
Elkins, AR 72727
Tel: 501/643-2622
Fax: 501/643-2249
Orders: 800/684-3734
email: info@hwildflower.com
web: www.hwildflower.com

Native and naturalized plants from east of Rocky Mountains. Seed mixtures to meet site-specific conditions available.

Pine Ridge Gardens
832-WG Sycamore Road
London, AR 72847
Tel: 501/293-4359

Native trees, shrubs, wetland species, native medicinals and native flowers and grasses. Plants (except some native iris) are container grown.

Ridgecrest Nursery & Gardens
3347 Highway 64 East
Wynne, AR 72396
Tel: 870/238-3763

Hundreds of southeastern US native annuals, perennials, shrubs and trees. Mostly container grown. No mail order. No seeds.

CALIFORNIA

Bountiful Gardens
18001 Schaefer Ranch Road
Willits, CA 95490
Tel: 707/459-6410

Open-pollinated flowers and herbs. An educational organization dedicated to sustainable agriculture and conservation.

California Flora Nursery
Somers & D Street
PO Box 3
Fulton, CA 95439
Tel: 707/528-8813
Fax: 707/528-1836

California natives, Mediterraneans, unusual perennials, vine shrubs and grasses. Propagated and grown on the premises.

Canyon Creek Nursery
3527 Dry Creek Road
Oroville, CA 95965
Tel: 916/533-2166

Heirloom flowers.

Elkhorn Native Plant Nursery
1957 B Salinas Road
PO Box 270
Moss Landing, CA 95039
Tel: 408/763-1207
Fax: 408/763-1659

Plants and seed including grass seed native to the central coast of California and natives that grow well on the central coast.

Far West Bulb Farm
10289 Candlewood Way
PO Box 515
Oregon House, CA 95962-0515
Tel: 530/692-2565
Fax: 530/692-2565

California native bulbs, and seeds of bulb-forming plants. Ships Sep–Oct only.

Heirloom Garden Seeds
PO Box 138
Guerneville, CA 95446
Tel: 707/887-9129

A source for seeds of old and almost forgotten herbs and flowers, with a highly informative catalog.

J L Hudson, Seedsman
PO Box 1058
Redwood City, CA 94064

Large selection of native seeds from around the world. Species for most habitats: prairie, woodland, wetland, alpine, cool and warm deserts, dry and moist tropical; chaparral, coastal and for a wide range of ecological niches. Also offers some rare and endangered plants. *See also page 186.*

The Living Desert
Palo Verde Garden Center
47900 Portola Avenue
Palm Desert, CA 92260
Tel: 760/346-5694
Fax: 760/568-9685

Comprehensive selection of plants and
wildflower seeds; promotes the landscape
use of plants indigenous to the deserts of
the southwest and Mexico.

Mockingbird Nurseries
1670 Jackson Street
Riverside, CA 92504
Tel: 909/780-3571
Fax: 909/780-4037

California natives specialist, growing without chemicals.

Moon Mountain Wildflowers
PO Box 725
Carpinteria, CA 93014
Tel: 805/684-2565
Fax: 805/684-2798
email: ssseeds@silcom.com

Seeds of plants native and naturalized to
North America.

Mountain Valley Growers
38325 Pepperweed Road
Squaw Valley, CA 93675
Tel: 209/338-2775
Fax: 209/338-2775

350 varieties of quality herbs and flowers,
some dating back to the 1600s.

O'Donnell's Fairfax Nursery
1700 Sir Francis Drake Blvd
Fairfax, CA 94930
Tel: 415/453-0372

Native seeds and bulbs, and a wide variety
of native plants, ranging from easy- to
hard-to-find.

Pacific OpenSpace
PO Box 744
Petaluma CA 94953
Tel: 707/769-1213
Fax: 707/769-1230
email: ecofixit@metro.net

Californian native perennials.

Roses of Yesterday & Today
802 Brown's Valley Road
Watsonville, CA 95076
Tel: 408/724-3537
Fax: 408/724-1408

200 roses, some modern, some antique.
Many hardy varieties and highly perfumed
rare roses.

Redwood City Seed Company
Box 361
Redwood City, CA 94064
Tel: 415/325-7333
Fax: 415/325-4056
email:rwc-seed@batnet.com
web: www.batnet.com/rwc-seed/juicy.gos-
sip.three.html

Seeds of vegetables and medicinal herbs,
sweetgrass plants native to North America.

**Santa Barbara Heirloom
Seedling Nursery**
PO Box 4235
Santa Barbara, CA 93140
Tel: 805/968-5444
Fax: 805/562-1248

Organic growers of heirloom herbs and
flowers with some seed stock from the
1800s.

Village Nursery
10994 Donner Pass Road
Truckee, CA 96161
Tel: 916/587-0771
Fax: 916/587-7439

Large selection of perennials native to this
area including some hard-to-find species.

Vintage Gardens
2833 Old Gravenstein Hwy S
Sebastopol, CA 95472
Tel: 707/829-2035

Nearly 2,000 roses, all rated for fragrance
and blooming habits.

Wildflower Seed Co
PO Box 406
St Helena, CA 94574
Tel: 707/963-3359
Fax: 707/963-5383
Orders: 800/456-3359
email: sales@wildflower-seed.com

Wildflower mixes for spring garden uses.
California native mix.

COLORADO

Edge of the Rockies
PO Box 1218
Bayfield, CO 81122

Seeds and plants native to mountains,
foothills and canyons of southern Rocky
Mountain region.

Western Native Seed
PO Box 1463
Salida, CO 81201
Tel: 719/539-1071
Fax: 719/539-6755

Specialize in seed for plants native to the
Rocky Mountains, western Great Plains and
adjacent areas.

CONNECTICUT

Select Seeds
Antique Flowers
180 Stickney Hill Road
Union, CT 06076
Tel: 860/634-9310
Fax: 860/684-9224
email: select@neca.com
web:
http://trine.com/GardenNet/SelectSeeds/

Flowers from the 18th and 19th centuries;
over 100 varieties of annuals and perennials. *See also page 84.*

Shepherd's Garden Seeds
30 Irene Street
Torrington, CT 06790
Tel: 203/482-3638

Specialty seeds plus unique varieties of
flowers and herbs from around the world
chosen for flavor, easy culture, quality and
high germination. Exclusive heritage sweet
peas.

Southern Exposure Seed Exchange
PO Box 170
Earlysville, VA 22901
Tel: 804/973-4703
Fax: 804/973-8717
web: http://www.southernexposure.com

Open-pollinated seed, encouraging seed
exchange by offering information and supplies. Herbs and heirloom flowers. *See also
page 187.*

FLORIDA

Hard Scrabble Farms
PO Box 281
Terra Ceia Island, FL 34250
Tel: 941/722-0414
Fax: 941/722-0414

Salt-tolerant freshwater aquatic and
marine Florida native plants, flowers and
seeds for restoration, stabilization and butterfly gardens.

Meadow Beauty Nursery
5782 Ranches Road
Lake Worth, FL 33463
Tel: 561/966-6848

Native plants only, specializing in butterfly-
and wildlife-attracting plants. Native wildflowers grown from locally collected seed.

Possom Hollow Orchards
10106 N.W 156th Ave
Alachua, FL 32615
Tel: 904/462-5455

Perennial and annual wildflowers for N
Central Florida. Plants only.

GEORGIA

Eco-Gardens
PO Box 1227
Decatur, GA 30031
Tel: 404/294-6468

Limited quantities of selected natives.
Ongoing research and breeding programs.
Slide-lecture programs and publications.

Flowery Branch Seed Co
PO Box 1330
Flowery Branch, GA 30542
Tel: 770/536-8380

Strange and unusual perennials and annuals from around the world. Lots of herbs,
including medicinals.

Goodness Grows
332 Elberton St. (Hwy 77 N)
PO Box 311
Lexington, GA 30648
Tel: 706/743-5055
Fax: 706/743-5112

Container-grown plants including a sub-
stantial collection of natives.

Wild Wood Farms
5231 Seven Islands Rd.
Madison, GA 30650
Tel: 706/342-4912

North American species that provide habitat for songbirds, hummingbirds, butterflies and other wildlife.

IDAHO

Buffalo-berry Farm
51 E Lake Fork Road
PO Box 749
Lake Fork, ID 83635
Tel: 208/634-3062

Specialists in propagation of plants native
to the intermountain region of the Pacific
northwest. Container-grown trees, shrubs,
wildflowers, and grasses are available for
restoration projects or wild gardens.

Seeds Trust – High Altitude Gardens
PO Box 1048
Hailey, ID 83333
Tel: 208/788-4363
Fax: 208/788-3452
Orders: 208/788-4419
email: higarden@micron.net
web: http://gardennet.com

Sells seeds hand-collected from more than
100 species at 6,000-10,000 ft in the
mountains of central Idaho.

ILLINOIS

Bluestem Prairie Nursery
13197 E 13th Rd
Hilsboro, IL 62049
Tel: 217/532-6344

Plants native to midwestern prairies and
savannas. Seeds are sold by packet, and by
custom mixes from November through
February. Plants are sold bare root in March
and April.

Midwest Wildflowers
Box 64
Rockton, IL 61072

Specialize in seed of more than 120
species. No plants or nursery.

Grandma's Garden, Underwood Seeds
4N381 Maple Avenue
Bensenville, IL 60106
Tel: 630/616-0268
Fax: 630/616-0232

Good selection of heirloom flowers plus
tips on seedsaving and organic growing.

The Natural Garden
38 W443 Hwy 64
St Charles, IL 60175
Tel: 630/584-0150
Fax: 630/584-0185

More than 200 species of plants of the
Chicago/Midwest region. Seeds and plants
from within a 90-mile radius.

INDIANA

Earthly Goods, Ltd
PO Box 614
New Albany, IN 47150
Tel: 812/944-3283
Fax: 812/944-2903
email: earthly@aye.net
web: www.earthlygoods.com

Wildflower seeds, mixtures, and native
grasses.

IOWA

The Flower and Herb Exchange
3076 North Winn Road
Decorah, IA 52101
Tel: 319/382-5990
Fax: 319/382-5872

Dedicated to the preservation of flowers,
wildflowers, ornamentals and herbs that
are family heirlooms, unusual or not available commercially. Listed members steward
such plants and share them with other gardeners via the Exchange. FHE compiles
one list each year that is mailed to members, who order directly from the member
offering the seed. There is an annual $10
membership fee ($12 Canadian, $15 overseas). See also page 94.

Heyne Custom Seed Service
26420 510th Street
R.R. I, Box 78
Walnut, IA 51577-9745
Tel: 712/784-3454
Fax: 712/784-2030
email: heyneseeds@netins.net
web: http://www.netins.net//showcase/
bluestem

ION Exchange
1878 Old Mission Drive
Harpers Ferry, IA52146-7533
Order: 800/291-2143
Tel: 319/535-7231
Fax: 319/535-7362
email:hbright@means.net
web: www.ionxchange.com

Over 200 species of native plant seeds and
over 100 species as plug and potted plants.

KENTUCKY

Dabney Herbs
Box 22061, Louisville, KY 40252
Tel: 502/893-5198

Specializes in herbs with some pre-1800
heirlooms. Organically grown and nursery-
propagated plants.

Shooting Star Nursery
444 Bates Road
Frankfort, KY 40601
Tel: 502/223-1679

Nursery-propagated wildflowers, trees,
shrubs, vines, wetland plants. Wildflower
and prairie grass seeds.

LOUISIANA

Natives Nurseries
320 North Theard Street
Covington, LA 704433
Tel: 504/892-5424

Trees, shrubs, vines, grasses, and herbaceous materials for various southern habitats. Plants for birds and butterflies.

MAINE

Eastern Plant Specialties
PO Box 226
Georgetown, ME 044548
Tel: 207/371-2888

Wide choice of native wildflowers, ferns, ground covers, shrubs, and trees

Fedco Seeds
PO Box 520
Waterville, ME 04903
Tel: 207/873-7333

Good selection of older varieties of flowers suitable for cold climates with short seasons.

Johnny's Selected Seeds
310 Foss Hill Road
Albion, ME 04910
Tel: 207/437-9294
Fax: 207/437-4290

Exceptional vegetable and heirloom flower varieties trialed in cold climates. Also medicinal herbs.

Pinetree Garden Seeds
Box 300
New Gloucester, ME 04260
Tel: 207/926-3400
Fax:207/926-3886
email: superseeds@worldnet.att.net
web: http://www.superseeds.com

750 varieties of seeds, including open-pollinated flowers and herbs.

Royal River Roses
70 New Gloucester Road
North Yarmouth, ME 04097
Tel: 207/829-5830

230 varietes of hardy uncommon roses that flourish when grown organically.

MARYLAND

Heritage Rosarium
211 Haviland Mill Road
Brookville, MD 20833
Tel: 301/774-2806

Large selection of old garden roses.

Native Seeds Inc
14590 Triadelphia Mill Road
Dayton, MD 21306
Tel: 301/596-9818
Fax: 301/854-3195
email: saund10449@aol.com

Wildflower seeds in packets and bulk. Individual plant seeds and mixtures.

MASSACHUSETTS

New England Wildflower Society
Garden in the Woods
1180 Hemenway Road
Framingham, MA 10701-2699
Tel: 508/877-7630

Native plants, retail only, April 15 to Oct. 15. Mail order seeds.

Underwood Shade Nursery
PO Box 1386
North Attleboro, MA 02763
Tel: 508/222-2164
Fax: 508/222-5152
email: shadeplant@ici.net

Choice perennial plants for shaded gardens, including ferns and grasses. All native plants are nursery-propagated.

MICHIGAN

Ensata Gardens
9823 E Michigan Ave
Galesburg, MI 49053
Tel: 616/665-7500

Iris specialist: 200 Japanese and Siberian iris varieties from 1880 to 1993.

Far North Gardens
16785 Harrison
Livonia, MI 48154
Tel: 810/486-4203

Rare flower seeds from around the world; specializes in Barnhaven Silver Dollar primroses.

Michigan Wildflower Farm
11770 Cutler Road
Portland, MI 48875-9452
Tel: 517/647-6010
Fax: 517/647-6072

Seeds of more than 55 Michigan wildflowers and grasses. Consulting service and wildflower planting installation.

Old House Gardens
536 Third Street
Ann Arbor, MI 48103-4957
Tel: 734/995-1486
Fax: 734/995-1687
email: OHGBulbs@aol.com

Old varieties of tulips, daffodils, hyacinths, crocus and other 'minor bulbs' plus lots of historical information. *See also page 56.*

Willard's Weigh Herbs and Heirlooms
4579 West E Ave
Kalamazoo, MI 49004

Collection of organic heirloom flowers and herbs, some dating back to 1700s.

MINNESOTA

Brand Peony Farm
Box 842
St Cloud, MN 56302

Founded in 1862; excellent source of heirloom peonies.

Feder's Prairie Seed Co.
12871 380th Ave
Blue Earth, MN 56013
Tel: 507/526-3049
Fax: 507/526-3509
email: feder@bevcomm.net

Wide selection of local ecotype native prairie grass and flower seed. Free price list and planting information.

Prairie Hill Wildflowers
8955 Lemond Road
Ellendale, MN 56026
Tel: 507/451-7791
Fax: 507/451-3812

Seed of wildflowers and grasses native to S Minnesota and N Iowa.

Prairie Moon Nursery
R R 3, Box 163
Winona, MN 55987
Tel: 507/452-1362
Fax: 507/454-5238

More than 400 species of seeds and plants native to the midwest.

Prairie Restorations
31922 128th Street
PO Box 327
Princetown, MN 55371
Tel: 612/389-4342
Fax: 612/389-4346
Orders: 800/837-5986

Central Minnesota seed (grasses and forbs) and plants.

Savory's Gardens
5300 Whiting Avenue
Edina, MN 55439
Tel: 612/941-8755

Over 300 varieties of organic field-grown hostas, including some traditional favorites dating to 1800s.

MISSOURI

Elixir Farm Botanicals
LLC, General Delivery
Brixley, MO 65618
Tel: 417/261-2393

Organically grown seed, many indigenous medicinals, also 55 Chinese medicinal herbs.

Gilbert Perennial Farms
2906 Ossenfort Rd.
Glencoe, MO 63038
Tel: 314/458-2033
Fax: 314/485-9722
email: nataq@primary.net

Specialists in perennials and water plants, about 20% native to the Midwest.

Hamilton Seeds and Wildflowers
16786 Brown Road
Elk Creek, MO 65464
Tel: 417/967-2190

Missouri native perennial wildflowers and warm-season grasses.

Manchester Gardens
614 Nandale Lane
Manchester, MO 63021
Tel: 314/227-5930

1,500 iris and 650 daylilies, including some from 1800s.

Missouri Wildflowers Nursery
9814 Pleasant Hill Road
Jefferson City, MO 65109
Tel: 573/496-3492
Fax: 573/496-3003
email: mowldflrs@sockets.net

Native plants and seeds with genetic origin in Missouri. Informative catalog.

American Daylily & Perennials
PO Box 210
Grain Valley, MO 64029
Tel: 816/224-2852

400 varieties of Hemerocallis, some heirlooms.

MONTANA

Garden City Seeds
778 US Hwy 93N
Hamilton, MT 59840
Tel: 406/961-4837

Specializes in quality heirloom flowers and herbs, especially hardy varieties for the north. All seeds are untreated, many organically grown.

Wild Flower Seeds
630 Wildlife Lane
Anaconda, MT 59711
Tel: 406/563-8048

Alpines native to N Rocky Mountains area, hardy for long, cold winters, snow cover, short summers. Some native flowers, forbs, and trees.

NEBRASKA

DiGiorgi Seed Company
6011 N Street
Omaha, NE 68117-1634
Tel: 402/731-3901
Fax: 402/731-8475
Orders: 800/858-2580

Seeds for ornamental grasses, perennial and annual flowers, herbs, vegetables, and wildflowers for all US regions.

Fragrant Path
PO Box 328
Fort Calhoun, NE 68023

Small but interesting selection of fragrant flowers, including herbs and vines. *See also page 83.*

NEVADA

Comstock Seed
8520 W 4th Street
Reno, NV 89523
Tel: 702/746-3681
Fax: 702/746-1701

Shrub, grass, and flower seed, primarily from the Great Basin, Mojave, and Sierras.

NEW JERSEY

Well Sweep Herb Farm
205 Mt. Bethel Road
Port Murray, NJ 07865
Tel: 908/852-5390

Excellent source for lavender: more than 50 species, some quite rare.

Thompson & Morgan
Box 1308
Jackson NHJ 08527-0308
Tel: 908/363 2225

Over 2,000 varieties, including many rare and unusual plants.

NEW MEXICO

Deep Diversity
PO Box 15189
Santa Fe, NM 87506-5189
Tel: 505/438-8080
Fax: 505/438-7052

Unusual catalog of heirloom flowers and vegetables. The list includes the seeds of many rare and endangered plants.

Desert Moon Nursery
PO Box 600
Veguita, NM 87062
Tel: 505/864-0614

Specialists in Chihuahuan Desert and desert grassland plants. Seeds and plants including wildflowers, cacti, succulents, shrubs, and trees. Garden design and consultation.

High Country Gardens
2902 Rufina Street
Santa Fe, NM 87505-29929
Order: 800/925-9387
Tel: 505/438-3031
Fax: 800/925-0097
email: plants@highcountrygardens.com
web: www/highcountrygardens.com

Specialists in xeric native plants from the Great Plains, Mocky Mountains, and the Southwest, including New Mexico. Winter-hardy cacti, succulents, herbaceous perennials, and woody shrubs.

Agua Fria
Route 6 Box 11A
Santa Fe, NM 87501
Tel: 505/438-8888

Little-known Indian plants and other cultivars that have adapted to the Southwest.

Seeds of Change
PO Box 15700
Santa Fe, NM 87506-5700
Tel: 888/762-7333
Fax: 888/329-4762
email: gardener@seeds of change.com
web: www.seeds of change.com

Over 400 varieties of open-pollinated seeds
for vegetables, flowers, and herbs, including many heirloom varieties, produced
organically.

Seeds West Garden Seeds
317 14th Street N W.
Albuquerque, NM 87104
Tel: 505/843-9713
email: seedsWest@ad.com
web: http://home.aol.com/seedswest

Mail order seeds specializing in heirloom,
open-pollinated and gourmet, organically
grown vegetable seeds for short growing
season gardening. Also an excellent traditional flower collection.

NEW YORK

Hillary's Garden
PO Box 430 Dept. FH
Warwick, NY 10990-0430
Tel: 914/987-1175

Wide selection of organically grown perennials, herbs and flowers.

Adrian Kencik
370 Frankhauser Road
Williamsville, NY 14221

Enthusiastic researcher, collector and grower of morning glories. See also page 65.

WildGinger Woodlands
PO Box 1091
Webster, NY 14580

Northeastern woodland wildflowers and
ferns and prairie species, retail only.

NORTH CAROLINA

Boone's Native Seed Co
PO Box 10363
Raleigh, NC 27605
web: http://www.nando.net/ads/boone-
seed

Open pollinated seeds of native plants of
the Americas, no hybrids. Native seeds
from plants indigenous to the Americas
prior to European settlement, non-native
wildflowers, vegetable seeds.

Elk Mountain Nursery
142 Webb Cove Road
Asheville, NC 28804-1929
Tel: 704/251-9622
email: elkmountain@circle.net
web: www.circle.net/elkmountain

Specialists in plants native to eastern US
perennials, shrubs, trees. Species for cooler
and warmer areas.

We-Du Nurseries
R R 5, Box 724
Marion, NC 28752
Tel: 704/738-8300
Fax: 704/738-8131

Plants only: woody natives and perennials,
ferns, trillium, iris and many wildflowers.

OHIO

Berlin Seeds
5371 County Road 77
Millersburg, OH 44654

Small collection of older flowers. Special
children's offers.

Homestead Farm
PO Box 946
Idaho Springs, CO 80452
Tel: 303/567-4886

Organically grown herbs and wildflowers.

Companion Plants
7247 N Coolville Ridge Road
Athens, OH 45701
Tel: 614/592-4643

More than 600 varieties of plants and
seeds, many turn-of-the century and settler
varieties.

OREGON

Cooley's Gardens
PO Box 126-AN, Silverton
OR 97381-0126
Tel: 503/873-5463

Large selection of tall bearded iris.

Ingraham's Cottage Garden Roses
PO Box 126
Scotts Mills, OR 97375

Heirloom and classic roses.

Nichols Garden Nursery
1190 North Pacific Highway
Albany, OR 97321-4580
Tel: 541/928-9280
Fax: 541/967-8406

Seeds of vegetables, culinary herbs and
some cottage garden flowers.

Russell Graham, Purveyor of Plants
4030 Eagle Crest Road N W.
Salem, OR 97304
Tel: 503/362-1135

Hardy herbaceous perennials and ferns
from Pacific northwest.

PENNSYLVANIA

W Atlee Burpee & Co
Warminster, PA 18974
Tel: 800/333-5808
Fax: 800/487 5530

Heirloom vegetables, herbs and flowers.

**Fox Hollow Herbs and
Heirloom Seed Co.**
Box 148, McGrann, PA 16236
Tel: 412/548-SEED

Quality organic heirloom varieties of herbs
and flowers.

Heirloom Seed Project
Landis Valley Museum
2451 Kissel Hill Road
Lancaster, PA 17601
Tel: 717/569-0401

Nonprofit organization working to preserve
plant material grown by Pennsylvania
Germans before 1940.

Heirloom Seeds
PO Box 245
West Elizabeth, PA 15088-0245
Tel: 412/384-0852
Fax: 412/384-0852

Seeds only of vegetables and flowers,
mostly of US origin.

Primrose Path
RR 2 Box 110
Scottdale, PA 15683

Hardy perennials including a good selection
of primulas and phlox.

TENNESSEE

Sunnyridge Gardens
1724 Drinnen Road
Knoxville, TN 37914
Tel: 423/933-0723

Older types of irises, daylilies and roses. Garden has 4,000 daylilies, 2,000 irises and a display from the Historical Iris Preservation Society.

TEXAS

Antique Rose Emporium
Route 5 Box 143
Brenham, TX 77833
Tel : 800/441-0002
Fax: 409/836-0928

250 old landscape and garden roses.

Kings Creek Gardens
813 Straus Road
Cedar Hill, TX 75104
Tel: 972/291-7650
Fax: 972/293-0920

Native and naturalized plants, both proven performers and new collections. Native perennials, trees, shrubs, aquatic plants plus fresh wildflower seeds.

National Wildflower Research Center
2600 FM 973 North
Austin
TX 78725-4201

Large selection of American wildflowers and extensive show gardens.

Weston Gardens
8101 Anglin Drive
Fort Worth, TX 76140
Tel: 817/572-0549
Fax: 817/572-1628

Plants and seed of many perennials and wildflowers; also bulbs.

VERMONT

The Cook's Garden
PO Box 535
Londonderry, VT 05148
Tel: 802/824-3400
Fax: 802/824-3027

"Seeds and Supplies for the New American Kitchen Garden" includes a nice selection of heirloom herbs and flowers. All seeds are untreated.

Countryman Peony Farm
RD 1, Northfield
VT 05663
Tel: 802/458-8421

Specialist in Victorian peonies.

The English Garden Emporium
Box 222, Manchester
VT 05254
Tel: 800/347-8130

Over 400 varieties of flower and vegetable seeds imported from Johnson's Seeds of England.

Perennial Pleasures Nursery
PO Box 147, 2 Brickhouse Road
East Hardwick, VT 05836
Tel: 802/472-5104
Fax: 802/472-6572

Field-grown perennials and herbs from the 17th, 18th and 19th centuries.

Vermont Wildflower Farm
Route 7,
Charlotte, VT
Tel: 802/425-3500
fax: 802/425-3500

Wildflower seed specialists, including specific mixes for different areas.

VIRGINIA

Andre Viette Farm & Nursery
Route 1 Box 16
Fishersville, VA 22939
Tel: 703/943-2315
Fax: 703/943-0782

Rare and exotic perennials from US and Europe.

Thomas Jefferson Center for Historic Plants
Monticello, PO Box 316
Charlottesville, VA 22902
Tel: 804/984-9821
Fax: 804/977-6140
web: http://www.monticello.org/shop

The Center collects, preserves, and sells historic plant varieties, many of which were grown by Thomas Jefferson in his gardens at Monticello. Also seed of some varieties of native American plants. *See also page 72.*

WASHINGTON

B & D Lilies
PO Box 2007
Port Townsend, WA 98368
Tel: 360-385-1738

Over 200 lilies, some rare and pre-1940.

Foliage Gardens
2003 128th Ave S E
Bellevue, WA 98005
Tel: 206/747-2998

Extensive selection of foliar plants including many N A. ferns.

Good Seed Co
Star Rt Box 73A
Oroville (Chesaw), WA 98844

Good selection of old flowers and herbs. Offers an organically grown colonial herb collection from the 1700s.

Lamb Nurseries
101 E Sharp Ave
Spokane, WA 99202
Tel: 509/328-7956

Hardy perennials, old-fashioned roses, daylilies, violets and kitchen herbs; 65 years in business offering quality plants.

WISCONSIN

Little Valley Farm
5693 Snead Creek Road
Spring Green, WI 53588
Tel: 608/935-3324

Native plants, seeds, shrubs and vines for the midwest and New England regions. Prairie, woodland and wetland species.

McClure and Zimmerman
108 W Winnebago, PO Box 368
Friesland, WI 53935
Tel: 414/326-4220

Quality flowerbulb brokers: bulbs suitable for restoration projects, and wild tulips and daffodils.

WYOMING

Wind River Seed
3075 Lane 51 1/2
Manderson, Wy 82432
Tel: 307/568-3361
Fax: 307/568-3364

Seed of native wildflowers, forbs, legumes, shrubs, trees and wetland species indigenous to the midwest, North, intermountain West, and Northwest.

CANADA

Aurora Biodynamic Farm
RR1 63-9
Creston
BC VOB 1G0
Tel: 603/428-4404
Fax: 603/428-4404
email: http://www.awinc.aurora

Supplies open-pollinated heirloom seeds of vegetables, flowers, and herbs. All seeds are biodynamically cultivated and untreated.

Gardens North
5984 Third Line Road North
RR3 North Gower
Ontario
Canada K0A 2T0
Tel: 613/489-0065
Fax: 613/489-0065

Hardy perennial seed for Canadian gardens.

Ontario Seed Company
PO Box 144
Waterloo
Ontario N2J 3Z9
Tel: 519/886-0557

Untreated open-pollinated heirloom seeds. Ships to Canada only.

Prairie Grown Garden Seeds
Box 118
Cochin
Saskatchewan S0M 0L0
Tel: 306/386-2737

A broad selection of herbs, vegetables, grains, and wildflowers, suitable for growing in the Prairies without irrigation, as well as those suitable for other cool climate areas. Seeds are organically grown. Ships worldwide.

Terra Edibles
Box 63
Thomasburg
Ontario K0K 3H0

Open-pollinated, organically grown vegetable and flower seeds, originating from many parts of the world. Specializes in heirlooms.

SEED EXCHANGES

The Flower and Herb Exchange
3076 North Winn Road
Decorah, IA 52101
Tel: 319/382-5990
Fax: 319/382-5872

See main entry page 181.

Garden State Heirloom Seed Society
PO Box 15
Delaware, NJ 07833

Seed savers organization and seed exchange. Membership $7.00.

Native Seeds/SEARCH
2509 N Campbell Ave 325
Tucson, AZ 85719
Tel: 520/327-9123
Fax: 520/327-5821

Members receive 10% discount on all purchases and workshops, and quarterly newsletter *The Seedhead News*. Dedicated to the preservation of endangered native plants, and to redistributing native crops, NSS hold various events at their trial gardens throughout the year. Membership $20.00, Family $35.00, Low income $12.00, free to Native Americans. *See also page 179.*

J L Hudson
PO Box 1058
Redwood City, CA 94064

Seed exchange open to anyone who would like to collect seeds from the wild or from unusual garden plants. Ask for Seed Exchange pamphlet, which includes directions for seed saving. *See also page 179.*

National Gardening Association
180 Flynn Avenue
Burlington, VT 05401
Tel: 802/863-1308

Offers an active seed exchange through its magazine, *National Gardening*.

Seeds of Diversity Canada
(formerly Heritage Seed Program)
Box 36, Station Q,
Toronto ON M4T 2L7

Membership scheme and seed exchange programs, founded by the Canadian Organic Growers in 1984, dedicated to preserving heirloom and endangered flowers, vegetables, herbs and grains. Members receive a quarterly magazine and annual seed listing. Membership: $18.00, Low income $15.00.

Seeds Trust
High Altitude Gardens
PO Box 1048
Hailey, ID 83333-1048
Tel: 208/788-4419
Fax: 208/788-3452
email: higarden@micron.net
web: http://trine.com/Garden
net: higarden.htm

Encourages and teaches seed saving, with programs and lectures.

Southern Exposure Seed Exchange
PO Box 170
Earlysville, VA 22901

Seed exchange and gardeners' seed bank for rare, endangered and heirloom varieties or herbs and flowers. Seed list $1.00.

United Plant Savers
PO Box 420
East Barre, VT 05649

Seed exchange. *See also page 89.*

PLANT SOCIETIES

The American Daffodil Society
1686 Grey Fox Trails
Milford, OH 45150

Publishes a quarterly journal that contains sources for heirloom daffodil collections.

American Dianthus Society
Rand Lee
PO Box 22232
Santa Fe, NM 87502-2282

The society encourages the enjoyment and cultivation of dianthus with special interest in heirloom pinks and fragrant pinks.

Canadian Gladiolus Society
1274 129A Street
Ocean Park (Surrey), BC V4A 3Y4
Canada
Tel: 604/536-8200

One of the oldest gladioli organizations. Annual publication of over 100 pages with a comprehensive rating of cultivars, including 'antique' types.

American Hosta Society
9448 Mayfield Rd.
Chesterland., OH 44026
Tel: 216/729-9838

Members are interested in modern and classic hosta varieties.

American Peony Society
Greta Kessenich
250 Interlachen R.
Hopkins, MN 55343
Tel: 612/938-4706

The only peony society in this country; members maintain many varieties from the early 1900s.

The Hardy Plant Society
539 Woodland Ave.
Media, PA 19063
Tel: 215/566-0861

A group devoted to increasing interest in hardy perennials.

The Heritage Rose Foundation
1512 Gorman St.
Raleigh, NC 27686
Tel: 919/834-2591

This group is dedicated to preserving roses by creating permanent collections that will be protected for future generations.

The Heritage Roses Group (Northeast Chapter)
RD 1, Box 299
Clinton Corners, NY 12514

Founded in 1975, it now has seven regional groups. Membership includes their quarterly publication *Heritage Roses*, which is very informative and entertaining.

Historic Iris Preservation Society
12219 Zilles Rd.
Balckstone, VA 23824

Similar to the American Iris Society, but devoted to preserving heirloom irises.

Marigold Society of America
PO Box 112
New Britain, PA 18901
Tel: 215/348-5273

Society for marigold collectors.

National Wildflower Research Center
44801 LaCrosse Avenue North
Austin, TX 78739
Tel: 512/929-3600

Nonprofit educational organization dedicated to the preservation of native wildflowers, grasses, shrubs and trees.

North American Lily Society
Dr. Robert Gilman, PO Box 272
Owatonna, MN 55060
Tel: 507/451-2170

Founded in 1964, the Lily Society publishes a quarterly bulletin and yearbook which includes a lily seed exchange for its members.

Pioneer Plant Society
Miss P. A. Puryear
798 Holland Street
Navasota, TX 77868

New society dedicated to collecting and maintaining old-fashioned medicinal and useful plants.

Solon Heritage Flower Society
Box 224
Solon, IA 52333
Tel: 319/644-2777

Founded by Antonia Russo and Winifred Ham in 1985 to increase appreciation and awareness of the old-fashioned Iowa flowers and shrubs.

Canadian Rose Society
686 Pharmacy Avenue
Scarborough, ON M1L 3H8
Canada

A group of enthusiastic rose growers, some with interest in old garden roses.

PLACES TO VISIT

Thomas Jefferson Center for Historic Plants
Monticello, PO Box 316
Charlottesville, VA 22902
Tel: 804/984-9821
Fax: 804/977-6140
web: http://www.monticello

Historic gardens growing many of the varieties grown by Thomas Jefferson in his gardens. *See also page 72* and *main entry on page 185.*

Landis Valley Museum and Heirloom Seed Project
Lancaster, PA
Tel: 717/569-0401

Living museum and historic gardens.

Old Sturbridge Village
1 Old Sturbridge Village Road
Sturbridge, MA 01566
Tel: 508/347-3362
Fax: 508/347-5375

Educational outdoor history museum. Vegetable and flower gardens demonstrate gardening practices and styles of the 1830s. Seeds of early 19th century heirloom varieties available.

Ebenezer Maxwell Mansion
200 W. Tulpehocken St.
Philadelphia, PA 19144
Tel: 215/438-1861

An authentic planting surrounding an 1859 house.

Longwood Gardens
Rt 1, Kennett Square, PA. 19348
Tel: 610/388-6741

First planted in 1906, this 350 acre estate is a showpiece of rare plants old and new.

Sonnenberg Gardens and Mansion
151 Charlotte St.
Canandaigua, NY F14424
Tel: 716/924-5420

A moon garden, a Japanese garden and an authentic carpet bedding scheme surround an 1887 mansion.

Antique Rose Emporium
Route 5, Box 143
Brenham, Texas 77833
Tel: 409/836-5548

Antique roses surround the nursery.

The Will C. Curtis Garden in the Woods
The New England Wildflower Society
Garden in the Woods, Hemenway Road
Framingham, MA 01701
Tel: 508/877-6574

A thoughtfully designed wildflower garden with an Endangered Species garden on the grounds

Dumbarton Oaks
1703 32nd Street NW
Washington, DC 20007
Tel: 202/338-8278

Designed by Beatrix Farrand, this is a masterful garden tucked in the midst of the city with heirloom plants included.

Old Salem
Old Salem Road and Academy Street
Drawer F, Salem Station
Winston-Salem, NC 27108
Tel: 919/723-3688

A Moravian community with restored and recreated buildings as well as plants grown from 1759 to 1847.

Mount Vernon House and Gardens
P. O. Box 110, George Washington
Memorial Parkway
Mount Vernon, VA 22121
Tel: 703/780-2000

George Washington's home is surrounded by authentically planted gardens.

Colonial Williamsburg Foundation
P. O. Box 1776
Williamsburg, VA 23187
Tel: 804/220-7255

A recreated colonial village complete with authentic plantings.

Harriet Beecher Stowe House
73 Forest St.
Hartford, CT
Tel: 203-522-9258

Part of the Mark Twain House grounds, an heirloom garden surrounds this house.

Bibliography

Andersen Horticultural Library: *Andersen Horticultural Library's Source List of Plants and Seeds* University of Minnesota, 1996

Andrews, Jonathan: *Creating a Wildflower Garden* Henry Holt & Co, New York, 1986

Betts, Edwin M. and Perkins, Hazlehurst Bolton: *Thomas Jefferson's Flower Garden at Monticello* The University Press of Virginia, Charlottesville, 1986

Bailey, L. H: *The Standard Cyclopedia of Horticulture* The Macmillan Company, New York, 1956

Beck, Joseph: *New Book of Flowers* Orange Judd Company, New York, 1879

Brickell, Christopher & Sharman, Fay: *The Vanishing Garden* John Murray, London, 1986

Coats, Alice M: *Flowers and their Histories* McGraw-Hill Book Company, New York, 1956

Coffey, Timothy: *The History and Folklore of North American Wildflowers* Houghton Mifflin Company, New York, 1994

de Bray, Lys: *Lys de Bray's Manual of Old-Fashioned Flowers* The Oxford Illustrated Press, Sparkford, Somerset, 1984

Fisher John: *The Origins of Garden Plants* Constable and Company Ltd., London, 1982

Genders, Roy: *The Cottage Garden and the Old-Fashioned Flowers* Pelham Books, London, 1969

Gordon, Lesley A: *Country Herbal* Gallery Books, New York, 1984

Gorer, Richard: *The Development of Garden Flowers* Eyre and Spottiswoode Ltd., Great Britain, 1970

Griffiths, Mark: *The New Royal Horticultural Society Dictionary Index of Garden Plants* Timber Press, Portland, Oregon, 1994

Harvey, John: *Early Gardening Catalogues* Phillimore, Chichester, Sussex, 1972

Harvey, John: *Early Nurserymen* Phillimore, Chichester, Sussex, 1974

Haughton, Claire Shaver: *Green Immigrants* Harcourt Brace Jovanovich, New York, 1978

Heiser, Charles B. Jr: *The Sunflower* University of Oklahoma Press, Norman, OK, 1976

Henderson, Peter: *Henderson's Handbook of Plants* Peter Henderson & Company, New York, 1881

Hyams, Edward: *English Cottage Gardens* Penguin Books Ltd, Middlesex, England, 1970

Jennings, Anne: *Garden Plan: A Detailed Guide to the Museum of Garden History's 17th Century Style Garden* The Tradescant Trust, London

Johnson, Lady Bird and Lees, Carlton B: *Wildflowers Across America* Abbeville Press, New York, 1988

Lane, Clive: *Cottage Garden Annuals* David & Charles, Devon, 1997

Leighton, Ann: *Early American Gardens: "For Meate or Medicine"* Houghton Mifflin Company, Boston, 1966

Martin, Tovah: *Once Upon a Windowsill* Timber Press, Portland, Oregon, 1988

Mohlenbrock, Robert H: *Where Have all the Wildflowers Gone?* Macmillan Publishing Co, Inc., New York, 1983

Newcomb, Peggy Cornett: *Popular Annuals of North America 1865–1914* Dunbarton Oaks Research Library and Collection, Washington DC, 1985

Nicholson, George: *The Illustrated Dictionary of Gardening* James Penman, New York, 1887

Rhodora: the Journal of the New England Botanical Club Vol. 98, No. 895, Summer 1996

Roots: Journal of the Historical Iris Preservation Society Vol. 2, Issue 1, Spring 1989

Royal Horticultural Society: *The Plant Finder* The Royal Horticultural Society, 1994

Skinner, Charles M: *Myths and Legends of Flowers, Trees, Fruits and Plants* J. B. Lippincott Company, Philadelphia, 1939

Slosson, Elvinia: *Pioneer American Gardening* Coward-McCann, Inc., New York, 1951

Stickland, Sue: *Heirloom Vegetables* Fireside, New York, 1998

Stuart, David & Sutherland, James: *Plants from the Past* Viking Penguin Books Ltd., Middlesex, England, 1987

Weaver, William Woys: *Heirloom Vegetable Gardening* Henry Holt and Company, 1997

White, Lyman N: *Heirlooms and Genetics* Lyman N. White, Cambridge, NY, 1988

Index

....

Page numbers in italic refer to illustrations.